OPENING DOORS

THE *ENORMITY* OF US

Printed in Australia
Cover design by Shawline Publishing Group Pty Ltd
Images in this book are copyright approved for Shawline Publishing Group Pty Ltd
Illustrations within this book are copyright approved for Shawline Publishing Group Pty Ltd

First Printing: February 2023
Shawline Publishing Group Pty Ltd
www.shawlinepublishing.com.au

Paperback ISBN 978-1-9228-5041-6
eBook ISBN 978-1-9228-5045-4

Distributed by Shawline Distribution and Lightningsource Global

 A catalogue record for this work is available from the National Library of Australia

More great Shawline titles can be found here:

New titles also available through Books@Home Pty Ltd.
Subscribe today - www.booksathome.com.au

OPENING DOORS

THE *ENORMITY* OF US

YVONNE FOGARTY

In Opening Doors, Yvonne Fogarty tells her story; a spiritual journey of courage, tenacity and love. In searching for truth, she learns to master the crippling, destructive and negative thoughts, behaviours and beliefs that influenced and dominated her existence. Yvonne's desire to live a whole-hearted life is revealed through her stories, as is her vulnerability as she bares her soul with the intention and desire of helping others with their struggles. Her story is living proof that we can be healed, that it is possible to learn to master fear, to trust, to love, to have faith and to live in truth.

Margot Storer

For my husband Graham, my anchor and love of my life.

In loving memory of our precious fur babies -
Karza born Feb 2004 died 2nd September 2020 and
Zoet born March 2007 who died suddenly on 22nd May 2021.
Both passed over during the final stages of this manuscript.

Acknowledgements:
I would like to express my heartfelt gratitude to my friends
Margot Storer, Ardathia Sulkowski, Marilyn Ardipradja,
Diane Spooner, Natasha Sawlani and Jeanette Johnson for
their ongoing encouragement, support and belief in me and
this book. A big thank you to my assessor Rosie Dub,
our family, friends and students who contributed to this book.

Please note: Chapter 52 – 'Keeper Of The Land'
mentions a deceased Aboriginal person.

'…Our greatness lies not so much in being able to remake the world… as in being able to remake ourselves.'

Mahatma Gandhi

CONTENTS

FOREWORD

PSYCHIC GIFTS AND OUR IMMORTAL SOUL

PSYCHIC GIFTS

The word 'psychic' is from the Greek word *psychikos*, meaning 'of the soul'.

We all have a personalised 'inner guidance system' readily available to empower and support us as we journey upon our own individual pathway. We are always utilising this inner power whether we are aware of the enormity of who we are or not.

WHERE DO THE PSYCHIC GIFTS AND INFORMATION COME FROM?

Some call this inner guidance God, Creator, Source of Life, Higher power, **Spirit** of Life or **Consciousness,** to name a few. This spiritual power is much greater than us, its frequencies and vibrations are everywhere present and always flowing through, around and within us, offering intuitive guidance, support and protection. Some call this power Spirit, because its energy is mostly unseen to the human eye and pervades the whole universe.

Please note: For ease of reading, I have used the word 'Spirit' or 'Consciousness' (with a capital C) directly relating to our Source of Life.

We all share Spirit's innate power and attributes through our immortal soul's interwoven relationship, and if this power and its attributes we live off didn't exist nor would we exist, including everything else in existence. For more detailed information refer to chapter 54 – A Soul's Associated Frequencies and Vibrations.

Below is an explanation of the inner guidance and psychic gifts that became available to me to support my own healing journey and my work as a spiritual intuitive healer.

Clairaudience – On extremely rare occasions, I have heard a name and received a message in my right ear, spoken by a family member who has passed over, along with an image of that person, offering support to a loved one in a time of need. The intention is for a specific reason and always uplifting.

Discernment – The ability to evaluate and understand through our senses. E.g. refer to chapter 35 – A Timely Coincidence.

Intuitive/Spiritual energy treatment – When working with a client, information sometimes flows into my conscious awareness. Sharing the messages I receive from Spirit opens a door for a distorted belief or a painful memory to surface into their conscious mind for a shift of perception to take place. E.g. refer to chapter 14 – Lower Back Pain and chapter 40 – Journey from Misery to Contentment.

Mediumship – Ability to see those who have passed over, residing in another realm, often referred to as heaven. They come to give a message to a loved one. This type of experience happens very rarely to me and only when necessary. There is always a direct link between me and the person the message is intended for. Refer to chapter 42 – Message for Loraine and chapter 51 – A Mother's Concern.

Past life – The act of going back to receive information and understanding regarding an unresolved past life experience that has been retained in a person's soul for healing. E.g. refer to chapter 20 – Stepping Forward, chapter 53 – Informative

Vision, chapter 64 – Paris, France, Late 1700s – Past Life Regression Session, chapter 65 – Paris France 2016 and chapter 68 – Completing a Frequency of Learning.

Remote viewing – The ability to project one's whole awareness to a distant place. This has only happened once when I was sending distant healing energy to someone who I didn't know was very ill in the hospital. Refer to chapter 25 – Saira's Experience In a Coma.

Spiritual counselling – Supporting a person through intuitive guidance. E.g. chapter 26 – Overprotective Mother and chapter 35 – A Timely Coincidence.

Visions overview – For me, visions appear first in my third eye, often called Spiritual insight. The images expand and I observe the images projected out in front of my eyes. Sometimes the visions flow as if I am watching short video clips. E.g. Refer to chapter 19 – Insightful Vision and chapter 20 – Stepping Forward.

Vision – clairvoyance – Also known as second sight or extrasensory perception. The ability to penetrate, 'see' deeper into consciousness. The image(s) I observe in a person's energy body is a key for a client to heal a troubling issue that represents an energy blockage, a solidified thought pattern (memory). E.g. refer to chapter 14 – Lower Back Pain, chapter 15 – Work Was Suffocating Him, chapter 28 – Kidney Failure and chapter 45 – The Healing.

Vision – pre-cognition – Knowledge of a future happening through extrasensory means. E.g. refer to chapter 11 – Hannah, chapter 21 – The Unexpected Guest, chapter 32 – Jakarta Riots 1998, chapter 38 – Mimi's Book and chapter 48 – Manifesting a Heart's Desire.

HIERARCHY OF CELESTIAL BEINGS

There are a hierarchy of spiritual beings from light and gold beings to spiritual helpers and angels that are around us all the time, residing in a higher realm. From my personal experiences, the ones whom I have encountered are mentioned below and their presence is always for a specific reason.

Angels (with wings) wear white loose-fitting robes. I see this type of angel prior to someone passing over and there are always four of them gathered together waiting to accompany a person 'back home' again after physical death. Refer to chapter 47 – Roy's Passing.

I have seen angels without wings. I call these angels 'the messengers/protectors'. From my observations, they can be seen in different coloured robes, sometimes with a simple cord tied around their waist.

White robe (without wings) – I saw two angels floating lengthwise on either side of a girlfriend's car just as we approached a toll booth at Bogor on our way back into Jakarta. A minute or two after we exited the toll booth, we found ourselves facing a sudden torrential downpour of rain. It was impossible to see any other car in front or on either side of our car and we were in the middle of an eight-lane highway, which was about to merge back into four lanes.

My friend, who was driving and had been living in Jakarta for many years, became very anxious. Then, all the windows suddenly fogged up and I couldn't locate the right button to activate the demister for her. I lowered my window and wiped the windscreen as best I could and I told her what I had seen and that we would be safe.

Blue robe (without wings) – Messengers often appear to give reassurance and/or to warn me to heighten my awareness.

I was out one afternoon, playing tour guide with friends who were visiting – all of us were from our home city of Perth, Western Australia. I had taken them to a heavily congested fabric market in Jakarta. Suddenly my body tensed and at the same time, I saw an angel wearing a blue robe appear, walking beside me. I looked back, calling out to my friends – who were walking close behind me with their husbands – to hang onto their bags and wallets. I then placed my left hand on my bum bag. I watched as three young men casually strolled towards me. Suddenly one attempted to rip my bag away from around my waist but to their dismay, I had attached the strap of my bag to the waistband of my jeans, with two large safety pins. If they wanted my bag, they had to take me with them.

'Heyyy!' I said in a light-hearted loud voice. They quickly dispersed in different directions and the angel disappeared. Similar incidents have happened a number of times whilst out shopping around Jakarta. Keeping the white light of protection around us heightens our senses. Refer to chapter 33 - The White Light.

Evolved gold being (without wings) – For receiving protection and/or information. Refer to chapter 41 – The Messenger.

Divine intervention – I use this terminology at times for other happenings I have encountered, which includes either seeing gold beings or spiritual beings. Refer to chapter 4 – A Life-Changing Experience and chapter 50 – Divine Intervention. These two experiences show clearly how spiritual beings can intervene to save someone's life.

Guardian angels – Spiritual beings assigned to watch over us. A highly evolved vibrational being's presence can be felt in our body, e.g. The Voice. When I have heard it, I experience the words spoken vibrating strongly throughout my whole body.

The Voice has guided me on rare occasions, since young. The Voice is mentioned throughout the book and has been a great source of encouragement to me.

Highly evolved light being (without wings) – While meditating outside on our patio the night before running a first degree Reiki training class, I saw what I can only describe as a 'light being'. It zoomed in extremely fast and stopped in front of me. The being's whole appearance was a very pale shade of bluish-white. It hovered above the ground in front of me in a lotus position for only a couple of seconds as our eyes met, and then it left in a flash. A spiritual leader once told me that it can also indicate an initiation of some kind when they purposely look directly into your eyes. This type of being has only appeared to me the once.

Animal beings – Pet lovers will be happy to know their beloved fur children definitely have precious souls. Refer to chapter 31 – The Power of Love and chapter 61 Fiona's Best Friend.

Spiritual beings – These beings wear day clothing. They either come to me to give a message to a loved one, seek help or give a warning. E.g. refer to chapter 4 – A Life-Changing Experience, chapter 6 – Trapped Between Worlds, chapter 12 – Those That Walk Among Us, chapter 42 – Message for Loraine, chapter 46 – My Parents' Goodbye Message, chapter 63 – Sid's Farewell Hug, chapter 51 – A Mother's Concern and another delightful gem, chapter 52 – Keeper of the Land.

The interactions I have encountered with spiritual beings communicate with me via mental transference of thought.

INTRODUCTION

One of the few things I excelled in at school was being a chatterbox. I engaged in all sorts of mischief just to avoid having to write an essay. I became an expert at avoiding; in fact, I left school without ever having written an essay of any substance.

One of my report cards states: 'If Yvonne could put in as much effort to learning as she does to talking, she would be an achiever.'

My regular homework was writing out 100 times, 'I must not talk in class'. A classmate taught me how to hold two pens together, thus creating two lines of writing for the effort of one. That lesson cost me a penny (in the days before decimal currency). I became so proficient at it, I wrote pages in advance.

One day, the teacher opened my desktop and discovered a huge pile of my 'homework', ready to hand in as required. I had made a big mistake one day by handing in my homework far too quickly. Sadly, all was confiscated, and in its place, I had to write out pages given at random from the current year's spelling book. *How unfair,* I thought. On the other hand, my spelling improved.

My mother's contradictory actions, her religious background and her outspoken aggression towards me, at times coupled with my seeing spiritual beings spasmodically became a huge stumbling block in my life, causing me mental and emotional confusion.

By the time I reached adulthood, my perception of life and my ability to interact easily with all around me had narrowed considerably. I blamed the world for my unhappiness. I desired freedom from the daily inner tormenting thoughts and afflictions.

I set to work with the aim of freeing my self-expression, fear of life and the many distorted beliefs I held within me. I slowly made headway in healing my various misperceptions through utilising inner spiritual guidance.

Over the years, I came to believe that we choose our parents, who best resonate with, our 'frequency of learnings'. Our frequency of learning refers to the choices we decide to overcome and the goals we set to achieve before returning back to earth with the intention of accomplishing in our current life cycle.

I know now without any doubt that my parents were perfect to help me face my shortcomings I carried into this life to overcome.

I enjoyed a successful career in the computer field through pure stubborn determination to prove that I was not totally worthless, as my mother believed.

My husband often helped me with writing business letters because at times I stumbled to find the words to express what needed to be said. My mind would go blank as if my brain had frozen. Unfortunately, the thought of expressing myself through writing overwhelmed me and any attempt to do so brought forth a deep-seated pattern of fear, self-doubt and inadequacy with a vengeance, resulting in anxiety and panic attacks. It sounds such a silly little thing, given I can be a chatterbox; however, expressing myself through writing terrified me.

One morning in March 1999 I heard The Voice (the inner support I have heard since childhood) suggesting I write a book. I froze. A book? Oh no! That was definitely something I was extremely reluctant to do. I couldn't understand why The Voice would suggest I do something that terrified me. I believed writing a book was way beyond my capabilities because I had a firmly implanted belief that I wasn't good enough and I 'logically' assumed my fear was based on the fact that I hadn't finished high school.

My husband Graham, seeing me in panic mode, gave me a writing exercise to do. 'Yvonne, instead of attempting to write a book, why don't you just write an essay on what you enjoy doing? Playing golf, for example.'

We both started playing golf after we were transferred from Perth, Western Australia to Jakarta, Indonesia through my husband's work.

An essay – *gulp!*

After thinking about Graham's idea whilst nibbling on my favourite comfort food – Cadbury's hazelnut chocolate – for a couple of days before sitting at my desk and writing. My short story, entitled 'Hellloooo Yoyo' (my caddy gave me that nickname as I would look up as I went to strike the ball and miss hitting that tiny thing) came into being. Despite my deep inner fear of expressing myself, to my surprise, the words simply poured out of me. That small, funny and quirky manuscript lies in a drawer at home. Maybe I will publish it one day. Writing that essay thrilled me and I was stunned to discover I really did enjoy writing after all.

I believe that when we have a deep desire in our heart to achieve something, despite our brain telling us we can't or it's impossible, it's our soul urging us forward, saying:

Come on, give it a go! You have the ability within you to achieve it, despite whatever has been programmed into your brain or whatever past experiences are blocking the way. Nothing is impossible to overcome.

When we have the courage to face life head-on and clear our buried fears, we walk through a doorway allowing inner spiritual guidance to support us to manifest our soul's desires and fulfil our chosen destiny in this lifetime, which can include a two-fold purpose, as in my case.

I began researching how our mind works in an attempt to gain clarity relating to my issues, which I believed at the time only stemmed from my childhood. I discovered later they were only the tip of the iceberg.

I came across an article that resonated with me which shed some light on my confused state of mind:

...A missing experience creates an inability to heal, yearning for

'unmet needs' while protecting against them. Just as we internally separate parts that seek connection from parts that seek safety, we push externally against whatever we need most in life because there is no agreement. At some level, we wait for the elusive experiential safety that will release us and reverse the process, bringing everything together.

Jeremy McAllister. Ma. IPCI: Ref Psychology Trauma. Substance Abuse and Mental H. Services 5/8/2014.

In retrospect, I can see that the fragmented aspects of my soul manifested themselves as phobias, panic attacks and extreme insecurity causing the ongoing stress and anxiety I harboured to escalate. From childhood to adulthood, I hated my life and myself. The psychological traumas I had been afraid to deal with in the past deeply affected how I viewed life. Trauma in one sense represents an ability to exist in pieces. I had locked the pains away, thus separating parts of myself from my whole 'self'.

The deep-seated desire within me to write a book kept nudging relentlessly at my heart to be set free, becoming the catalyst, encouraging me to take a much deeper journey within to heal traumatic memories buried deep within my soul with the aim of setting my imprisoned self-expression free. I had no idea back then that this book would become my memoir. A soul's frequency and its associated vibrations create our energy body (our subconscious mind) and physical body. Therefore, every memory, past or present, we retain creates an imprint in every cell in our body. That's how an intuitive healer can 'see' a memory thread that links to a physical illness. For example, chapter 14 – Lower Back Pain and chapter 45 – The Healing.

I was a distrustful and very reluctant participant on what has turned out to be an astonishingly eye-opening journey that I never believed possible until I experienced it for myself. My journey lead me deep into the recesses of my mind, back to two past life traumas I had buried, both of which were connected to the fears I was currently experiencing in this life cycle.

Now as I look back, I am grateful I never remained a sceptic; instead, I opened the door to our inner world accepting this wonderful connection to inner guidance. As you will read in the book, I do not believe in coincidences. If you have picked up this book it's for a reason.

My life experiences also occurred for a reason, with the aim of guiding me along a shrouded pathway, towards achieving the deepest desire of my heart – freeing my soul's self-expression, my fear of people and of life itself.

One of the most exciting discoveries on my journey, which is explained through various experiences in my memoir, is that we definitely **DO NOT DIE.** Many believe, as I used to years ago, that when we die, that's the end of our existence! Yes, it's a fact our physical body stops functioning and decays, but our soul definitely doesn't – we are immortal. Refer to chapter 47 – Roy's Passing. We simply step out of our physical body and **LIVE ON** in our soul's spiritual body and we retain all our accumulated knowledge to date.

I believe we all come into this world with a specific gift(s) to share. How our soul urges us to express our self is our own unique gift to the world, which can be of benefit to others in wonderful ways. Do whatever causes your heart to sing and don't be afraid to let go, be yourself and shine.

I likened my journey to the hare and the tortoise story… sometimes I was the 'very' slow tortoise, meandering along and at other times I raced ahead, exhausting myself, then wandered off, distracted, snoozing on the job.

In hindsight, I recommend being the tortoise on this inward journey… slow and steady wins the race and my journey was an extremely slow one. In fact, it has taken me over twenty years to face and heal my fears, clearing the way for me to complete this book.

Some readers may find some of my experiences inexplicable to believe.

All experiences in this book are the truth. Some names have been changed in respect for those whom I have lost contact with, or who wish for anonymity, in those cases I used a fictitious first name only.

I've had the privilege of mixing with many different cultures whilst my husband and I resided overseas through his profession in the construction industry. In the motivational training workshops I've conducted here and in different parts of the world, I have supported many people to open their 'inner door' to heal aspects of their life that were holding them back.

Our inner guidance has different ways of supporting us to uncover our authentic self; we are all unique and individual. Our heart will always lead us towards building upon and expanding our own foundation of truths. When a desire doesn't give up on us and persists until acknowledged and acted upon, it's our soul encouraging us not to give up.

Why? Because it's directly connected to our current life cycle's frequency of learning we chose before birth to accomplish in this life cycle. Our soul and heart are our doorway to our inner world for receiving protection, guidance, support and thankfully… encouragement.

We all have the ability to free ourselves from any encumbrances that we may sense/feel are holding us back or hidden away in the recesses of our minds.

As I share my life journey, may it encourage and support you as you journey towards manifesting your dreams and purpose in this life cycle. My desire for you and others is to recognise the enormity of who you are, shouting out loud for the entire world to hear…

'Yay, I have done it. I have uncovered my soul's authentic voice.'

I assure you the journey is worth it.

We are never alone.
Receiving support and guidance
is a natural aspect of our existence.
Spirit's consciousness is readily available to
support us all and encourage us to recognise
the enormity of who we are.

Yvonne Fogarty

CHAPTER 1

EARLY YEARS

A trauma occurred early in my life that I had no conscious recollection of: an event that became 'indelibly' imprinted within my psyche. The experience, combined with an unsettled childhood, gave rise to some very strong patterns of insecurity in my formative years and beyond. It was many years before I uncovered the cause of that psychological trauma.

When I was about four years of age, I turned within, seeking comfort escaping to an imagined, joyful place, in an attempt to shut out the unhappiness I was experiencing in our home. I have often wondered if that's why I started seeing a person wearing a white robe occasionally at night standing near my bed. The person disappeared as soon I looked at them. Did they come to comfort me? If that was their intention, it didn't work! Seeing them terrified me.

I remember waking in the early hours one morning, running to Mum, telling her I was scared because I saw someone standing in my room before disappearing. She made me go back to bed, telling me it was just a bad dream and/or I had imagined it.

Her words led me to doubt myself. I wondered if these people were real or imagined. If real, they must be evil, I reasoned, as I was often told by Mum when I did something wrong that I had the devil in me; I was bad and good for nothing. At the time, I assumed the people I saw occasionally were sent by the devil. As an adult, I now understand that these spiritual beings came to support me, not hurt me, as you will discover further on in the book.

I was an over-sensitive, naïve and lonely child. If I didn't obey my mother's demands, I experienced her very harsh wrath, mostly in the form of verbal abuse, causing me to feel frightened and nervous around her. If I accidentally spilt a drink, I was yelled at and sometimes smacked for being careless. I lived in fear of doing the wrong thing.

I was not allowed my own voice. I quickly worked out a way to survive in our home environment by keeping my mouth shut and my feelings to myself. I restrained my inquisitiveness by living and behaving within the restrictions of our home environment, well, most of the time, except when my impishness couldn't contain itself. No wonder I became a chatterbox outside of home.

Each time I experienced my mother's abuse, I swallowed the painful words.

Over time, they slowly gathered together forming a solid hard crust, an impenetrable wall of self-protection, creating within me a judgmental attitude and resentment towards the outside world. I also know there were many times where I tested my mother's patience with my antics and behaviour. Eventually, I buried any claim to thoughts or feelings of my own. It was safer that way. The consequence of that decision affected my ability to freely express myself. I had unknowingly shut the door on my authentic voice. I had given away my inherent power, becoming a mindless puppet.

I was unaware back then that the unresolved issues and unhappiness between my parents caused my mother to unleash her own built-up disappointments in life onto my older sister and me. I was too young to understand that her outbursts weren't anything to do with me. Due to my sensitivities, my mother's own inadequacies were transferred to me. I took on board someone else's issues and beliefs, making them mine.

Isn't hindsight wonderful? Looking back, I can see that my mother's own unresolved beliefs, such as believing she was unlovable and unworthy, often caused her to react angrily towards loved ones around her. I believed that I must always 'obey' and respect authority figures and whatever was said to me by my parents was true.

During my younger years in my need to feel loved and accepted in our home, I took on the responsibility of trying to make everyone else feel happy around me, I became a people pleaser. Little Miss Fix It. I exhausted myself attempting to make everyone feel loved, firstly within our home and then spreading my unmet needs towards others, especially by rescuing stray dogs. I knew that feeling of believing you're not loved and it hurt.

It was a few months after my seventh birthday when I first experienced a strong vibrational presence and heard a Voice speak to me as I was walking home from school, which I aptly named 'The Voice'. I can even remember the clothes I wore that day – a tartan skirt, red jumper, white socks and black lace-up shoes. My hair was straight without a curl or wave in sight, except when Mum rolled up my hair in rags, twisting them into a knot before tying them off. I hated it being done because it hurt. It didn't help that I kept wriggling and pulling my head away from her, only causing me more discomfort.

I was walking along our street, swinging my brown school case. As I approached our next-door neighbour's house, I suddenly stopped walking and looked up, observing the clear blue sky. I still have no idea why I stopped! I just stood there searching the sky when suddenly this warm loving Voice spoke clearly to me...

'Yvonne, you are going to leave something to the world to be remembered by.'

The words echoed around and within me simultaneously, creating a quivering throughout my body, before leaving a tingling sensation in my heart. I remained still until the warm sensation subsided. It felt very comfortable and surprisingly, I wasn't frightened at all.

To this day I can still remember how I simply smiled and accepted what happened without questioning it, shrugged my shoulders and tucked the experience away, becoming a treasured memory that I have never forgotten.

Once again in hindsight, I can only surmise my very warm acceptance of The Voice was because no one suddenly appeared in front of me to frighten me, or maybe it was the warmth and comfort I felt from that experience that left no room for fear to creep in, only love.

One morning, months after my encounter with The Voice, while I was eating my breakfast at the small kitchen table – as our formal dining room was only used for special occasions – my mother said, 'Yvonne. YVONNE, look at me.'

With a feeling of trepidation, I raised my head slowly before looking at her.

'I don't want you talking to the lady down the road who lives in the house with the green picket fence. She is crazy. She sees ghosts and hears voices!'

I stopped chewing my food as her words registered in my mind. *Oh no!* I thought. Her words churned over in my stomach.

Why? Because I was made to go to church every Sunday and I believed being a good Christian meant I was not supposed to 'see' or have these experiences I encountered. I pondered over her words and came to the conclusion that I really was evil and the people I saw occasionally at night were evil too.

A few years later, one Sunday the minister confirmed my mother's words from the pulpit, saying, 'Anything that is occult is of the devil.'

I sat bolt upright from my slouching position on the church pew, looking up to see if his eyes were zoomed in on me.

What did he just say? Uh oh… I'm doomed to hell, I thought. *I really must try to block out seeing these people visiting me occasionally at night.*

My parents were both born in the United Kingdom. My mother's father was a Minister who preached the old-fashioned hellfire and brimstone God-fearing sermons. My mother's parents had both died before I was born, yet my grandfather's dictatorial manner lived on in our house. Although my mother stopped going to church years ago after an argument with her father, the tone of her words when she passed on his preaching only reinforced my fear of the unknown.

I felt a shudder run through me and I purposely shook my shoulders, laughed and said out loud 'Oooooooo!'

It's a wonder I didn't feel the earth shake when my mother used to repeat her father's words. I tried hard to be a good Christian yet my attempts to shut the door on seeing these night visitors that suddenly appeared by my bed didn't work. I continued to keep these experiences to myself. Who would have believed a child anyway! I felt it was safer to stay quiet; Mum might think I was evil and crazy. In fact, I genuinely had doubts about my own sanity at times.

I can laugh now, but as a child and into adulthood I feared the unknown. These days I occasionally see various spiritual beings when I am supporting a person to heal an issue troubling them, using my inner gifts that slowly unfolded. That is when I finally found the courage to give myself permission to acknowledge them.

That first encounter with The Voice left a profound impression within my psyche, becoming deeply embedded in my heart. Many years passed before I realised The Voice had given me a gift of inner strength, which encouraged me to keep going and not give up when life became extremely difficult to handle.

After all these years I can still easily recall experiencing the comforting, joyful feeling that The Voice left in my heart that day. It was a feeling that was unfamiliar to me at the time, but I know now I was embraced and touched by our Source's vibration of unconditional love.

As I grew older, my fears turned to anger and resentment towards my misperception about God. I continued going to church as I was searching and reaching out for something, I just wasn't sure what. Thinking about it now, all I wanted was to be loved and accepted and told I was an okay person.

I laugh now at how the Bible was interpreted back in the early 1900s and sadly passed on to my mother by my grandfather's bone-rattling fear-based religious teachings.

All throughout my close association with the church, I believed as many others did back then that this so-called person named God sat on a throne, had a beard, stern beady eyes and carried a big stick, which I believed was always pointed directly at me. I was terrified of this God. I believed this God was not loving; instead, he was cruel and harsh. For many years I was frightened of what could be lurking in the dark. No wonder I was often at the doctor's with stomach issues due to nervous tension. I now know that this power is not a person but a power so much greater than us, which the European Organisation for Nuclear Research (CERN) named this mysterious element 'The God particle'. Refer to chapter 12 – Those That Walk Among Us.

Mum and Dad were both honest hard-working people. Although we were not financially well off, I was well looked after physically but not emotionally. One minute, Mum was cuddling me telling me she loved me and the next minute berating me, leaving me frightened and confused. They both loved and cared for my sister and me with all their heart, from their level of understanding of love, which was conditional. They didn't know anything different; nor did I back then.

If we are not shown unconditional love and do not experience the effects of this vibration for ourselves, how can we pass it on to others? It is very difficult. We are incapable of expressing clearly what we do not understand in our own hearts.

I can see how I came to believe only in a love that hurt instead of a love that embraced and nurtured. My mind had selectively blotted out all the thoughtful things Mum did for us and there were many. I had unknowingly closed my mind off to anything that didn't fit in with my negative and narrow view of life. Although my life was very challenging at times, Mum was a very caring person and always home when I arrived back from school.

My mother, who was 1.4 metres in height, overweight and had brown permed hair, was the dominant controlling authority in our home, yet it was my father who took me to marching girls' training, state competitions and gymnastic events. My mother never once came with us. Dad was a kind and gentle person, always very quiet in our home.

By the time I reached my teens, I couldn't see beyond my pain and anger. I was often very moody and I carried around a huge chip on my shoulder. I was looking out at the world through eyes that could only see resentment and bitterness towards life. I had taken on board a 'poor me' attitude and carried a heavy load of emotional baggage.

To live was a struggle. I feared being hurt by what life might shower upon me. I did the only thing that I could see would secure my survival and safety: I shut the door on my feelings. As a result of that decision I often felt confused as to what emotion I was experiencing. I lived on the surface of life. I had lost my connection to discern my own inner feelings and gave up seeking to have my own needs met. Even in high school, I had an 'I don't care' attitude towards study. Something I deeply regretted later.

Standing outside the door of my high school classroom one day, I listened in on a private conversation between my mother and my second-year high school form teacher. Who said listening to other peoples' conversations about you isn't always a wise thing to do! In this instance, I was so pleased to have excellent hearing. What I overheard my mother say changed the direction my life was heading.

'What am I going to do with Yvonne? She doesn't care about study. She sees life as one big joke. Do you think it's worth keeping her on at high school for another year?'

'Well,' the teacher said. 'In my opinion, if Yvonne keeps up this "I don't care about school" attitude towards her studies, I don't see her gaining anything by staying on at school for another year.'

As a result, my mother informed me it would be a waste of money paying for me to go to business college as she had done for my sister, who was nearly five years older than me. Instead, she was going to put me to work in a clothes factory making shirts, as a neighbour's granddaughter was doing.

That conversation proved to be a blessing in disguise. Out from deep within me burst forth with gusto a defiance I didn't know existed, along with a stubbornness I did know existed. I finally had a purpose in life and something to strive for. I was determined to succeed and prove just how wrong my mother was.

I was aware my two older cousins had received cadetships to go to a prominent business college, so unbeknown to Mum, after school the following day with my determination egging me on, I cycled the few kilometres to my mother's sister's home and told her everything in between sobs.

My aunt, who was always very loving and kind to me, said, 'Yvonne, I will ring the college and find out if they have plans to take on any cadets next year and then I'll speak to your mother.'

I reluctantly cycled very slowly towards home, delaying the inevitable as long as possible, knowing I was in big trouble for not going straight home after school. Turning into our street, I could see my mother hanging over the front gate looking for me. I slowed down even more, which in hindsight only infuriated my mother more. When we stepped into the house and out of sight of neighbours, Mum let loose her fury. I was smacked across the back of my legs with a wooden spoon many times for being home late.

Looking back now, I understand Mum was worried that something may have happened to me, yet she was so happy to see that her precious child was at last home safe – she smacked me so hard, I thought the spoon might break! I'd have preferred to have been smothered in kisses, as kisses don't hurt. Well, except when Mum hadn't plucked out the prickly whiskers above her upper lip. Nonetheless, my defiance was worth it.

Thanks to my aunt, I secured the cadetship for the following year. I left school at the end of the school year, just prior to my fourteenth birthday (30 December 1961).

I commenced in the January, working my way through business college, cleaning classrooms before school started, making morning and afternoon teas for the teachers, running errands and doing odd jobs in the office every day between classes, assisting the very strict head of the college, Miss P. I was terrified of her; in fact, I was terrified of any authoritarian figure.

One afternoon after classes had finished for the day, Miss P was called to the staff room, leaving me in her office to complete some filing. I glanced over my shoulder, noticing her small purple hat (that she wore every day) which had small, different-coloured flowers all around it, hanging on the hook behind the door. An idea flashed through my mind and a thought quickly followed... *Yvonne, don't do it.* My curiosity won. I walked over plopped her hat on my head, held my head up high, stuck my nose up in the air, copying her stance and turned my head from side to side, looking at myself in the mirror. I heard a sudden noise behind me as the door creaked open. I hesitantly turned around, craning my neck back I looked up. *Oh no!*

There, towering over me, stood Miss P's skinny body, with her glasses perched on the end of her nose and her arms crossed in front of her.

I thought, *oh, why do I do these things? I'm in big trouble now.* To my surprise she didn't say a word nor reprimand me; instead, she very quickly told me I could go home now. I'm sure I saw her lips twitching, attempting very hard not to laugh. I, in turn, was trying very hard not to wet my pants. I concluded that day that she liked me.

I topped the school in typing, which I attributed to the daily practising on the piano I had been forced to endure since young. I failed in shorthand and passed in bookkeeping.

When I was older and a little wiser, I realised Miss P's worth as a mentor. I attempted to locate her to thank her for the wonderful training she instilled in me. I laughed out loud and sat straight up in my chair as I typed the word 'instilled' because that was exactly what she did. I learnt to be responsible, thorough, respectful and loyal, and to do a job properly whether it was going to be seen or not. Sadly, she passed over before I could thank her.

After I graduated, the company that owned the college employed me in the December of that year. I commenced work not long before my fifteenth birthday. It was illegal in Australia to employ anyone before they turned fifteen, so I was told to keep my employment a secret until January. I was so excited to be working and getting five pounds a week. Wow! But… keeping my mouth shut took all my willpower. It was a huge undertaking for a chatterbox.

My boss saw my potential and in mid-February I was trained to use an accounting machine. The first time I sat behind one, I was amazed. It was huge. The machine was bigger than me. (Did I tell you I am small in stature?) I strained to see what I was doing; I couldn't see over the top of the monstrosity. When they raised my chair for better access, my feet dangled in the air. They solved that problem by putting a small box under my feet and a cushion behind my back.

It was the only time I grudgingly appreciated having size (with a s-t-r-e-t-c-h) 32 breasts. It meant I could sit very close up to the machine to operate it and still look down easily to see the keyboard without anything of 'great' substance blocking my view. My only problem was when I was required to roll a new A3 sheet of paper into the machine; I had to stand on the wobbly box to accomplish it successfully. I loved the job, possibly because I felt needed and valued.

A couple of years later I saw my dad after he died, opening a door in my consciousness that would never be closed again…

CHAPTER 2

MY FATHER'S DEATH

In January 1968, I was 20 years of age when my father died of bowel cancer. It was a sad eighteen months prior to his death as we were never allowed to talk to him about his illness. Mum was adamant that neither the doctor nor any of the family was allowed to tell Dad, as she said he would drop his bundle. Sadly, I suspected that was not the reason at all. He was a very intelligent man. He was approximately 1.7 metres tall, solid build, grey hair with a receded hairline. Being unable to talk to Dad upset me as I wanted to tell him how much I loved and appreciated him. Watching a loved one deteriorate before your eyes is very difficult.

For a few days prior to his death, we all sat with Dad at the hospital every day while he lay in a coma, then on this particular night, we kissed him goodnight and left. After arriving home, I retired early to bed. My medium-sized bedroom held a single bed, dressing table and a built-in wardrobe. Besides a bedroom door, I had two French doors on the other side of the room that opened out onto an enclosed-back veranda with louvred windows across the length of the upper part of the wall. Being a warm summer's night I had the French doors and louvres open to capture any sea breeze that happened to find its way in. It was a clear night and beams of moonlight filtered in, creating a broken display of light on the floor and one wall of my room.

That night I experienced what I call my first vision-dream where

I seemed to be awake and asleep at the same time.

I saw my father, in his striped pyjamas, walk into our home straight through a large window at the front of our house into my parents' bedroom. He stood by the side of the bed, looking down at Mum. He then walked into my bedroom and stood at the end of my bed, staring at me and I saw myself sitting up in bed wearing cotton pyjamas and rollers in my hair, gazing back at him with my eyes wide open. Dad then walked into my sister's room, pausing there for a moment before leaving out the back of the house straight through a solid brick wall.

I came out of the vision-dream with a jolt. I went to sit up and realised I already was. I looked at my bedside clock. It read 4.06 a.m. I lay back down and promptly fell back asleep. The telephone woke us just after 6 a.m.; it was the hospital informing us that dad had died at approximately 4 a.m. It saddened me that no one was with him when he died. I now know from my own personal observations when supporting a dying person that there are always four angels (refer to chapter 47 – Roy's Passing) waiting to accompany them back home. I didn't see Dad again until 2004.

After his death, I realised he had been the only element of stability in my life, even though deep in my heart I felt I never really knew him. He kept to himself, working long hours to avoid my mother. He was a quiet unassuming man and was well-respected in the community. Behind closed doors and out of sight of family and friends, we lived in a turbulent environment.

I can only recall us having two family holidays together and the last one was the year I turned five. After that, Dad changed. He became withdrawn; he hardly spoke at home and never came away with us again. Dad would take me for a drive some Sundays; it was always just the two of us. I often wondered why. It was only after my mother's death in 1992 and a trip to England a few years later to meet Dad's family that I discovered Dad's secrets and all that was behind the animosity held between my parents: they had both, in different ways, betrayed each other.

Sitting in a park having lunch weeks later, I realised it was the first time I had seen someone who wasn't living anymore that I had known. That realisation caused me to question if there's more to life than just this external existence. That thought disturbed my indoctrinated beliefs and I quickly attempted to close the door on that idea as I had done previously. Even so, the impact of that thought continued niggling at my curious mind.

Despite my religious upbringing, I battled to close the door on the idea that life could possibly exist elsewhere other than the life I could see and touch in front of my eyes. I surmised it was possible that I believed the times I saw spiritual beings standing by my bed were not real, and I had left a door open to the idea that I had imagined them as Mum had told me. But seeing my father was different, he had physically lived and seeing him after he died etched a deep impression in my mind. I couldn't let go of this notion and it continued to infiltrate my thoughts. Even though the church spoke of angels, from my limited understanding they didn't mention that it's acceptable and logical for us humans on earth to see angels and people after they had passed over.

I read that people eons ago were condemned to death by the church for believing in anything that was not in accordance with their religious doctrines. I knew without a doubt I had seen Dad after he died; therefore, there had to be more to life than what I had been led to believe. Seeing Dad convinced me that I hadn't imagined the other encounters I experienced growing up either. Yet, my mind battled to move beyond the indoctrinated beliefs I inherited.

I tried to logically explain away these happenings but no matter how hard I tried they continued to torment my thoughts. I liked everything to fit neatly into a little box; I didn't like having unsolved questions hanging around me – it unnerved me. I felt out of control and insecure. I never invited these 'happenings' and I believed I would be a much happier person if they didn't occur. Even though Dad's death had opened a big door in my consciousness, one that would never be closed again, I shelved as best I could those niggling thoughts to the back of my mind.

Thinking back to my youth, I came to understand my mother was saddened by how her life had unfolded. Mum once told me that her father's sister, who was rich, asked her brother if she could pay for Mum to go to a London conservatory of music as Mum was very gifted on the piano. He refused to allow it.

Not long after Dad's death, my mother's pain from losing Dad and her inner struggles caused her to become even more resentful and bitter towards life in general.

My sister Nancy deeply loved Dad and only tolerated my mother for his sake. She told me once that Mum was a manipulator, but I couldn't see it back then. Nancy, a high school teacher, transferred to the country a great distance from home and Mum couldn't understand why she stopped having any contact with us after Dad died. My sister's decision triggered hostility within Mum and her outbursts and behaviour towards me escalated.

As an adult now, I can understand that Mum was hurting; she had not only lost her husband but she had also lost a daughter, and my heart went out to her as she feared losing me too.

My mother and I argued often, as she believed I didn't love her; sadly, she couldn't see that it wasn't true. All I desired was to voice my own individuality. I vacillated between loving and immensely disliking her and at times hating her, yet I couldn't turn my back on her, as my sister had done for her own survival, which I begrudgingly understood.

On rare occasions when I was extremely distressed, I felt two arms encircling me, and the hairs on my arms would stand up as goosebumps popped up all over my body. I liked to believe it was Dad comforting me, which left me with a smile on my face.

I understand now from experiencing the passing of other close family members that this sensation is definitely a spiritual being's vibrational presence touching me. A person's bodily reaction to these feelings is connected to our soul's energy body, which surrounds our physical body. When contact is made, it can cause a physical reaction such as goosebumps or shivers. Refer to chapter 63 – Sid's Farewell Hug.

I was 24 years old when I heard The Voice for the second time. I had hit rock bottom emotionally and life was a daily struggle. I desperately wanted freedom from the negative tormenting thoughts that bombarded me day and night. I was looking for a way to escape my pain by ending my life.

One lunch hour, I was standing at a crosswalk at a wide intersection in Perth CBD waiting for the lights to change. Glancing to the right, I saw a large, fully-loaded, fast-moving truck intent on making it through the green traffic lights before they changed. I thought, *all I have to do right now is just step out in front of this approaching truck and end it all. Go on do it. Do it! Just step forward right now. DO IT!*

At the precise moment I went to step forward onto the road The Voice spoke, distracting me… *'Yvonne, remember.'*

Only two words were spoken, yet, in that instant, I experienced the same sensations again as the Voice's vibration spread throughout my body. My memory flooded back to the previous encounter I experienced when I was seven years old. The vibrations touched my heart once again as they had done so long ago. Besides comforting me, it triggered a curiosity within me to understand how I came to hear and feel this Voice so strongly. The Voice had given me a reason to keep living. It had opened another door in my curious mind.

The following year I started questioning my family's hand-me-down beliefs and what my strict religious training had taught me. I realised as admirable as their view of life was, it was far too narrow a perspective of how I was literally seeing life.

By the age of 25, I was heading towards a successful career in the computer field for a very large well-known Australia-wide company. I discovered I had a gift for analysing a company's existing workflow systems to improve their efficiency as they prepared the transition from a manual system to computerisation. I worked with contracted consultants and computer programmers prior to the changeover, testing the new diverse programs before implementing the new systems. I was involved with the choice of a computer system to purchase after I found the courage to tell the accountant that I didn't believe the one they were going to purchase would be efficient enough to handle the workload.

This new and innovative system was later adopted interstate. I loved the work. My work colleagues nicknamed me 'Bubbles' as I always appeared happy and vibrant. On the surface, life was going well for me or so I thought.

When I was 27, suddenly overnight, my life took a turn for the worse. I went from a woman who appeared to be confident and somewhat carefree to a very frightened one. The door to the freedom I was enjoying slammed shut in my face. I kept up a persona as if I didn't have a care in the world, although it felt as if there were two very different people residing in my body, fighting with each other. The aftermath of my father's death and the build-up of negative emotions that my body had amassed and buried over the years, suddenly, without any warning, released their load, bringing on acute anxiety and terrifying panic attacks. I believed life was scary, the world a dangerous place and everyone was out to get me.

Over the past ten years, I had broken up with two wonderful men after they asked me to marry them. The first – we drifted apart after being together for five years. The second – I couldn't handle exposing my flaws to him. I had been living a lie.

I felt as if I might implode and I started having difficulty coping with how the tormenting fears affected me. I often felt extremely insecure and threatened in certain situations. For instance, I sometimes found it difficult to relax when I was sitting in a chair without side arms in the middle of a restaurant, surrounded by other patrons. I used to grip onto the sides of the seat with my fingers whenever I felt myself becoming dizzy and thought I might faint from the inner pressure that built up in my body. I preferred to sit with my back to a wall to feel secure and safe.

When I experienced moments of insecurity, I unconsciously triggered flashbacks of intense fear, overwhelming feelings of dread along with a deep sense of hopelessness. I had no idea what was causing these feelings to suddenly burst forth without warning, crippling my ability to function rationally at times. I couldn't see any logical reason for these occurrences.

I just wanted to scream and escape from my inner struggles. I added to my stress by not allowing anyone to know about my issues. I was so embarrassed and ashamed of what was happening to me. I hated myself immensely. My negative attitudes towards life started showing up in the form of small health issues.

One night my car was hit by a drunken driver, which resulted in severe whiplash, leading me to take a prescription relaxant tablet to reduce muscle contractions in my neck and back. I became addicted to the drug Serepax. I discovered these tablets helped me cope with my anxieties and the underlying discomfort I felt, especially when I was at a restaurant.

I kept up a facade at work and amongst friends that life was a breeze, creating even more inner stress. I slowly increased the dosage, blindly remaining ignorant of the effects the tablets were having on me. They became my crutch. I couldn't go anywhere without having them on hand. If I did forget, I panicked and would have to return home to collect them.

A few months before my 28th birthday, I started to seriously question my life and the teachings handed down to me. I had no intention of turning my back on The Voice – that door remained open. I still yearned to understand how I came to hear it. On the two occasions I'd heard The Voice, the words spoken felt so very loving and kind.

I recalled reading that many people were persecuted and some burnt to death by churches in a long-ago era when their beliefs differed from the strict religious doctrine of those days. I could see the connection between my dilemma back then and the people who were persecuted. I realised my indoctrinated religious beliefs were my mother's inherited concept of religion and misconstrued as true, as were some churches' beliefs long ago. My past beliefs no longer fitted with how I was 'literally' seeing life.

While typing this, I feel a surge of heartfelt compassion for the younger me, her inner struggles and her bravery by choosing to pursue her own concepts about life.

Thank goodness, the days of the hellfire and brimstone approach to religion are mostly a thing of the past. Many, like me, were part of an era that was coming from an overzealous approach in their desire to save us. Unfortunately, my mind still clung on to a negatively ingrained view of life and beliefs that had been instilled into me that I couldn't shake off.

I still had many issues to resolve and I needed space to unravel my confused religious beliefs and the inner turmoil I experienced daily. In order to create the space I desperately needed, I made a big decision that I knew would bring consequences, yet at the same time, it opened another door in my life…

It's our beliefs that can hinder or free our soul.
It's our own understandings and choices in life
that can expand or stagnate our growth.
It's our acceptance of inner guidance that can
enhance our experiences.
It's Spirit's vibrational presence within and around
us freely offering support when we choose to listen
to the inner Voice of wisdom and truth.

Yvonne Fogarty

CHAPTER 3

STEPPING OUT

I was pondering over how to untangle my confused beliefs, how to decide my truths for me and how they may differ from what had been instilled in me. I needed to spread my wings and investigate whatever was behind our existence and change my outlook on life to a more positive one. That thought excited me and also filled me with fear of the repercussions I might encounter by taking such a bold action.

I found a lovely two-bedroom apartment with a balcony and views of Perth city and informed my mother of my decision to move out of home. Having to wait a week until my apartment was ready was difficult. Mum was extremely angry and upset. The night before I moved out, she informed me to take all my belongings; I wasn't to leave anything behind.

The following weeks were heart-wrenching. At first, my mother disowned me, refusing to have any contact with me. If I rang to check on her, as soon as she heard my voice, she would hang up. I stopped calling, which left me feeling torn inside with guilt.

Then Mum began telephoning me at work every day, chastising me and asking, 'What have I done to deserve such a selfish and ungrateful daughter as you? You are no good.' Then she would slam the phone down, causing pain in my ear. Her cutting words and actions caused me to feel sick and disloyal, like an ungrateful daughter. Guilt would wash over me.

I had been called to a meeting and a work colleague Ann Thompson walked into my office to see me as my telephone rang. She picked up the receiver and before she could say anything my mother began her daily ranting, unaware it wasn't me on the other end of the phone. When I returned to my office, Ann was waiting, her face full of concern.

'What's wrong?' I asked.

Ann turned, closing my office door. Turning back, she said, 'I answered your phone and heard your mother yelling abuse, thinking it was you.'

'Oh,' I said. 'I'm sorry you had to hear that.'

'How long has this been going on?' Ann asked.

My eyes welled up. 'Since I moved out, nine weeks ago.'

I moved past Ann to sit behind my desk and collapsed into my chair, feeling exhausted.

'Ann, I had to move out for my own sanity. I feared I might end up having a nervous breakdown if I had stayed.'

'Yvonne, that's mental abuse! Don't allow yourself to be a scapegoat for someone else's unhappiness any longer, do something about it.'

Ann's words stunned me. I couldn't see at the time that what I was experiencing was actually mental abuse. How could I not have seen that? It had always been a part of my life. I didn't know any different. Funny how these things just become 'normal' until you realise they are not!

Pondering over what Ann had said to me, I realised I had allowed myself to become a doormat. I likened myself to a short spindly weed being blown about in all directions by the wind. I needed to learn to stand firmly in my own power.

Reflecting back as I type this: the mental abuse was aimed at controlling me and came from a sense of need.

I felt for Mum. It took all my courage to disobey her. Eventually Mum realised I had no intention of backing down and finally accepted my decision and our relationship became somewhat amicable.

I had a belief in my little screwed-up head that I had to 'obey' everyone else first, ignoring my own needs and when I didn't comply, I felt guilty. The word obey kept niggling at me. I checked a dictionary, discovering the word 'obey' also means *'honouring yourself, obeying unselfishly the highest good for you in a situation'*. In certain circumstances it means, saying 'no' to a loved one. Gradually I learned to listen to the voice in my heart and know whether to say yes or no.

I realised only I could deal with my past instead of expecting everyone else to fix my problems for me; otherwise, I may have stayed on a pathway towards self-destruction.

Within a few months of moving out, I found a psychologist to support me regarding my anger, resentment and the overwhelming feelings of guilt I carried, believing I was a bad person. I was an expert actress at hiding my inner problems – only Ann and another friend knew of my struggles. I perceived myself to be weak because I had an addiction to a relaxant drug and suffered from severe anxiety attacks. While I have always been a deep thinker, I appeared shallow to many friends and lived on the surface of life. I laughed and joked a lot, pretending life was easy. I made sure I always appeared perfect on the outside; I wore mostly designer clothing, my accessories were always coordinated and very stylish, my hair immaculate. All with the aim of hiding my flaws – to convince everyone I was okay and had my life together.

I realised years later that hiding my anxiety from others only caused me more anxiety. It's not a weakness, as I used to believe, to speak about my affliction. It actually shows strength, courage and honesty.

I know now that our appearance doesn't define us; for me, it was camouflage. I felt like such a hypocrite and that truly bothered me. I desired to be the same person, inside and out. I was tired and fed up with living a lie. In saying that, these days I still enjoy wearing coordinated outfits; the difference now is my decision to do so is coming from choice not insecurity.

After a year I stopped seeing the psychologist because I sensed I was ready to continue alone. I slowly commenced working on my misperceptions, one at a time. The false beliefs I inherited began nudging at the door of my heart to be acknowledged and transformed to resonate with my inherent nature.

Why did my misperceptions start showing up? Firstly, I made a conscious choice to take sole responsibility for my life by re-evaluating all my beliefs and stop blaming everything and everyone else for my problems, expecting others to fix my life for me.

Secondly, the strong desire I harboured to heal my life grew in intensity, encouraging me to 'let go' of the pains I held onto. I realised I had used my pain as a crutch, an excuse to blame others for my unhappiness and hide from the world. In a nutshell, I saw myself as a victim.

Thirdly, the best decision I made was to connect within asking for inner spiritual guidance to assist me. The false beliefs and negative behaviour patterns niggling at me were not mine to own. They were inherited.

Why did these false perceptions start nudging me for attention? Because my desire for inner freedom was stronger than my desire to hang on to them any longer. I set to work dealing with them one at a time.

The 'hare' disappeared and the 'tortoise' took over as I slowly plodded along, dealing with each distorted belief as they rose up for a shift of perception to take place. I still had many (that's putting it mildly) personal issues to unravel yet; this next stage of my journey excited me.

Why? Because I no longer saw myself as a 'victim' of my circumstances. I'd turned a corner, opening another door. I had 'taken charge' of my life and started reaping the benefits from my earlier decisions.

Slowly I began experiencing the odd joyful and spontaneous

moment. In those moments there was no need to pretend I was happy; it flowed forth naturally. Seeing and experiencing the results of my inner work spurred me on and I was determined to overcome my issues using inner guidance alone.

I commenced meditating daily. I would direct my conversation within, focusing on my heart, as if I was chatting with my best friend. Then I would sit in silent appreciation for a few minutes, knowing I had been heard. In the past when praying for guidance, focused out there in space, I was looking for answers outside of myself (an old childhood pattern).

Sometimes, in the shower or when doing some menial task, an idea would pop into my mind in answer to a request for guidance. Or occasionally the small voice of intuition would speak to me quietly in my heart, giving encouragement or guidance. The more I opened up listening to the inner guidance my efforts to heal my life became exciting... I was growing in self-confidence.

I read some self-help books. Two books in particular helped me considerably. One was Louise Hay's book 'You Can Heal Your Life'. That wonderful book took me a long time to read. It stirred up issues that required addressing and some issues were confronting to face.

The other book was 'Creative Visualization' by Shakti Gawain. That book explained that we are creative beings. I never knew we could direct our life by using our focused intention coupled with Spirit's attributes to support us in creating and manifesting the life we desired to experience. E.g. refer to chapter 24 – Why We Ask Three Times and chapter 48 – Manifesting a Heart's Desire.

That focusing technique opened another door; I realised I alone had the power within me to create the life I desired. Both books complemented each other beautifully.

Each time, I cleared a false belief about myself; I emerged a little stronger. Through my perseverance, I made a wonderful discovery: I wasn't a 'selfish and no good' person as I had been told and believed.

My close friends had been telling me for years that I was a loving and kind person, yet I hadn't been able to see it for myself. The false perceptions deep in my mind had blocked my ability to clearly see this truth for myself. I still hadn't come to accept that I was a kind person as a truth deep in my heart. I hadn't anchored that truth as a deep inner knowing and cleared the root cause.

There is a big difference between knowing 'of' something (head knowledge) and knowing something as truth and internalising and embodying it, leaving no room for any doubt. Heart knowledge empowers and uplifts us; it's a very different vibration. When my soul resonates with the frequency and vibration as a truth and aligns with my inherent nature, I feel lighter and joyful. Heart knowledge is a positive comforting vibration.

Whenever I grasped a new concept with clarity by changing a false perception to truth for me, it automatically resonated deep within my whole being and I grew internally stronger. I felt encouraged even though I was still taking relaxant tablets to calm my anxiety and panic attacks. The inner guidance became easier to hear. I gradually discovered life was stimulating, exciting and fun. What a turnaround! I was able to clear some issues easily while other more ingrained patterns were a much bigger challenge and I struggled at times to cope with the turmoil and buried feelings of panic that rose up from deep inside me during the process.

When I noticed myself being drawn into the turmoil, I imagined myself taking a gigantic step back in my mind where I could 'observe' the uncomfortable feelings that rose up without getting hooked in by their strong negative emotional pull. Sometimes I forgot and I activated umpteen negative thoughts and I was drawn into them, feeling as if they were real and true. The key here is to remember to observe the discomfort and not tune into it.

I used to believe because I experienced these strong feelings and beliefs that I owned them and they were there to stay. Not true.

They were only a protective belief pattern formed when young in my subconscious mind and I knew I now had the ability to change any thought I chose, by 'inserting' a new thought. Our soul knows the vibrational difference between a truth and a falsehood. A falsehood carries a low vibrational disturbing energy pattern.

I remember one particular morning when I suddenly had a wonderful 'aha' moment. A big smile spread across my face when I realised I was 'not' my thoughts, I was only 'experiencing' these repetitive thoughts as they flowed in and out of my conscious awareness and when I stopped believing in these negative belief patterns, they slowly lost their power over me.

Why does a false belief appear to become stronger after a decision is made to transform it or let it go? A psychologist friend once told me that this inner resistance happens when a conditioned belief, a mentally formed belief pattern is rising up from our subconscious to the surface of our awareness for refining that distorted belief. It's exciting when we see a distorted belief through new eyes and our soul's energy body responds and our physical body feels lighter.

I used to believe the old pattern was fighting for survival, causing me grief. No! Not at all. From my experience, it is simply a natural part of my healing process. Although at the time it can feel as if the opposite is true, and a battle is going on within. I had to continually remind myself each time a distorted belief rose up to only observe the disturbing feelings and not get hooked by paying attention to the uncomfortable feelings.

Why? Because energy will follow our thought.

I had a strong belief that I was unlovable. To support myself to change that distorted belief, I commenced saying an affirmation every time I looked in a mirror, to reinforce a new belief pattern, such as I love you instead of I hate you. (Keep affirmations very simple.) At first, I would hear my mind answering back immediately with comments like, *That's not true, it's a lie. You are a monster.* Or *no, you don't love yourself; you hate yourself. You are a bad person.* Refer to chapter 8 – Rebirth.

These mental comments caused a deep disturbance within me and a strong resistance would rise up. I persisted and one morning, I looked at myself in the mirror and I realised I wasn't repulsed by what I saw anymore. I knew I had begun making inroads towards accepting and loving myself.

A couple of weeks later before leaving for work, I stood in front of the mirror to say my affirmation with conviction and I was overjoyed to hear myself reply, *Yes.* When that happens it's a wonderful joyful feeling and most of all you know without any doubt that you have spoken and heard the truth reflected back to you at your 'level of understanding' at that time.

Reflecting back over the years, when I was working on changing a deeply ingrained issue, e.g. loving myself, I felt I was clearing the same issue repeatedly, even though I thought I had cleared it months or years earlier. Please do not get discouraged if this process happens to you; it's because some issues are not only deeply ingrained, but they can also be multi-layered, requiring each layer to be removed gently until the root core of the belief is exposed and cleared. In my situation, clearing this issue became a very slow process. Our inner guidance knows and does not give us more to cope with than what we are capable of handling at any one time. I learnt to be patient trusting the process.

In 1978, aged 30, I had broken down my shell of protection enough to face life head-on; I discovered life was so much fun, although I still battled internally with panic attacks in certain situations. I bought a small house and continued playing squash and netball, travelling abroad yearly and dabbling in interior decorating when work allowed. It felt great to be alive and embracing life again.

During an overseas trip in late 1978, I met my future husband Graham. We were both part of a large group of about 60, made up of Australian rules football umpires, wives, girlfriends and hangers-on:

'me'. I was invited to go along by a female work colleague who asked me to accompany her sister on a trip to Malaysia and Hong Kong.

The men were playing their own version of volleyball in the pool of our hotel in Penang against the women. I was enjoying a leisurely swim when I saw the ball heading towards a garden bed behind me. I jumped up, flicking the ball back to them, and continued swimming.

'Hawk eye' (I still call him that at times) Graham, swam over to me and said, 'You can put that away any time you like.'

I looked down to where he was looking and to my horror, one of my boobs (most definitely a size 32 now) was floating on top of the water. One breast had popped out of the top of my bikini when I'd stretched for the ball.

Later, we had a drink together and Graham commented, 'You punched me on my arm and told me off and all I was innocently attempting to do was save your dignity.'

'Really, is that right? Well, if that was your intention, why were you smirking?'

'I didn't see myself smirking. I was simply being a gentleman.'

I chuckled.

We became friends 'without benefits', catching up occasionally for a drink or if we were without a partner for a function.

Four years later, our friendship deepened, and we became very good friends 'with benefits'.

One evening I rang Graham at his home (20-plus kilometres away from me), asking him if he wouldn't mind coming over for a 'sleepover'. Of course, what hot-blooded male could refuse such an invite? He was extremely accommodating by very quickly agreeing. When he arrived, I explained to Graham my gift and that I had begun having more episodes of seeing deceased family members when they passed over. I told him I had an uneasy feeling and I didn't want to be alone tonight as I still feared seeing a spiritual being.

We were sitting enjoying a glass of wine when I suddenly saw my aunty (who was in the hospital) appear in front of me before quickly disappearing. I jumped up, telling Graham 'I think my aunty has just died.' Although he appeared calm, I suspect he may have felt a little rattled by it. A short time later my uncle rang, informing me she had died.

A year later, seeing a spiritual being saved our lives…

*There is a vibrant reality beyond this physical world
and we all belong to it.*

Yvonne Fogarty

CHAPTER 4

A LIFE-CHANGING EXPERIENCE

During the month of August 1983, Graham and I had both been extremely busy with our professions and decided a week's holiday away together was what we both needed. We each lived in our own homes, both of which were mortgaged, so where we chose to go was determined by our budget. We decided on a beachside holiday town about 600 kilometres north of our home city Perth, Western Australia.

We were experiencing a pleasant spring and the thought of lying on a beach, soaking in the sun and doing some fishing, amongst other 'activities', sounded wonderful. We decided to leave for our trip around 1.30 a.m., travelling throughout the night so we would arrive in the morning and have the whole day ahead of us to enjoy.

I arrived at Graham's house early in the evening. His sister Lorraine King was staying with him at the time and with Graham out at a meeting, I proceeded to sort out our food. I turned to walk out of the kitchen and stopped in amazement at what I saw forming…

A mass of white snow appeared (like what was visible on an old analogue television screen) a few feet in front of me. The energy was swirling noiselessly and excitedly as it developed rapidly in size and shape. The more it expanded, a sense of peace surrounded me. The energy changed and in front of me stood an elderly man. So real I could have reached out and touched him. He was dressed in old-fashioned khaki shorts and a short-sleeved shirt. He looked at me then moved his head slightly to one side, placed the palm of his right hand under his chin, bringing his left hand over in front of his body, supporting his raised right elbow. His movements appeared to have a definite purpose to them. Then as quickly as he had appeared, the energy began shrinking as he slowly disappeared, until all I could see were his sandalled feet until they too disappeared.

Even after the man had vanished, surprisingly I still felt very calm and peaceful, which was the exact opposite of what I usually felt when I 'saw' things, as my mind struggled to grasp logically what had just taken place.

Unbeknownst to me, Lorraine had been standing watching my face from the passageway. 'Yvonne, what have you just seen? You look alarmed.'

'I'm finding it very hard to comprehend what just happened. A man formed in front of me. He looked just as real as you do,' I replied, shaking my head in bewilderment.

'Do you know him?'

'I have never seen this man before and it's the first time I've experienced a spiritual being manifest this way.'

After I described him, Lorraine explained that she had felt that an energy has been present in the house for the last few days. While Lorraine did not 'see' the same way I did, she had a strong intuition and was very open-minded to things that could not be explained.

In the past when I had seen someone who had passed over, other than my occasional night visitors, it was usually a loved one and in those instances, their form appeared quickly before disappearing. But never before had I seen swirling energy manifest into a person in front of me, especially a person I didn't know. I still inwardly struggled to accept these happenings. I still had a fear of the unknown, especially a new experience like this one. This experience was very different to what I had been used to seeing. My stomach churned. Even though I had grown in understanding, I obviously still held doubts in my mind about whether these beings were coming from good or bad energy.

When Graham arrived home, I told him about the incident. He just shrugged his shoulders and treated it with scepticism. I could understand his reaction and I accepted his approach without question or frustration. Well, perhaps I was a little disappointed.

We lay down to rest before heading out on our seven-hour journey, the subject closed for Graham at least and he quickly fell asleep. My mind was far too active to sleep. I kept asking myself, *Did I imagine this? Did it really happen? Am I going crazy?* I couldn't rest as I kept replaying the incident over and over until I woke Graham at 1.15 a.m. We packed up the car, said goodbye to Lorraine and settled ourselves in for the journey.

As Graham reversed his car out of the driveway, the hairs on my arms stood up and goosebumps covered my body. I intuitively turned my head in the direction of the back seat. There he was again. The same man I had seen earlier and he was looking directly at me.

Darn it, I thought. I quickly turned back around. I didn't know whether to say anything to Graham or not because he might think I was crazy. Even I was beginning to question my sanity. I didn't have that all-important ring on my finger yet either. I wondered if there was a danger of scaring Graham off if I pointed out that there was a man sitting in the back seat of his car.

Then a thought flashed into my mind: *I have to be myself if I intend to spend the rest of my life with this man; I cannot hide anything from him, no matter how incomprehensible it might seem to him.*

I attempted to soften the impact by cautiously and slowly saying, 'Darlinnggg.'

Graham picked up on the tone of my voice and answered, 'Yesssss, what is it?'

'Well, you know that man I told you about earlier, well... err... mm, he's sitting in the back seat,' I blurted out nervously.

I saw Graham's shoulders tense as his hands gripped tighter on the steering wheel. He took in a deep breath before glancing in the rear vision mirror. Of course, he didn't see anything. Then when I looked around again, I didn't see anything either. The man had once again disappeared.

Graham sighed, and with the great dry sense of humour that endeared him to me, said, 'That's okay, I won't charge him petrol money.'

We both laughed and relaxed as the tension subsided. As I sank back into the seat, the understanding as to why I had seen him came tumbling into my mind. It was a warning of danger ahead. 'Graham, we have to be extra careful on the road tonight; I think we are in danger, that's why I've seen him. Even though you find it difficult to accept what I have seen, please stay extra alert.'

It was an overcast night – not one star was visible and there were no streetlights to illuminate the dark country road. The only indication of the direction the road curved were the strategically placed reflectors on each side of the road, red on the left and white on the right-hand side.

About 50 minutes into our journey, Graham asked me to turn on the interior light and look at the road map to give him an indication of how far we still had to travel before we turned off onto the highway that would take us all the way to our destination.

Oh, this is a challenge, I thought. I am not very good at reading road maps. I attempted to look intelligent as I studied the road directory. (I wish we had a GPS in our car back then). Finding the correct page was easy, yet none of it made any sense. Unfortunately, navigational skills are not one of my attributes.

I started to mumble some words to give the impression that I could navigate when all of a sudden Graham yelled out, 'Yvonne, turn off the interior light, quick, turn it off.'

As I did so, Graham brought the car to a sudden stop. The road directory fell to the floor as my hands flew to the dashboard to help brace myself against a possible impact. I scanned the road ahead; I couldn't make out anything untoward. I continued to stare out through the windscreen, searching the road for the cause of our abrupt stop. As my eyesight adjusted, I saw something moving in front of our car as a form slowly began taking shape. All I could make out at first was the outline of what looked like a pendulum swinging from side to side. As the whole image came into focus, there, standing in the middle of the road was a black cow swishing its tail as it turned its head back around again, looking curiously at us.

I love cows.

'Oh no!' I said. 'What are you doing standing on the road? You're a naughty girl. You could have been killed.' Then it dawned on me and I added quietly, 'Oh! We could have been killed too.'

I could see her huge beautiful brown eyes still looking back at us, happily chewing her cud. We both took a deep breath and sank back into our seats. Neither of us spoke for a few seconds then we looked at each other, realising just how close we had come to possibly becoming tomorrow's news, informing the public of a fatality on our roads overnight. If we had hit the cow at the maximum speed of 110 kilometres per hour we were travelling, we most likely would have been killed. Glancing around at our surroundings, I saw many large gum trees close to the winding road.

'Yvonne, I didn't see the cow. The only reason I stopped was because the white reflection I saw bouncing off the cow's eye didn't appear to be in continuity with the reflectors on the right-hand side posts,' Graham explained, his voice still sounding shaky from the near miss.

I truly believe, because of the warning, Graham's awareness was heightened; he was fully alert and concentrating on the road. After my legs stopped shaking and my heartbeat slowed, I tapped the cow on its rump as I used to do on my cousin's farm and shooed it off the road and we recommenced our journey. As our car started gathering speed, I suddenly saw a bright white light appear down the centre of the road before vanishing into the horizon.

'We were very lucky, weren't we?' Graham said softly.

'Yes,' I said, then quickly changed tack. 'Actually, luck didn't have anything to do with it; we were being protected by a spiritual being.' I told Graham what I had just seen appear before me. I stretched over the console and planted a big kiss on his cheek. 'We are out of danger now; we're not meant to become angels just yet.'

We finally arrived at the junction and turned left towards the resort town of Kalbarri. We weaved our way down the long winding road catching glimpses of the ocean. It was just before 9 a.m. when we tuned the car radio to the regional station.

As we got closer, refreshing sea air filled our nostrils. Rounding the bend, we saw the clean white sandy foreshore with the waves creeping back and forth cooling the already warming sand. The sun was bouncing sunbeams off the water; it looked very enticing and we looked forward to having a swim until we heard the lead news on the radio. We both gasped in horror and pulled the car over to the side of the road. Sadly, a young male motorcyclist had been killed instantly after hitting a cow on a dark stretch of road in the early morning. We heard the tragedy happened not long after we had travelled through that same section of road.

'The cow must have moved back onto the road,' I murmured.

We both felt extremely sad at the loss of a young life as thoughts plagued our minds with 'what if' scenarios.

Upon our return to Perth, we told Lorraine about the incident. Within a short time, it was soon forgotten as our lives were once again consumed by our professions.

A few weeks later at Graham's house, I sat down to enjoy a chat and coffee with Lorraine. During our chat, Lorraine remembered she had been meaning to show me the family photo album. 'Have a look through this album and meet our relatives.'

As I studied the photos in the album, unbeknownst to me, Lorraine was watching my face for any reaction. I came upon a photo of a group of three elderly men. My eyes widened. I had difficulty believing what I was seeing. I quickly sat forward. My voice sometimes goes up an octave when I become excited and I squeaked, 'That's him, Lorraine. That's the man I saw before we left for our holiday.'

'Yes, I thought it might be him from the way you described him to me.' Her face was full of acceptance.

'And Lorraine, his hands and arms are in the same position in the photo, just as he had demonstrated when he was standing in front of me. And he's wearing shorts with a short-sleeve shirt.'

It was Graham's Uncle Tom who had died many years before.

I do not believe in coincidences in life and after that incident where a spiritual being intervened, Graham simply accepted that there was more to life than what he had previously been aware of. I, on the other hand, still struggled to accept it. It frustrated me that Graham just accepted and got on with his life. Even though I knew I 'saw' things, I still battled internally to accept anything that I couldn't logically understand.

These happenings played havoc with my brain, leaving my analytical mind baffled. I didn't like having unexplained incidents in my life. I felt out of control because I couldn't easily explain them away. Another reason I believe I had difficulty accepting these happenings was because these experiences came through me. Ugh!

Why? Because I struggled to believe in myself. On the other hand, I definitely believed there was a spiritual power supporting me to heal my life and I was so grateful for the warning that saved our lives. Although I had done so much self-growth work, some residue of fear still remained deep within my psyche.

In hindsight, I now know these firmly embedded fears were connected to not one, but three traumas I experienced over a long period of time.

CHAPTER 5

WITH THIS RING

When Graham asked me to marry him in October 1983, I eagerly responded with an excited 'YES!' After the excitement wore off, I became confused and afraid of commitment.

Upon arriving home from work one evening, I kicked off my shoes, padded across the carpet, put on a Richard Clayderman album, went into the kitchen to the refrigerator and retrieved the block of Cadbury's hazelnut chocolate kept for emergency situations. I lay down on one of my two large sofas in the lounge room, placing a cushion behind my head and the chocolate within easy reach on the coffee table. I asked myself *why am I afraid to marry him?* I knew I loved him so what was my problem? Why the hesitation?

I sent out a plea for help to The Voice asking the question out loud. 'Please indicate to me clearly if I am to marry him?'

A while later whilst munching on the chocolate, savouring the taste of the combined flavours one bite at a time, I sensed a stillness emerging from deep within my heart and The Voice came through so powerfully that the words again vibrated throughout my body.

'Yes, Yvonne.'

The powerful response from The Voice took me by surprise and I sensed a presence in the room. I felt the presence so strongly, I was too scared to open my eyes in case I saw a spiritual being standing near me.

I thought to myself, *Oh no, here I go again. This fear of the unknown is raising its head.* I quickly placed my hands on my stomach in an attempt to give comfort to the now-familiar sickening reaction I experienced when I was scared. I logically knew clearing some misperceptions could be a slow process and seeing spiritual beings occasionally still affected me, more so if I was alone.

I waited a couple of minutes before opening my eyes and quickly looking around. I was relieved to see no one standing in the room, the sun had crept out from behind the clouds and its rays were streaming in through my large lounge room window. Since a child whenever the sun found its way into my bedroom, I believed its warm rays had come to comfort me.

Putting what was left of the chocolate aside, I quickly sat up as clarity came into my awareness as to why I had hesitated to get married. It had nothing to do with my relationship with Graham at all – it all stemmed back to my home life and the verbal abuse experienced in our home.

My thoughts drifted back to our home and I recalled a vivid image of Mum just before she let her fury loose. She would clench her jaw and purse her lips tightly together. It wasn't so much her actions as the scary tone and loudness of her voice that caused me to shudder and feel frightened, especially when her words were extremely hurtful and belittling to hear, causing me to feel insecure and worthless.

Her harsh words were coming from her own undealt with issues or from jealousy, causing her to feel out of control, resulting in her speaking so cruelly at times. This often happened after my boyfriend said goodnight and left to go home. Sadly, because those words came from my mother, I believed what she said about me must be true. 'You are not good enough for him. He will dump you.'

Isn't it interesting how buried memories can suddenly pop up, bringing confusion and hesitancy with them, resulting in us having second thoughts regarding a good decision we have made?

Our marriage in June 1984 opened a door for both of our careers, setting in motion a chain of events that would totally change the direction of both our lives and where we were to reside in the future. We sold both our homes and within a year we had built our dream home in a new subdivision in a lovely undulating area south of Perth city, Western Australia, with a park adjacent to our property.

Three years later our family had quickly grown to six. No! I definitely didn't give birth to two sets of twins. Sharing our home with us were our four beautiful fur children – two Lhasa Apso dogs, Kouchi and Sharza and two cats, Cammy and Sasha.

Our dogs Kouchi and Sharza loved running through the natural bushland, exploring and enjoying a sense of freedom, and often our cats would jump over our back fence, joining us on our walks around the neighbourhood. When our neighbours saw the cats walking alongside the dogs, they were amused at the sight. On rare occasions, Cammy would take over holding Kouchi's lead, carrying it in her mouth until we arrived home.

Cammy, who was only a few months old when Kouchi came along at six weeks of age, had taken on the task of washing Kouchi's face after every meal. If Kouchi objected, Cammy would clamp her paw down more firmly on top of Kouchi's head. They also used to sit on a window ledge together, catching moths until Kouchi got bigger and fell off whenever she tried to swipe at a moth. When Sharza came along nearly three years later, Kouchi took it upon herself to wash Sharza's face, which became a more frustrating task as Sharza grew bigger.

I had commenced writing down all my experiences and feelings. One evening I wrote that through my past experiences, I had withdrawn, shutting myself away from the world to protect myself from harm. When Graham came into my life, I felt a part of me was slowly emerging from my cocoon of protection.

I commenced writing the date and time on each box of Serepax tablets when newly opened. I made sure it lasted longer than the previous box. Even if only by an hour at first. Gradually one box lasted me a year. Through this transformation, I was slowly able to get my dependency on the tablets reduced to only requiring a tablet on rare occasions. A few months after stopping the tablets I could feel an inner disturbance building up within me as if I wanted to break free of something. The cause of that disturbance wasn't uncovered until later.

CHAPTER 6

TRAPPED BETWEEN WORLDS

In 1986 I changed companies, becoming the manager of information systems for a large diverse organisation. My immediate boss, the managing director, requested the company's accountant and I go to Adelaide to check out Point of Sale software, which was recommended by our consultant for one division of the company.

After spending a few days outside of Adelaide observing this particular software in action and after many meetings with consultants, we concluded we had seen and gained enough information to satisfy us. We were both happy to finally be returning home the next afternoon in time to spend the weekend with our families.

After dinner, we returned to our rooms in the motel. I was eager to quiet my mind from all the conversations and ideas floating around in my head. I sat on the bed meditating for quite a long time.

I turned off the light and settled down to sleep. I woke up suddenly, rolling onto my left side and turning my head slightly to the right before opening my eyes. By the side of my bed, I once again saw energy swirling around excitedly before a young man formed in front of me. He was maybe in his late twenties, tall, with short dark brown hair. He just stood there wearing long trousers and an open-neck long sleeve shirt. His head was bent down and his eyes were closed. I sensed a deep sadness around him, and then, as quickly as he had formed, he disappeared.

Oh s... I thought. *I don't need this right now.* With my heart thumping in my chest I lay back down, leaving my bedside lamp on all night. I tossed and turned – sleep was spasmodic as seeing spiritual beings still scared me.

The next morning, we had one more business meeting in Adelaide prior to flying home. When checking out, I was tempted to ask if someone had died in that room and I quickly disregarded that idea as the company's accountant was standing next to me.

After returning home I was unable to shake the image of the young man from my mind. At odd moments he would come into my awareness and I could still sense a deep sadness around him. I wondered what had happened to him. Had he committed suicide? Was he murdered? Did he die from an illness?

After two weeks of having his image coming in and out of my mind, I went to see an acquaintance, Ron, a psychic, who had been attempting to help me gain more understanding of life beyond our physical world.

I walked up the pathway to Ron's open front door where he greeted me warmly and showed me into his meditation room. Ron was English and very handsome with thick wavy black hair.

I sat down and Ron could see I was twisting my hands together nervously. He gently said, 'Why don't you tell me what's troubling you?'

I explained the spooky experience to Ron with a shaky voice and said that I thought he was still around me somehow and it was spooking me.

'Is that possible or am I imagining his presence? Sometimes I think I am going crazy having these experiences.'

'There is nothing to be afraid of, Yvonne, and stop thinking you are crazy. You are not. You have a strong connection to the other side and it shows in your energy body.'

'I truly wish I didn't see things; I don't like these experiences happening to me.'

'Your connection is there for a reason and eventually, you'll understand.' He sat very still, looking at me for some time through his penetrating deep blue eyes.

Finding his stare quite unnerving, I squirmed in my seat, looking anywhere except at him.

Then he spoke, still looking at me intensely as if he could see right through me. 'I'm going to give you the telephone number of a friend of mine – Ruth. I think she can help you.'

'Why do I need to go and see this person?'

'Yvonne, please promise me you will go and have a chat with her. She may be able to help you.'

When I went to see Ruth, she told me she was a medium and straight away her words unnerved me. My brain connected with the word medium and the associated word that popped into my mind was 'evil'! I felt extremely uncomfortable; I had never met a medium before. Ron was the only spooky person I knew. After sharing my experience and feelings regarding this young man, Ruth shocked me by describing him to me.

I raised my eyebrows, saying in a surprised voice, 'Yes, that's him.' Then I leaned forward, whispering, 'How do you know what he looks like?' I guess I whispered because I didn't want him hearing me. Duh!

'He is standing right behind you.'

Yikes. I was already on edge! That did it, I freaked. I jumped up out of the chair and grabbed my handbag, ready to bolt out the door.

Ruth quickly stood up. 'Yvonne, Yvonne, please sit back down and relax, there is nothing to be afraid of. The spiritual being will not harm you; he is seeking help.'

My mind began quickly replaying all the scary movies I used to watch with girlfriends, with our eyes half-hidden behind cushions. 'Well, I'm sorry but let him seek help elsewhere, not through me.' Then I felt mean for having such a thought and I reluctantly sat back down.

'You have a wrong impression of a spiritual being.'

I sure have, I thought. I guess I had images of a spiritual being jumping out in front of me, waving their hands around, screaming *boooooo!* I was truly freaked out at her words that a spiritual being had attached itself to me and what made it worse, I could 'sense' his presence.

'I have enough of a challenge accepting seeing spiritual beings appear occasionally but this is a new experience, that's why I'm frightened. It has truly upset me.'

'I can see that. He has attached himself to you because of your strong light and connection to the other side. He committed suicide and is trapped between worlds, and he knew through the strong light around your vibration, he could move on.'

By the time she had finished explaining this to me, I was feeling lightheaded and dizzy and I started perspiring.

Then she casually said, 'Let's pray.'

This woman prays! I thought.

Ruth prayed out loud, calling for Jesus to come forward and take his hand and guide him home. When she finished praying, she said, 'Jesus came and guided him to the Light. He's home now.'

My religious upbringing kicked in. Jesus was sacred and wouldn't just appear like that. I admit thinking at the time *Gee, I thought I was crazy; this woman is a real weirdo!*

The experience was way beyond my capability to accept or understand. I seriously doubted if what she said and did was even true. Before I left, I asked her why I have this so-called connection to the other side when I am scared of it and I prefer not to have it.

Ruth became very quiet for a while, deep in thought, before answering. 'I believe it's connected to your future work. I am not to tell you what it is. It is for you to grow towards it yourself.'

I let her words wash over me because my work was in the computer field and I couldn't see any connection.

The next evening, I told Graham about the whole experience over dinner.

He looked at me and said, 'I think you're overthinking this.'

'Really! I wonder how you would handle seeing a spiritual being and having him hang around you all day, then hear a woman call Jesus forth.'

'Yvonne, listen to me, just put aside your conversation with the woman and—'

I felt my face go red. I raised my voice, saying, 'It's easy for you to say. You weren't there and I was frightened by the experience. This has really unnerved me, love. Do you und—'

Graham put his hand up firmly in front of me to stop me rambling on. 'Yvonne, stop. Please let me finish what I started to say.'

I huffed and puffed.

'Listen to me,' he said. 'Take a deep breath and tell me how you're feeling right now, not what you're thinking.'

'Huh,' I replied.

'How are you feeling now, compared to before when you visited the woman?'

'Ohh!' That stopped me huffing and puffing. *Good question*, I thought. I sat back, focusing in on myself, realising the sadness and heaviness I felt around me had gone.

'I feel light again,' I admitted very reluctantly. 'And he isn't coming in and out of my mind. I am only reminding myself of the incident, not sensing him anymore.'

'Uhh well, that answers it then, discussion finished,' he said, all matter-of-fact (Graham is a very pragmatic person), which of course annoyed me. He stood up, pushed his chair back and left the table heading towards his office, leaving me sitting at the table with my mouth open.

Of course, big mouth couldn't let it go. I jumped up and started ranting. 'Hang on, stop! It doesn't answer anything, Graham. Why do these things happen to me? When I don't want them to – they really upset me.'

Graham stopped and turned back, staring at me deep in thought before saying in a quiet voice, 'I can see that these occurrences continue to upset you. I think your strict religious upbringing is in the way of you being open-minded.'

Wow! Those words stopped me in my tracks. I hadn't thought of that. He was right again! Darn it. His words definitely shut me up and gave me something else to think about.

I thoughtfully added later as we were preparing for bed, 'Thank you. You and your wonderful wisdom. I think you need a medal at times, being married to me.'

He replied, with a cute smirk on his face, 'Mmm, well I confess, being married to you is definitely never dull.'

I really didn't like these 'happenings' as they unsettled my equilibrium and triggered old fears as to whether these experiences were coming from a good or bad place. I might end up in hell as our Minster once said. What a screwed-up mind I had back then, hey! I don't believe that there is a hell out there as described in the Bible. I think hell resides within and is created by our own negative beliefs and actions.

One evening after Graham and the four fur kids had all gone to bed, I sat up in our family room praying, asking for help regarding my inner fears. Suddenly the leaves on a large indoor plant swayed, creating a rustling noise in the room, causing me to look over at the plant sitting in the corner. As I looked over at the plant, it happened again. It freaked me out as my fear of the unknown raised its head. I knew there were no doors or windows open to cause the large plant to rustle its leaves and I wanted to run down the dark passageway to Graham's comforting arms but I was too scared to move.

Then, The Voice spoke, saying, *'Yvonne, that is real fear you felt. Open your hand and see your fear.'*

With my heart pounding in my chest instead of opening my hand, I clenched both hands into tight fists, afraid of what I might see. The Voice gently asked me again…

'Yvonne, open your hand.'

When I did, I looked down at my hands and said out loud in a very surprised voice, 'Empty. They're both empty. There isn't anything in my hands.'

'Yvonne, your inner fear isn't real, it's an illusion.'

Wow! Those words stunned me. The Voice's response was so powerful it left me speechless and in awe at The Voice's wisdom. I sat there for some time, just staring down at my open hands and replaying The Voice's words in my mind. Then the strangest thing happened. In my mind's eye, I saw a bright, bluish energy surrounded by gold shoot in through the top of my head down my right arm resulting in a tingling sensation in my hand.

The Voice told me to go and place my hand on Graham's head. I went into the bedroom and because Graham was sleeping on his side, I found it difficult to place my right hand directly over the top of his head without waking him. My hand ended up slightly to the side of his head for about a minute and I didn't feel anything at all when I did that.

The next morning, Graham said to me over breakfast, 'A strange thing happened to me last night. I partly remember waking up and feeling a lot of tingling sensations in my head.'

I answered in a surprised and excited voice. 'Oh, really! Did you really, Graham?'

'Yes, it was a strange sensation. It felt as if I had pins and needles in my head.'

I told him excitedly what had taken place, but neither of us had any idea at the time why I was told to do that and it baffled us. I truly believe the energy was healing something in his head. I just hoped they weren't giving him any more brains as I already had enough trouble keeping up with him.

The next evening, I recalled an incident on a flight to Malaysia the previous year: as the plane was coming in to land, Graham suddenly developed a terrible pain in his head. It intensified as the pain drained his face of colour. I saw a lump appear on his forehead and the air hostess noticed Graham's distress and sat with us until the plane landed. Both the hostess and I were very concerned. After the plane landed and taxied along the runway coming to a stop, the lump and pain slowly disappeared. It never happened again.

I knew I had a deep driving force inside me guiding me towards something, but what? It was so easy a few years later, whilst living in Jakarta, to wipe my whiteboard clean when I commenced running motivational training workshops in 1994. But erasing deeply inground, painful memories often happens gradually until the root cause is revealed and cleared. Although, I did experience the odd moment where peace and joy bubbled up from my heart before quickly disappearing again. I knew deep in my heart that it was possible to have this feeling of inner peace present all the time, no matter what transpired. Living daily with this depth of connection to our Source was something that still eluded me.

Why? I still held on to beliefs that I was unworthy and not good enough!

I thought, *I want to be enlightened just like Buddha was while sitting under a tree.* He got what I imagined was a little tap on the head and in an instant, he received total enlightenment. I was after the easy way out without having to deal with my screwed-up mentality and a pile of debilitating attitudes. I felt I was going backwards instead of forward. I had moments where I felt sorry for myself, the mountain too high and the work to get there too hard. I was tired.

That's what I'm after. I thought. *Yes, just a little tap on my head will do, please, and then my mixed-up emotions will be gone. Instant enlightenment is what I'm after. Thank you.*

However, it didn't eventuate that way for me and I found out it didn't happen that way for Buddha either, he had done a lot of work on himself before he received total enlightenment. I told Spirit that I was willing to go back to meditating, I'll keep working on my attitude and I'm truly grateful for all the positive changes so far in my life, but no more 'hangers-on', please.

I realise the more my misperceptions were cleared and I embraced a truth, the more my conscious awareness expanded making it easier for me to receive inner guidance.

Later on, Spirit utilised my psychic gifts of pre-cognitive visions and clairvoyance to assist other people in different ways. I would like to add here that I never do readings. My psychic gifts come through only when required and always for a specific purpose. I made a pact with Spirit to only use my gifts in this way after foreseeing the death of a man which happened a couple of days later in Australia in 1994. That experience will be shared in my next book.

If I had maintained the belief that life was very challenging and problematic, that's what I would have continued to reinforce and experience in my life because...

Energy follows thought.

We are all on an inner journey of unfolding our truths for us. It is an ongoing process.

Yvonne Fogarty

CHAPTER 7

UNCOVERING THE TRAUMA

Graham and I had just celebrated our third wedding anniversary in June 1987. I had grown in confidence and I could clearly see the positive changes from where I had started out to where I was now. It was a joy to see the growth I had made over the years.

One warm evening Graham, me and our fur kids were all dining outside on our patio and I was talking about how far I had come in healing my ingrained feelings of self-doubt and inadequacy.

'Graham, these feelings and anxieties are still sadly hanging around no matter how much inner work I've done to clear them. I don't seem to be able to pull out the root cause to heal the issue completely from my psyche. I yearn for my expression to flow freely and unfortunately, it doesn't. You still have to help me write business letters sometimes because my mind goes completely blank and panic rises up.' (I call them a 'brain freeze'.) 'I know this may sound strange but there are times when I'm meditating and it feels as if I have chains around me holding me back.'

Graham just nodded and listened.

I added, 'I need some help to understand where these feelings are coming from as they don't make any sense. I am getting impatient to break these invisible chains I sense are in the way of expressing myself freely.'

I am the sort of person who likes to do a job properly. I don't like to leave a job half-done. I know I won't give up until I am totally free.

After chatting about my concerns in depth, Graham, in his wisdom, understood as he too believed there was something holding me back and suspected it was related to my mother. He chose to keep that suspicion to himself.

Soon afterwards, my inner guidance stepped in and I 'coincidentally' met a young doctor whom I was seated next to at a wellness seminar at the University of Western Australia. Over lunch, we each shared why we were attending the seminar. Later that afternoon, she handed me the phone number of her friend Edith, who was a retired psychiatrist. I telephoned Edith and after a long discussion, she kindly invited me to her home to see how she might help me with my puzzling dilemma.

Pain is the breaking of the shell
that encloses your understanding.

Khalil Gibran

CHAPTER 8

RE-BIRTH

*Please note: This experience contains details
that a reader may find distressing.*

Re-birthing is a form of psychotherapy, where the subject 'relives' an experience to heal an emotional disorder.

I had no idea at the time that Edith specialised in re-birthing (I had never heard of it before) and she also had a gift of clairvoyance, which supported her work with clients. As it turned out, both of us had similar inner gifts and we could both simultaneously tune into the same images of what was taking place. If I had known beforehand what lay ahead, I may not have gone through with it. In saying that, I am glad I didn't know because the re-birthing session slowly opened many more doors for me.

I lay down on the carpeted floor in Edith's large office and watched her close the curtains. I could still see slivers of sunlight penetrating into the room from the sides of the curtains. I found the warm streams of light comforting.

'Yvonne, because of your sensibility I sense you will be able to observe and experience what took place during your gestation in the womb. The images you capture in your mind's eye will represent how you conceptualised any trauma you may have experienced. Unfortunately, some of the intrinsic memories we form when young affect how we see and react to life when older.'

Edith settled herself on the floor behind me, placing my head on her lap, she slowly guided me through a deep breathing technique, whilst I repeated a Sanskrit mantra she gave me to say, which slowly opened a door into the deep recesses of my mind. Edith continued reinforcing that I was safe and that no harm would come to me during the process.

In my mind's eye I saw a swirling purple mist flowing towards me, enticing me to follow it along a tunnel to relive my time in the womb of which I had no conscious recollection. Slowly, images began appearing as the purple mist disappeared with a subtle whooshing sound and the minuscule amount of purple mist that I had been able to see was now gone.

Thoughts raced through my mind... *What's going to happen? I'm feeling vulnerable and confused; my brain feels spacy, my breathing feels restricted or am I just feeling anxious?* I wondered.

As I attempted to settle my racing thoughts and relax my body to this new experience, an image quickly formed in my mind and my senses instantly alerted me to impending danger. My heart began beating faster as I saw the first image of a very tiny form squirming. I couldn't offer it any comfort all I could do was look on...

I saw the baby quickly curl up to protect itself. *What's happening? I thought. Why does the baby appear to be panicking?* Then I saw it. Something was being poked around in an attempt to get to the baby. As the experience unfolded, I began feeling more anxious. It was heartbreaking to watch. I was very aware I was observing what was happening to the tiny form yet, as Edith had warned, I felt I was the baby. Reliving it was very frightening.

I started to panic as I watched the poking intensify. *Why are we being poked at? Someone is attempting to destroy us. But why?* I thought. As I looked on, my body started to shake. I observed what appeared to be a very smooth wooden stick. Whoever was on the other end of this stick was desperately manoeuvring it in all directions, attempting to locate the baby. My body stiffened, my heart rate rapidly increased and I gasped in horror as the person on the end of the stick was moving the stick around in fast, sharp, jabbing motions. I felt helpless. I got so caught up with what was happening I wanted to scream out to warn the baby to stay still and not move.

Why are they doing this to us? Suddenly the whole experience became too real and I thought I was going to die. Oh no! I was in shock. Panic quickly rose up and I tried to scream out but I couldn't, my throat had tightened up. Adrenalin poured in and I could feel my heart pounding loudly.

Seeing the way the baby squirmed in distress pained my heart. I deliberately slowed down my breathing, hoping it would help me relax. I sighed with relief when I saw the stick had been withdrawn. No matter what age, survival is our first instinctive response.

In a flash, the scene changed and I desperately wanted to step in to protect us from further harm. I shuddered in horror when I saw the stick was back, like a prowling animal looking for food and the baby was the food. *Here it comes again,* I thought. The stick seemed to be penetrating deeper with more urgency this time. The tiny form sensed the danger and curled itself up as we both lay tense and anxious. The stick seemed as if it had eyes of its own waiting to pounce, as it attempted to sense where the baby was in order to destroy it.

I know I am okay. I'm alive, I mentally told myself, *I survived this ordeal.* Unfortunately, I couldn't separate myself from the frightening images. I started to tense up again until I realised the stick was still out of reach. I took a deep breath and thought to myself, *We're still okay.* I physically let out a long deep sigh when the prodding ceased and the stick withdrew. Even though I was experiencing the trauma through images, it felt so real as I relived what had transpired.

I felt Edith place a blanket over my shaking body as I slowly calmed myself down then all went quiet within. Some disturbing thoughts rose up. *Why did my mother try to abort me? Did she hate me? No, that's not true, how could she hate me when she hadn't yet seen me?*

As I pondered over those thoughts, another image of the baby broke through into my awareness. I looked on more intensely at the image of the baby's naked form; I was appalled at how my adult mind perceived myself to be. I was looking at a horrid image of a scrawny monster. I felt sick. *How could I possibly believe that about myself? Did I? Is that what I still see subconsciously when I look in a mirror?* I squeezed my eyes shut and turned my head away in an attempt to shut out the image. Of course, closing my eyes didn't stop the image from tormenting me. I took another deep breath and faced myself again. The image was frightening to look at. My eyes appeared larger than my head, my body appeared out of shape, my face was ugly and worst of all, I had vicious sharp black pointy teeth protruding out from my mouth. I was a monster. The image reminded me of something out of a horror movie.

The mental imprints my mind created from the trauma coupled with the mental abuse growing up had concreted a negative perception of myself – I am bad. I am no good. I am unlovable. I am a monster. Realising this, I started to cry again as pain welled up in my heart. I looked on in horror as I couldn't stop that monstrous image from replaying vividly in my mind. My body succumbed to the moment, sinking deeper onto the carpeted floor. I felt as if I had been shattered into a thousand pieces. My thoughts kept repeating the same words over and over: *I am a monster. I am a monster! It is better that I stay isolated from the world emotionally to protect myself from being hurt by people.*

Another scene flashed in my mind and I succumbed mentally, melding in with the baby, who was curled up in a corner of the womb.

Another image formed and I saw the baby wake up to the sound of crying. Then I saw a flash of a woman sobbing. It disturbed the baby and I could sense her discomfort. I started to cry too. Shortly after I saw the entrance partly open and in flooded a thick liquid, quickly filling the cavities as its fumes slowly seeped through the protective walls of the womb.

Seeing what was happening I wanted to scream out to the baby to warn it. I watched in horror as fumes continued to seep in. I automatically gasped for breath; I watched the baby move, wrapping its scrawny little arms around itself.

I couldn't take anymore. I curled my body up into a ball as my voice broke the silence in the room and I started screaming out loudly to Edith, 'Stop. Stop. Edith, please stop this, it's too frightening to watch. I don't want to continue this re-birthing session any longer. I can't bear to look at myself. It's just too horrid, I can't take anymore.' I sobbed.

I opened my eyes to see the warm sunlight still penetrating into the room as far as its rays could reach. I found seeing the light was again a comfort to me as I lay drained, staring at the constant streams of light. I couldn't stop my physical body from shaking as I continued releasing the pain that I had absorbed at feeling the baby's distress. *How could I not?* I thought to myself. *The baby IS me.* The memory thread had embedded itself so deep within my psyche that the experience was too traumatic to ever forget, affecting how I saw myself and life.

I had done so much work on being able to see myself as a loveable person, but neither the mirror work nor the affirmations could reach the depth required to clear this root cause.

Edith spoke ever so softly to me, moving her hands from my shoulders to my head... she began gently and lovingly wiping the perspiration from my forehead and stroking my damp hair, reassuring me that I was safe.

After I relaxed and calmed down, she gently said to me, 'Yvonne, can you still see the tunnel?'

'No, NO!' I said, shaking my head from side to side indicating by the tone of my voice that I didn't want to go back there ever again.

'It's important to continue the session as we cannot postpone it at this stage and we haven't quite finished yet,' said Edith. 'I want you to take a deep breath, repeat the mantra as before and journey back to your memory of your time in the womb... You are safe, nothing is going to happen to you.'

'But I don't feel safe. It's so frightening.'

Again, Edith reassured me with her gentle yet firm voice, reminding me I would be okay. After much persuasion by Edith, I reluctantly followed her guidance and once again repeated the mantra. I found myself floating back as before, coaxed by the slowly swirling purple mist, drawing me like a magnet deeper into the recesses of my mind. I let out a deep sigh as my body started to relax. I found myself floating along peacefully following the mist. Slowly pictures appeared in my mind, this time to my amazement and relief, I wasn't in the womb.

Oh, it's beautiful and peaceful here. Where am I? I wondered. I vaguely saw a tall, thin, distinguished-looking man dressed in a suit and tie with silver streaks either side of his short hair. Is he my father? Who is he? Whoever he is, I know he cares about me. I can sense it. He radiates love.

Suddenly, in a flash, the image changed and I was looking down upon a house. It was made of wood, painted white, with a wide veranda surrounding the whole house. I looked around at the breathtaking view. Vivid-coloured mountains, lakes, green valleys, very brightly coloured flowers and birds flashed through my mind. A deep serenity washed over me as I watched the scenes flash before me.

In an instant, the scene was replaced with the image of the man again. He was standing in front of me. I again felt unconditional love emanating from him. I felt comfortable and safe. As he spoke to me, his warm yet authoritative voice very gently penetrated my whole being.

'Yvonne, would you like to know inner freedom?'

His words echoed over and over in my mind and I felt a deep stirring within. *I feel free, or am I?* I instinctively knew that wherever I was, there existed an invisible barrier that I couldn't move beyond. Such a simple question had stirred up a deep longing in my heart to expand my horizons to see how far I could venture. My curiosity was aroused. I desired to step out, and I mentally replied, *'Yes.'*

The scene changed and I saw myself talking to a group of people, including the man. Some were wearing robes in a huge room with high ceilings and long narrow windows. It reminded me of a library and journals or books appeared to be very old and were scattered open on a very long table, when suddenly my feelings of joy and excitement were interrupted by Edith's voice...

'Yvvooonnnnne, Yvvonne, can you hear me?'

I could vaguely hear a voice gently repeating my name. It sounded so far away and I didn't want to acknowledge it. I wanted to stay wherever I was as it felt so peaceful and comfortable. There it was again – this time the voice was much louder, drawing my attention away from what I had been observing.

'Yvvoonnnne, can you hear me?'

I reluctantly nodded as I slowly acknowledged Edith's weary voice.

'Where have I just been?' I asked as I opened my eyes, looking up at Edith. I could again see the warm rays of the sun still shining through the gaps in the curtains.

'Yvonne, focus on my voice, follow my voice. Are you aware enough to do that?'

'Yes, I think so but where had I gone to just now?'

'Yvonne, you are safe. You drifted off.' Edith let out a deep, tired sigh.

I was still feeling very spaced out and wondered if I had fallen asleep and if what I experienced was a dream!

Edith spoke again. 'Now, I would like you to take yourself back to connect with the memory again. Can you do that now, please?' Edith's voice was sounding very tired.

I started to panic again. 'I don't want to. I don't want to continue this re-birthing session. I don't want to look at myself.'

'Yvonne, can you feel the warmth and comforting sensation of my hands on your head?'

'Yeesss,' I mumbled.

'Breathe in slowly, draw in the warmth from my hands. You are safe. We are nearly finished. It's important for you to see yourself born; nothing is going to happen to you,' she said, reassuring me.

'Alright,' I mumbled. A comforting warm sensation flowed in through my head and my body began to relax.

'Yvonne, you are safe. You have been very courageous and we have almost finished. Listen to my instructions and let's proceed for just a few more minutes. Can you do that for me?'

'Yesss, I think so,' I replied in a shaky voice.

'Take three slow deep breaths for me from your abdomen and repeat the mantra three times breathing, in and out. Good. Take one more deep breath for me and continue repeating the mantra. Can you do that for me?'

I nodded in reply as I slowly inhaled and exhaled, silently repeating the mantra. I could feel myself sinking down into my body.

Once again, my inner mind's eye began searching the darkness until the swirling passageway reappeared, encased in a purple mist. I watched the mist coming towards me before fading away almost out of sight, then suddenly reappearing, encircling my mind and tempting me to let go and flow with it. I slowly began sinking deeper into myself as the purple mist faded completely. I could hear voices.

'I can hear a male and female yelling at each other,' I whispered to Edith just as the arguing stopped. *What was that all about?* I wondered.

A scene flashed through my mind. I saw an image appear and I was again looking at the baby. *Oh, the baby has grown,* I thought. As I focused in on the baby, another image formed and I could hear voices. I looked on cautiously as my heart started racing again. I listened intensely, straining my ears as I tried to hear what was being said. I waited, expecting them to burst in and grab me from that opening.

They didn't, they tricked me. They came for me in a different way.

On the 30th of December 1947 in Perth, Western Australia, I observed myself being quickly removed, whimpering, from my mother's abdomen. Edith too could see the baby in her mind's eye and told me to place the image of the baby onto my stomach and give it love and comfort every day. I followed Edith's instructions and placed the baby on to my stomach as requested, without feeling any love for it.

My reaction to the baby both shocked and repulsed me. I didn't want to comfort it. I despised it. I wanted to shove it away out of sight and not have anything to do with it. I told Edith what I was feeling and she suggested every day I say an affirmation by using my imagination, holding the baby in my arms, nurturing it, saying, 'Everybody loves me, I am perfect just as I am.'

Unfortunately, I didn't do that. I simply couldn't love the baby; instead, I rejected it. I didn't realise at the time I was really rejecting myself!

Edith had given me clear instructions with the intention of changing the negative perception I had of myself in my subconscious mind to a positive one. Through my ignorance, I didn't realise the importance and value of following through on her instructions, which would have supported my healing. Instead, I distanced myself from it. I still couldn't face my buried pain. I shut the door on the experience. Unfortunately, as a result of that decision, my inner journey continued to challenge me due to my distorted beliefs.

I don't know how I managed to drive home that day; my mind and body appeared to be separated from each other. I felt numb, in shock and washed out. I knew I had an important business meeting the next day, so Graham and I walked the streets around our neighbourhood until I felt somewhat coherent again.

Graham told me a few days later that he had sensed the issue was very deep and connected to my mother and her outward hostility towards me at times.

'Yvonne,' he said, 'I believe sometimes when your mother looks at you, she feels ashamed and guilty as your presence reminds her of what she had tried to do, which could explain why she treats you the way she does sometimes.'

That husband of mine amazes me with his wisdom. I thought I now knew where the root cause of the feelings of anxiety, panic attacks and my struggles expressing myself originated from. I also believed at the time the root cause of my self-doubt and inadequacy was solely connected to the trauma in the womb and my upbringing. How wrong I was!

I discovered later during my research that a hot mustard bath produced an odorous liquid that was used years ago with the aim of bringing on a miscarriage. One more thing – my mother's monthly period cycle was very erratic. I believe she was unaware of her pregnancy until she was possibly four months pregnant.

I asked Mum once how I came by these scars near my ankle and calf. She told me I was very underweight at birth and nearly died. I stopped breathing and turned blue three times and was placed in an incubation unit for a couple of weeks, prior to being taken home from the hospital. Then a short time later I was returned to the hospital as I wasn't keeping the bottled milk down and they had to feed me intravenously.

I wondered what may have been going on in Mum's life at that time that caused her to attempt to abort me.

The re-birthing helped me immensely by, slowly, over the following years, opening many doors for me.

Door one. Surviving the abortion attempts affected my psyche so strongly growing up. Because of that experience and the imagined perception that I held seeing myself as a monster had extremely distorted how I viewed life. No wonder I feared life and partly isolated myself from people; I believed life didn't play fair as I looked out upon the world through negative eyes.

At last, I understood why certain thoughts repeatedly played in my mind. I had set up some protective ground rules to ensure my survival. *Don't trust anyone. Life is dangerous. Stay alert. Protect myself. Be suspicious of people. Make them prove their worth before allowing them into your life, otherwise you could get hurt.* I had built a high impenetrable protective barrier around myself.

Door two. Within a few weeks the anxiety and panic attacks disappeared. I began clearing away the deeper, more ingrained misperceptions I held about myself that had been locked away. I didn't have the courage to ask my mother if she had tried to abort me. I was still afraid of her and, through embarrassment and guilt, I don't believe she would have admitted it.

Door three. Released dormant healing gifts, which slowly revealed themselves as I grew in understanding.

Door four. Is huge. I discovered years later as I journeyed deeper into the recesses of my consciousness that I had carried painful memories, deep-seated feelings of self-doubt and inadequacy with me into this current life cycle.

Through my spiritual growth work, my soul's stored memories gradually revealed their buried secrets and the past life memory threads slowly began rising to the surface of my conscious awareness, firstly through visions preparing me to acknowledge and heal a past life trauma.

I know without any doubt our Soul contains all past experiences, especially anything unresolved from our previous reincarnations and commences recording anything of significance from conception in our current life cycle.

Door five. Whether it was a dream, a vision-dream I had experienced during the re-birthing session, or I actually did slip back between life cycles prior to my conception, I cannot say with any certainty. In saying that, if it's true and I had slipped back between life cycles, it was no coincidence. Because the spiritual being's (the man in a suit) decisive words and my excited reply imprinted a deep seed of desire within me to continue my journey. I wondered if he is The Voice I hear and if he is my guardian angel? It's very possible.

I'm confident through inner guidance I am going to know 'inner freedom' by the end of this life cycle. We all grow in understanding when we choose to step outside of the comfort zone of our mental boundaries and our walls of protection.

CHAPTER 9

SHARZA'S HEALING

Late 1987, we discovered our five-month-old Lhasa Apso dog Sharza had a degenerative condition in the joint of his front right leg.

The vet believed the problem happened due to too much in-breeding. The vet rang the breeders, who then telephoned us offering to give us another dog if we put Sharza down.

I couldn't believe what I was hearing. I was shocked and I said to the breeder, 'We cannot do that, Sharza is our child.' I asked them to think about what the vet had told them because continuing to breed knowing of this condition would only bring pain to the little puppies and heartache to owners like us.

The vet reset Sharza's tiny leg by placing a stainless-steel pin in it. Unfortunately, a week or so later the pin broke.

After a couple of months of going back and forth to Murdoch Veterinary Hospital, the vet said in a concerned voice, 'If the leg doesn't start healing within the next six weeks, we will have to do a bone graft.' His words caused my heart to cry out to the universe for help.

Following my instinct, I sat in our lounge room on the carpet with Sharza on my lap every morning and night, giving thanks for the healing, believing it would happen, although back then I had no idea what I was actually doing. I placed one hand over his injury and the other hand a few centimetres above. A few nights later I felt my hand connect with a slight springy sensation and both hands became warm.

Within a short time, my raised hand was tingling; it felt as if I had a very mild electric current flowing through it. I discovered later that the springy sensation was his soul's energy body (also known as our aura) I had made contact with and the buzzing in my hands was the Spiritual life force's healing energy flowing through me to Sharza.

I refused to allow any negative thoughts to enter my mind. I only focused on seeing Sharza healed without a cast or bandage on his leg and once again racing around the house, chasing his big sister or running away from the cats. The cats knew he was scared of them and they took every opportunity to gang up on him. Many a time I heard him crying out for help and I would find him cowering in a corner. I would pick him up and carry him back to wherever I was working. He was such a delightful little wuss.

The healing energy I felt in my hands has many different names given to it e.g. Reiki, Pranic or ki (chi) energy. It doesn't matter what we call this life force energy; it exists and we all live off Spirit's attributes.

Six weeks later I left Sharza at the vet's for another x-ray. On my return, the staff greeted me excitedly. The vet showed me the x-ray pointing out where the bones had started connecting. I continued treating him until the vet said Sharza had fully recovered. For months afterwards, we nicknamed Sharza 'Tiles'. All the money we had saved to buy the Italian floor tiles I had set my heart on went to pay Sharza's veterinary bills. We were grateful to have the money readily on hand to pay for his recovery.

The vibration of unconditional love is a powerful healer. That experience opened another internal door, one of deeper acceptance and appreciation of life, reminding me we are all definitely connected to a power that is truly there to support us. My inner gifts continued to slowly unfold, eventually leading me into my life work of supporting others and myself, just as the medium had told me.

Energy follows thought.

CHAPTER 10

TILES

I kept a sample of the floor tiles we required in the boot of each of our cars. We visited other tile companies, hunting for suitable tiles to no avail. We occasionally called back into the tile shop where we had originally found our favourite tiles, asking if they were planning on getting more of this particular tile again. The staff always responded with the same negative answer.

In my heart, I never gave up hope that we would find the tiles we preferred. I sensed intuitively deep in my heart it would happen. I kept reassuring my husband it would all work out.

After months of searching and still being unable to find suitable tiles for our home, we continued to live on painted concrete floors in the uncarpeted areas of our home.

One evening when I was preparing dinner, Sharza and Kouchi skidded past me playing chase, followed by the cats, which was a regular nightly routine around 5 p.m. between the four of them before dinner. As I quickly moved out of their way, laughing as I watched them all racing back and forward down the passageways, my eyes focused in on Sharza as an idea formed in my mind. I had sat focusing daily on Sharza's healing and I believed in my heart he would recover. Why not on something else? I thought. Why not focus daily on seeing the tiles on the floor?

I mentioned earlier a book I had read 'Creative Visualization' when

I first started on my spiritual journey. I recalled reading that we can use our minds to create our desires through our focused intention on a desired outcome.

Then my integrity popped in. *Is that using this power in the wrong way?* I wondered. *No.* My desire and intent are pure and would not harm anyone else, actually, my husband would be very happy (his patience was wearing thin). I was still learning and it was important to me to respect this power.

I got to work, visualising daily the tiles I desired for our home, which were elegant and had a faint finer shades of beige drawn into the plain off white tile (toning in with our beige carpets), perfect for the large walk-through traffic areas. I even started imagining, when working in the galley kitchen and surrounding areas, that I was walking on them.

Almost a year later I was returning to my office after meeting with a client when suddenly I felt an 'inner urge' to divert my car and call in once again to the tile shop. Of course, my logical mind stepped in, attempting to tell me it was a waste of time. I am so glad I listened to the voice in my heart that day and ignored my logical mind.

Walking into the now familiar shop, the owner/manager 'coincidentally' walked out of his office greeting me, instead of one of his staff. They were all on their lunch break. I explained to him in great drawn-out detail (poor guy) my dilemma. He asked me if I had a sample. I quickly retreated to my car returning with my precious item.

My tummy flip-flopped in excitement as he stood looking at the tile for a few seconds before saying, 'Just give me a few minutes. I will make a call to my supplier to see if I can help you to get these tiles.' After a short while, he poked his head out of his office door, yelling out, 'Hey, how many metres do you require?'

I excitedly replied, 'Only seventy-eight metres!'

He came back with a big smile on his face, whereas my smile was so much bigger.

'My supplier in Italy has enough tiles in stock to fill your order and they have room in my container to add them to my shipment. Here is the name of a floor tiler, they will be here in about eight weeks.'

I was so elated I couldn't contain my excitement. I ran around to his side of the counter and kissed him on the cheek. I then thanked my inner guidance for answering my desire. As soon as I arrived back at my office, I rang Graham with the good news.

A couple of months later, much to Graham's relief, we walked on those tiles. Our inner guidance supports us no matter how big or small our request is, because...

Energy follows thought.

My gifts continued to unfold and I experienced my first precognitive vision.

CHAPTER 11

HANNAH

One Sunday afternoon just prior to Christmas, it was a beautiful warm day; the clear blue sky coupled with a slight breeze removed the sting out of the sun's rays.

We were returning home after walking our fur kids (including the cats) when we stopped to chat with our close friends Elizabeth (Liz or Lizzie as I affectionately call her), her husband David Pretsel and their young son Cameron. Like many of our neighbours, they were in their garden, taking advantage of the beautiful warm day. My senses heightened as I looked at Liz and after we left them, I said to Graham, 'I have a feeling Liz is pregnant.'

The sensation stayed with me and that night I experienced my first precognitive vision.

Someone was ringing our front doorbell and when I opened it, Liz was standing there with a baby in her arms, wrapped in a pink baby rug, and the baby's head was covered by a large mass of black hair standing up on end. I placed my little finger up to her hair and said, 'Oh my, her hair is as long as my little finger.'

I always kept a notepad by my bed at night and I wrote down what I had experienced, including the date and time, and then I waited. And waited. No word from Liz. By Thursday morning my curiosity got the better of me and I rang her.

We chatted for a few minutes then I said, 'Liz can I ask you something very personal?'

'Yes, of course, Yvonne.'

I took a big breath and blurted out, 'Liz are you pregnant?'

'Nooo, but I would like to be. Why do you ask?... Oh!' She hesitated. 'Oh, Yvonne, do you think I am?'

'Well... yes, I do, but I am nervous mentioning it to you as I don't want to get your hopes up. I could be wrong and I know it took you a very long time to fall pregnant before.'

I proceeded to tell Liz about the very vivid vision I had, purposely omitting the gender. Liz told me that she had hurt her little finger playing netball and it was very painful and she was planning on seeing a doctor.

Liz explains in her own words the results of the insight:

My husband and I had always known we would have difficulty having a family and would not be following in the pattern of our parents who had four children each. So after a series of disappointing fertility treatments, we were overjoyed when I gave birth to our son in 1988. We were satisfied that our one child was to be the extent of our family.

Life went on enjoying parenthood in the suburbs of Perth. I even went back to work part-time as a social worker, as my husband, then a teacher, decided to change careers and went back to university, studying for his law degree.

The neighbourhood we lived in was very new and many homes were being built and gardens established. We were getting to know the neighbours when passing each other on walks around our streets. It was through one of these casual encounters that we met Yvonne and Graham Fogarty as they walked their dogs past our home. The chats were easy and we soon began having dinners and holidays together. Yvonne and I developed a particularly close friendship. She knew how much we went through in our trying-for-a-baby years.

Our son, Cameron, was around eighteen months old and had just started sleeping through the night. Life was getting back to one that was not sleep-deprived. On yet another encounter with the Fogartys and their entourage of pets, Yvonne must have had one of her 'feelings', because a few days later she rang me and asked if she could ask me a personal question. For a moment I wondered what such a question could be as we'd shared many personal stories before!

Anyway, she asked me if I was pregnant. 'Don't be silly,' I said. 'I don't get pregnant without a lot of help!'

'Well,' she said, 'last Sunday when I saw you, I sensed an aura around you and I thought you were pregnant. Then that night I had a vision that you came to my door, smiling, with a baby wrapped in a blanket in your arms, and the hair was sticking up on end and it was the length of my little finger.'

I was mystified. I told Yvonne I doubted I was pregnant, adding, however, that it would be wonderful if I were. I had never experienced anyone saying anything 'spooky' like this before so I was intrigued, excited and sceptical at the same time. It kept replaying in my mind.

Earlier that same week I played a game of netball and injured my little finger. It was bruised and painful and even though I was at work and not near my regular doctor, I was able to get an appointment to see a local doctor. I showed him my finger and he suggested getting an x-ray. Yvonne's prediction popped into my head and so I told the doctor I didn't really want an x-ray.

He gave me an enquiring look and said, 'Oh, do you think you are pregnant?'

I answered, 'I am not sure, but I have a feeling I might be!'

He gave me a questioning look and I just smiled at him. He suggested that I have a pregnancy test first and wrote out a pathology referral. I paid the bill and left.

Now this was December 1989 and our work Christmas lunch was that day. As I had used my 'lunch money' to pay for the doctor's visit, I *had to find a Medicare office or a bank before I went to lunch. On my way to the Medicare office, I had debated whether or not to have the pregnancy test, as all the years of negative test results played back in my mind, and I had all but decided not to do that to myself again.*

Well, I got to the Medicare office to secure my refund and lo and behold a pathology clinic was right next door. It was then I let my curiosity get the better of me and I marched inside. The pathology nurse was lovely. She saw I was having a pregnancy test and something about her made me share with her that it was my spooky girlfriend who thought that I was pregnant, not I!

She too became curious. 'What a pity,' she said. I would have to wait till Monday to get the result. The nurse looked at me as if to weigh up my trustworthiness and wrote a telephone number on a piece of paper.

She said, the results would be ready on Saturday morning (the next day) and to ring this number saying you're calling from the pathology collection clinic. When they say 'patient's name', give them your name and they will give you the result.

We shared a conspiratorial smile.

So the next morning arrived. I was working in the city and eventually made the call.

'Patient's name?' asked the receiver.

'Elizabeth Pretsel,' I replied. I could hear papers shuffling, then, 'Greater than 250mg, positive.'

'So she's pregnant?' I asked.

'Yes. Greater than 250mg, positive,' came the emphatic reply.

'Thank you,' I said in my most controlled attempt to sound casual. Well, my heart was beating fast, my palms were sweaty and I was in a whirl. This is quite a challenge when your job includes answering the phone!

My natural instinct was to share the news with my husband; however, being a careful person I thought I'd better double-check with the pathology centre. The man on the phone was amused when I told him why I needed to confirm the result.

I told him, 'I could kiss you!'

He was kind enough to say he'd send me a copy of the result to my home as well as the doctor's office. It was then I phoned my husband with the news.

'How did that happen?' he asked.

'In the normal way, apparently,' was my reply!

It was wonderful to share the news with Yvonne and Graham, and surprise, surprise, in August 1990, our beautiful baby girl, Hannah, was born, her voluminous hair sticking up straight, just like Tina Turner.

I cannot explain how Yvonne knew I was pregnant before I did. I can only attest that she did know. Our close relationship enabled her to read my ovaries better than I could, and I entertain the thought that my daughter was somehow waving to Yvonne during the vision of the aura that sunny day in the garden. I am so glad that I didn't have that x-ray while I was pregnant!

Liz Pretsel

After Liz received the news that she was pregnant, she walked to our house. I opened the front door to find her standing there with a huge beaming smile on her face. She didn't say a word; her radiant smile confirmed it all. We both cried.

On the evening after Hannah's birth, Graham and I made a quick trip to the hospital to see little Hannah. I headed straight to the crib and put my little finger alongside her big mop of black hair and sure enough, it was the length of my little finger. I gave her a kiss.

Hannah is now in her thirties and a beautiful person. Whenever I communicate with her, I always jokingly remind her that I 'saw' her first!

We are always watched over and divine intervention will always step in when we are open to receive. In saying that, sometimes things do happen that are so very difficult to understand and accept, but in the big scheme of things there is always a reason behind why certain things transpire.

The responsibility of parenthood can never be underestimated. Children learn by example and the young people of today will become the parents of tomorrow. A home is a place where a child needs nurturing and, most of all, to be accepted and loved unconditionally.

That experience with Liz touched me deeply and knowing her history, she could have easily lost the baby if she had had an x-ray not knowing she was pregnant. Through that experience, I opened another door in my mind towards being more accepting of my gifts.

This experience was the result of having a 'precognitive' vision – knowledge of a future event through extrasensory means.

There are those who walk among us every day.
At times, we may sense a spiritual being's presence,
yet rarely do we physically see them.
On those occasions when their presence is visible to us,
it is usually only for a brief moment.
During that fleeting encounter, they can leave a deep
and lasting impression within our consciousness.
From my own personal experiences,
their appearance is never at random.
It is always for a specific purpose.

Yvonne Fogarty

CHAPTER 12

THOSE THAT WALK AMONG US

After setting up my own small consultancy company the previous year, I had another encounter with a spiritual being while in Sydney on a business trip.

The year was 1989 and I had been in Sydney for five days, sourcing suitable software for a client. By Friday evening I had achieved a successful outcome for my client.

I thought to myself, *tomorrow I have the whole day to myself before flying home to Perth on Sunday. I'm going to go and visit some local boutiques and purchase a new outfit to wear home.*

After breakfast, I walked outside and saw that a circus had been set up over the road. I hadn't been to a circus since I was a child and decided to walk back through the expansive park with its trees and lush gardens and enquire what time the evening performance would start.

After sitting in meetings most of the week, I walked down towards the shops with a spring in my step and the sun shining down brightly. I explored the local shopping centre for a new outfit. Disappointed at not finding anything suitable, I decided to get my hair done instead. After enquiring around, I found a salon that could accommodate me. The hairdresser asked what I would like done.

'Well, I want something that will get my husband's attention.'

'Why is that?'

'Well,' I said with a sigh, 'my husband has been so busy at work lately. I'm feeling neglected.'

The hairdresser rolled her eyes and gave me a knowing look.

'Why don't you have a rinse put through your hair?'

'Yes,' I said. 'That's a great idea. I want a colour that will get his attention.'

With that thought in mind, I kept looking at the chart for quite a while. I finally chose a colour that matched my husband's newly replaced company car. The assistant checked with me twice before going off to mix the colour. I assured her on both occasions that it was definitely the colour I wanted.

I walked out of the salon with my head held high in the air, feeling very smug – until I saw the sun reflecting off my hair in a passing window. I gasped in horror; it was my husband's car colour, all right, but I didn't expect it to look this bright.

As I walked back up the street, I noticed I was on the opposite side of the road to the park. A 6-foot-high brick wall enclosed one large section, running adjacent to the footpath. At one end, the wall jutted up against a shop wall and finished at the corner diagonally opposite the boutique hotel where I was staying. To get access into the park I needed to cross over and walk further up the road to a large old-fashioned wrought iron gate.

I waited at the crosswalk for the lights to change then proceeded to cross along with everyone else. I was suddenly aware of a person walking close to me. I felt quite uneasy. I stepped up onto the footpath and turned my head to glare at this person who was invading my space. The lady gave me a beautiful smile. She appeared to be in her sixties, dressed in a tan skirt and a pale blue jumper. She was of average build with light brown hair; her skin was flawless and she wore no makeup. It was her eyes that caught my attention; they were clear blue with a sparkling gleam to them.

We both stopped walking and stood staring at each other. I couldn't turn away; it was as if her eyes were holding me in place and my glare quickly melted into a soft smile.

The woman spoke in a gentle yet imposing voice. 'My dear, do not walk through the park. If you do, you will be robbed of your new sports shoes and all your money.'

I was dumbfounded. I stood staring at her with raised eyebrows. Without saying another word, she smiled at me again, turned and walked in the opposite direction to where I was headed.

As I stood there recalling her words, I immediately looked down at my white sneakers as my mind quickly analysed what I'd heard. *How did she know I planned on walking through the park?* I thought. *The gate into the park is a further twenty metres away.*

I turned back around to look at her and in those brief couple of seconds it had taken me to digest her message, she had simply disappeared from sight. I searched the area, looking to see if a car had stopped to pick her up; I checked to see if she could have walked the distance past the wall of the park into a shop. No, that wasn't possible either.

I thought, *maybe she has crossed back over the road?* Glancing around, I realised that wasn't possible. The busy traffic was flowing and the 'don't walk' sign was still flashing. I thought, *there isn't anywhere for her to go unless she just simply vanished!*

As those thoughts hung in my consciousness, a shiver ran down my spine, then goosebumps popped up over my whole body. I moved away from the crowd that started gathering, waiting at the crosswalk for the lights to change. I leaned back against the high brick wall, reliving the incident over and over in my mind whilst my eyes continued searching for her.

What were the words she used that struck me as odd? I am very analytical and I again replayed the experience slowly taking in everything I could recall about our encounter. The lady used the word 'new'. That's it. That's what grabbed my attention. I glanced down at my expensive sneakers again. I had purchased them about six weeks earlier; I guess they could still pass for new, although I had worn them every day since on my early morning walks with Liz and from my observation, they weren't shiny clean. They appeared to have some scuff marks.

More thoughts poured in as goosebumps once again popped up over my arms. *There was one more thing about her that struck me as odd. She was not carrying anything, not even a handbag, and she had a warm motherly presence about her.*

That thought triggered another startling thought, *Oh! Was I being protected by a spiritual being?* I was certain of it. The goosebumps and shivers again appeared and I remembered when a spiritual being had appeared to warn Graham and me before travelling on the road to our holiday destination a few years ago. Refer to Chapter 4 – A Life-Changing Experience.

Trusting the spiritual being's message, I decided not to walk back through the park and returned to the hotel via the footpath. Upon arriving back, I walked into the reception area where the owner's wife was doing some paperwork and she looked up and said in an enquiring voice, 'Is there anything I can do for you?'

'Oh, yes, um, oh – by the way, have you heard of any problems in the park, like robberies for instance?'

'Oh, my goodness, I hope you didn't run into any trouble?' she asked with an anxious look on her face.

'No, nothing like that,' I responded quickly.

'We have been meaning to put a sign on the noticeboard suggesting that guests refrain from taking a shortcut through the park as there have recently been some teenagers robbing people to support their drug habits.'

I asked her if it was okay to venture over the road to the circus tonight and was told that this end of the park opposite the hotel was in an open exposed area and quite safe. I had lived in Perth all my life and compared to Sydney, Perth was a small country town and to my knowledge, I could walk in the daytime anywhere without incident. I picked up a circus brochure from the reception desk and went to my room.

Recalling the incident as I lay resting on the bed, I realised once again I had been protected from danger by a spiritual being. Yes, I went to the circus and joined in on cue along the crowd as we either gasped in shock, held our breath and laughed or clapped in unison. I also thoroughly enjoyed eating a large bag of popcorn.

Arriving back in Perth, I was waiting to collect my luggage when I saw my husband rush into the airport terminal. He swivelled his head around, scanning the terminal for me but of course, he didn't see me. His eyes were looking for his perception of me that had left home a week earlier. The impishness in me let him look around for a couple more minutes before I took pity on him, waving my hand high in the air to get his attention.

He hurriedly walked over with a big frown on his face, saying, 'Hell, Yvonne, what have you done to your hair?'

'Oh, hello, darling. I missed you too. Does my new hair colour remind you of something?'

'Yes,' he said in realisation and resignation. His facial features softened. Taking a deep breathe he lowered his eyes from my hair back to my eyes and said in a quieter voice, 'My new maroon car.'

'Get the message?' I asked with raised eyebrows and a cheeky grin.

'Yes, but it's definitely not as bright as your hair!'

He gave me a big juicy kiss, then added, 'Yvonne, promise me you won't do that again. That colour really looks terrible.'

It was quite a few weeks before the colour completely faded; even so, it made a good story at dinner parties.

When I am able to move beyond the doubts that bombard my mind, I can sense a deep inner knowing in my heart that Spirit's vibrational presence is always protecting me. I have been saying an affirmation ever since the near encounter with a cow back in 1983.

'I am always guided, always protected and always supported by Spirit.'

I was receiving what I believed I would receive and that was protection.

If a person had observed me standing on the footpath, the spiritual being would not have been visible to anyone else. Just as Graham's sister Lorraine couldn't see Uncle Tom when he appeared before me. Refer to chapter 4 – A Life-Changing Experience.

Even with all the encounters and support I and others have received, why do doubts still creep in? It is easy through our busy daily life to get caught up in thinking that everything we can see and touch in front of our eyes as being our only reality.

I slowly became more aware that life had so much more to offer me, other than what I had previously perceived. My past limited thinking had restricted me from experiencing a much broader reality.

In ancient times people believed that the world was flat and there was nothing beyond the horizon. As they expanded their understanding of life around them, their perception of how they saw life changed as they opened their minds to accept that life did exist beyond the horizon of their original understanding and their world was much larger than they were first led to believe.

Since then scientists have continued to expand upon our understanding of life and all that we can see and touch, including everything else on Earth and beyond, is made up of energy and Quantum physics is referred to as the study of matter and energy at a fundamental level – the atomic and subatomic level – the building blocks of nature.

For a few years, scientists at the European Organisation for Nuclear Research (CERN) on the France/Switzerland border have been attempting to uncover the elusive fundamental element of creation. They named this mysterious element 'The God Particle'. I read a while ago that they are working on creating a super smasher upgrade, which they expect to be ready for operation in 2026, replacing the Large Hadron Collider, with the aim of unlocking more information about our existence. Our inner reality will continue to remain a mystery to scientists until they can explain the inexplicable and how it takes place. I wonder if the inexplicable is meant to remain a mystery!

I ask myself, 'If this elusive God Particle were uncovered, could humanity lose the importance and value of this unseen element required to stretch our minds to look beyond our current beliefs to expand our conscious awareness with the aim of refining our soul? *I wonder.* I believe my heart would be filled even more so with love, gratitude and appreciation towards this unseen power.'

I can only attest to the fact that my life has changed in a very positive way through believing in this unseen 'element', as scientists call it, enriching my life. I remember reading years ago a book by Wayne Dyer titled 'You'll See It When You Believe It.' A great title and so very apt.

One more thing, just because scientists cannot physically prove beyond any doubt the existence of life elsewhere, e.g. spiritual beings, it doesn't mean that they don't exist! I know we are not alone and our lives definitely do carry on after physical death. A hierarchy of spiritual beings exists throughout the whole universe and there is always guidance available. Refer to Foreword.

The way Spirit responds to us can differ greatly and sometimes it comes from those who have previously made the journey. I battled internally to accept that life carries on after death until I saw my father after he died and I had the courage to question the beliefs that were handed down to me. Refer to chapter 2 – My Father's Death.

Spirit understands the challenges that we face here on Earth as we continue journeying towards expanding our awareness, which is a vital element in our soul's development.

CHAPTER 13

JAKARTA, INDONESIA

In February 1990, I sensed that our time in our home with its beautiful, landscaped gardens was coming to an end and I sensed we were possibly going to be moving away.

Later that same year, Graham's company transferred us to Jakarta, Indonesia. We rented our house and, in the whirlwind that preceded the move, my self-growth was put aside. Sadly, we could only take our dogs with us as we were advised it wasn't wise to take our cats. Fortunately, friends willingly adopted them.

Mum and I had gradually mended our relationship, even though at times it was challenging being with her. Yet, I cared deeply for her and it pained me that she wouldn't have any immediate family around her when we left. All she ever wanted in life was to feel loved. Sadly, Mum couldn't see that the love she was seeking was right in front of her.

Graham and I would bring my mother over to our home every couple of weeks to spend the weekend with us; unfortunately, it still left her yearning for her family to be around her all the time so she felt loved. Her attitude caused us to feel stifled at times; Mum couldn't see that her attitude and resentment she carried through life was the only thing that stood in the way of her own happiness.

The hare is back racing ahead a few years... during a trip to England, we discovered things that shocked us, which gave me a better understanding regarding my mother's outbursts at times. Refer to chapter 30 – Discovering a Family Secret.

By March 1991, the four of us were settled in a beautiful house which overlooked a winding river, lush green fields, rice fields and many kampongs (villages) were nestled amongst the distant hills. This was our first overseas posting and we were suffering from culture shock and also excited at this new adventure. We had a lot to learn, especially about renting houses in a third-world country. The electricity would go off if one of our staff accidentally turned on an iron or toaster while we were showering.

The spacious house, spread out over three levels, was paid for by Graham's company. Two days after settling in, I opened up our bedroom sliding doors and walked out onto the large balcony, enjoying the expansive view towards Bogor. I glanced down at our back garden, yikes! I was shocked to see all our washed underwear and clothing spread out on top of or hanging off all the shrubs and draped over the adjoining neighbours' fences. I hurried downstairs and the maid informed me we didn't have a clothesline. That was quickly rectified.

One morning I walked into the only store back then, named Kem Chicks, that carried a good variety of food from different countries. I was looking at all the different bags of flour. Unfortunately, all the information on the packets was written in Bahasa Indonesian. I couldn't find a bag with the words 'self-raising' flour written on any of them. It was such a silly little thing, but in my frustration, my eyes welled up and the odd tear escaped, rolling down my cheeks. I felt overwhelmed and frustrated.

An American expatriate walked over to me. 'How long have you been in the country?' she asked.

'Two months,' I replied, sniffling.

'I thought so. Culture shock affects most of us when the thrill wears off and reality sets in.' She kindly showed me the type of flour to buy.

The next day I asked our cook Suti, who spoke fairly good English, to make a chocolate cake for us. She set to work mixing the ingredients.

I happened to walk back into the kitchen, glancing at the mixture and said, 'Suti, that mixture looks a strange chocolate colour. Are you sure you used cocoa?'

'Yes, Madam, I have used all the right ingredients.'

I noticed the mixture had a yellow-brown tone to it instead of being a deep chocolate colour. I walked out, thinking something didn't feel right. After a few minutes, I walked back in and tasted it. UGH! I asked her to bring out all the ingredients she'd used. Bless her. She had mistakenly used the container of Gravox (for making gravy) instead of cocoa. I suggested throwing it all out and starting again. She wouldn't hear of it.

'Please, Madam, I will cook this cake and the staff will enjoy it.'

I thought, the end result will be interesting to see. To my surprise, that darn gravy cake had risen so high; the top of the cake was at least 30mm above the deep round cake pan. I tasted a tiny bit; it was very salty and dry, but the staff enjoyed it. When our chocolate cake came out of the oven, it was less than half the size of the gravy cake.

Living in Jakarta gave me the opportunity to have time for myself. For the first time in my adult life, I wasn't working. I joined the Australia and New Zealand Association (ANZA) and became heavily involved in the social welfare side of this wonderful organisation. Some experiences we encountered really shocked us. We all worked tirelessly fundraising for various projects, including paying for the building of toilet blocks to accommodate up to 700 people in many small villages dotted around Jakarta.

Prior to the villages having these facilities, which consisted of a well, toilets, showers and an area for washing their clothing, 'everything' was taken care of in the local river. Many children and adults died from the diseases that quickly spread throughout the villages, partly due to the contaminated water.

I soon learnt to always go to the toilet before leaving home or prior to returning home. Needing the toilet urgently fortunately only happened once to me when our driver and I picked up Graham from the airport after he had been away on a business trip. We had travelled about eight kilometres on the toll road when we came across a huge traffic jam. A bridge had collapsed and we found out later, sadly, a number of people had been killed. It was a very slow, anxious and uncomfortable journey back into the city. I told Graham I needed the toilet urgently and he could see I had become extremely fidgety. Graham asked the driver to divert the car to his office.

As we pulled up outside his office building, Graham said, 'Quick, off you go. I'll wait here.'

I let out a big sigh. I slowly turned to face him with a look of horror, shock and embarrassment plastered on my face and said quietly, 'Oh, Graham, I am so sorry, but it's too late.' I squeaked the words out in a pathetic voice.

He looked down at the car seat and then looked back up at me. His shocked expression and the look on our driver's face (who spoke excellent English) was something I wished I could have photographed. Silence followed. I let out another big slow sigh, waiting with my head down, attempting to look extremely embarrassed and not fidget or grimace at the discomfort I was feeling.

Then Graham said in a shocked voice, 'Are you for real? You're not serious, are you?'

Pursing my lips together and biting my tongue to stop from smiling, I glanced up into his eyes giving him a pathetic look and after pausing for effect as I watched his eyes grow big and his eyebrows rise up under his hair...

I said to Graham in a loud voice, 'GOT YOU!'

He blew out a sigh of relief and said, 'Oh s—Yvonne, that's the first time you've been able to fool me!'

I bounded out of the car, racing up the steps into the building, giggling. The look on my face quite possibly held a mixture of amusement and agony. That was the one and only time I have ever been able to trick him (so far) and I thought it was worth mentioning in the book. A high five to me. Yay! Instead of taking approximately one-and-a-half to two hours on average to get home, that night it took us over four hours.

Whenever our driver took us down a narrow road full of unavoidable deep potholes (in Australia, we would call them craters), my husband would say, 'Uh oh, hang onto them, love. We are venturing along Jalan (road) tits wobble!'

I was not endowed with large breasts but they did wobble and bounce around ever so slightly when we travelled along very bumpy roads, which always brought a smirk to my husband's face. A saying came to mind as I typed this… 'small things can definitely amuse small minds.' I wondered why some 'sensitive things' very valuable to the male species didn't wobble around as well causing them discomfort too.

In Indonesia back then, there was no welfare system available to anyone. If a person was seriously ill and couldn't afford a doctor, they often died. No one received fortnightly cheques from the government if unemployed or unable to work through sickness.

One time we had been away for a few days and upon returning home late at night from the airport, we found our houseboy sitting on the back steps waiting for us. With tears in his eyes, he explained his second wife (who had just turned fifteen years of age) needed a caesarean operation to save her and the baby's life. He didn't have the money. Tragically his first wife and baby had died during childbirth. The doctors in the local hospital near his village (a minimum of six hours or more by car from where we lived) wouldn't perform the operation until he had the cash to pay them. Fortunately, we always kept money for an emergency in our safe and our driver drove him back to his village. Thankfully, they arrived there in time to save his wife and the baby.

Not long after we had settled into life in Jakarta, I woke one morning sensing a familiar inner excitement that something good was about to happen. The decision I was about to make would open a door to my future life's work. We were invited to attend a fundraising dinner and we were 'coincidentally' seated next to an expatriate lady, who told me about a healing energy called Reiki and that she was attending a first-degree Reiki training course in a few weeks. (The word Reiki means universally guided life-force energy). It resonated with me and I decided to join the class in this natural healing technique, thinking it would enhance and ground the healing gift I had discovered when our dog Sharza had his injury. Refer to chapter 9 – Sharza's Healing.

Prior to attending the training course, I went to the Reiki Master's home to meet her. I walked through the gate of her home and as I turned to relatch the gate, I heard that warm loving Voice that I had come to recognise and cherish since I was young come vibrating through my body, saying,

'Yvonne, welcome home.'

I was overcome with the emotion that welled up from deep inside me. I introduced myself to the Reiki Master through a flood of emotion.

The training course went over two days and after the last initiation (four in total), I couldn't control my hands. Whenever I focused my mind on giving energy to someone, it automatically activated the energy. My hands would take off in all directions as they scanned someone's body, they would begin tingling as the energy poured, giving me a variety of sensations. Over time, I came to discern what the different sensations I experienced meant. It felt as if my hands were plugged in to a powerful electrical circuit and had taken on a mind of their own as they moved over a person's body, supplying me with information via my internal senses.

Reiki not only accelerated my healing gifts but it also deepened my connection to receive inner guidance. My gifts of insight increased and through word of mouth I found myself supporting other expatriates.

My belief that this healing technique may open a door for me proved to be accurate. My participation in this first level of Reiki was a major turning point in my life, setting me upon a journey I never imagined myself ever taking...

Energy follows thought.

CHAPTER 14

LOWER BACK PAIN

I have never forgotten the first time I saw an image form in front of my eyes when I unknowingly tuned into a person's energy body while giving them a treatment.

I was sitting with a group of expatriate ladies at an ANZA morning tea when an acquaintance, Gwen, who happened to be sitting beside me, suddenly stood up saying, 'Please excuse me for a few moments. I have an annoying back pain and I need to get up and stretch.'

Gwen, a tall, slender woman, came back a while later telling me the pain had started shortly after her return from Sydney a month earlier. We decided to meet at my house to see if a Reiki treatment could support her desire to uncover and heal the cause of this sudden back pain.

As the energy worked on her back, a picture formed of a little girl, maybe three years of age. I saw the image in my mind's eye, yet at the same time, the image appeared to be projected out in front of me. Trusting my inner guidance and her keenness to heal this issue, I hesitantly asked Gwen if anything had happened to her around that age.

'Yes, a couple of days before my fourth birthday, my father left my mother.' Then uncontrollable tears burst forth as the buried emotions came to the surface.

I thought, *Did Gwen blame herself for her father leaving, believing she was the cause of them separating?*

As the realisation dawned on her, she cried out, 'Oh! Did I blame myself for Dad leaving? If so, after forty years how can that incident be connected to my pain now?'

'Well, there has to be a subconscious "memory thread" linking the two experiences together somehow. What transpired while you were in Australia? Could something have happened, triggering this memory to manifest now?'

Gwen told me she had taken her son to boarding school in Sydney. She felt extremely sad and guilty for leaving him there.

I suggested she write about the two incidents and when ready, come back for another treatment. It is so rewarding if a client can connect the threads together themselves. The 'aha' feeling they experience is a life-changing moment for them when they connect the dots, impacting their awareness and a shift of perspective takes place.

To paraphrase a wonderful Wayne Dyer quote: 'When the thing you perceived as a truth changes, the way you see that truth changes.'

Writing out our feelings regarding an issue can clear our heads and can help considerably in releasing suppressed emotions. I use it if I feel stuck; it can open a door for understanding and clarity to manifest.

During the next treatment, Gwen said, 'When I wrote about the two incidents and my feelings, I came to clearly understand the connection between the two experiences – it was guilt! I had no idea an old memory could sit dormant for so long in my body, then suddenly cause this back pain.'

I explained, 'Trauma can do that if an upsetting situation forms a strong disturbing emotional memory and remains unresolved. It would have been difficult at your young age to understand that your parents' separating had nothing to do with you, especially if your mother was deeply upset and distressed over his leaving. The pain of leaving your son triggered the unresolved trauma to manifest in your body, which had been buried in your subconscious mind.'

While giving Gwen a treatment, she felt the pain in her back become stronger as we talked. In my mind's eye, I saw a very tiny speck of grey energy as it started moving around slowly to different areas in her back as my hands followed. It was the first time I had experienced seeing energy (subconscious memory pattern) moving around. I saw that as a good sign.

At one stage she called out, 'The bloody pain keeps moving as if it's trying to hide from us.'

'Gwen, take a deep breath and relax; the pain will find its own way out when ready.'

A short while later, she again felt the pain as it moved. She became quite impatient and yelled out at it in frustration. 'You get the bloody hell out of my life now, you bastard.'

I wondered if the words she said out loud at the energy mass were coming from her or a memory. Maybe she was recalling her mother's words to her husband! Gwen opened her green eyes, looking up at me in frustration, pushing her long brown hair back behind her ears as a tear trickled down her face before letting out a big sigh.

I suggested she take some more deep breaths, relax her body, open her heart and repeat the following words with deep heartfelt feelings three times.

'I willingly and lovingly release and let go of this emotional disturbance.'

Gwen cried at the relief she felt as the energy mass moved out through her hip joint, making its way down her right leg before flowing out through her foot.

We chuckled afterwards at her colourful outbursts.

Gwen telephoned me the next morning to thank me and to let me know the pain had completely gone and her body felt light and she felt peaceful.

Every vibrational energy healer has their own way of working that is unique and perfect for them.

When I work with someone, I have repeatedly seen that once the energy blockage is acknowledged, a shift of perspective takes place and the energy will find release through a joint in the body. Sometimes when energy is being released, a client can feel numbness, tingling or heaviness in their arms or legs during the process. Then finally relief. It is a normal occurrence for some.

If a person isn't mentally willing or ready to let go of their issue, I do not receive images. Well, in saying that, sometimes I do, yet I also instantly sense not to say anything and wait. Timing is a very important element in healing work.

Why? Whether I see images or not is the result of a person's freewill choice, as we each have total control over our own healing and what we are willing to experience. When receiving a treatment, the client draws the energy through the practitioner's hands, not from her, as the practitioner is a channel for this healing energy to flow through her and the client will draw in the perfect amount of energy they are open to receive.

If the person isn't ready mentally, it may take a few sessions before a door opens in their consciousness to clear an issue. When the root cause of an issue is cleared, deep healing can take place.

Reiki reconnects and/or strengthens our connection to Spirit and aligns our soul with our inherent spiritual gifts, heightening our awareness of our existence to all life around us and the energy that flows through our hands can be felt and experienced by the client. It is a vibrational healing therapy.

To paraphrase a wonderful quote by Mahatma Gandhi:

'We have to be the change for any change we desire to manifest in our lives.'

Energy follows thought.

CHAPTER 15

WORK WAS SUFFOCATING HIM

A friend's husband, Michael, came to see me regarding a health issue. He was in his mid-forties, medium height and weight with short light-brown hair. He had been living in Jakarta for six months, working as a project manager on a new complex.

He analysed his condition logically, saying, 'It must be the high level of pollution here in Jakarta causing my asthma to flare up after thirty-plus years of being free of it.'

'That's a possibility,' I murmured.

As I treated him, focusing in on his chest area, my hands stopped moving as an image of two men formed in my mind's eye. I asked him if he was having a particularly challenging time at work. He told me that the two owners of the project had obtained an unsecured loan from an Indonesian bank and immediately pocketed half of the money between them.

As the project manager, he felt a responsibility towards the contractors when he discovered that there was insufficient money left to pay for the work done so far and the project still had a long way to go before it was completed. Michael was the type of person who took his responsibilities to heart and the situation troubled him deeply. He told me he was not only feeling cornered and pressured; he felt as if the job was suffocating him. He couldn't see a way out. While talking, he realised for himself that this issue could be the cause of his asthma.

Slowly, the energy that had built up in his energy body around his chest area cleared and the tightness he felt in his lungs eased off, allowing his lungs to breathe more freely. After the treatment was finished, we discussed setting a goal of focusing only on the desired outcome. I suggested he not focus on the situation he saw happening in front of his eyes. Things have a way of turning around if we can stay positive and I know from firsthand experience it is not easy to do when confronted with what appears to be an overwhelming situation.

'Michael, no matter what is taking place around you right now, keep your eyes on the end goal only; make that your reality. Every day, sit quietly, picturing the end result and saying, "Thank you. The project is now completed." Repeat that affirmation three times to yourself. Energy follows our thoughts, especially when it is coupled with a picture and a clear intent held in our minds. A few times a day confidently repeat the affirmation, anticipating the end result. Don't surmise how this may happen, just believe it will turn around.'

I gave Michael time to allow his thoughts to ponder over what I had suggested. Later, I again reminded Michael, 'Do not dwell on the situation. It's important to acknowledge and accept the situation for what it is at that moment, then focus only on what you desire to see transpire.'

'Yes, I can see where you're coming from. I'm going to focus on seeing the project completed, not on what I don't want to see happen.'

'Yes. That's it.'

I quickly explained why we repeat an affirmation three times. The number three represents Spirit's natural doorway of creation.

Instead of feeling disempowered as he felt when he arrived, Michael left feeling empowered. The project was stalled for a short time, then another party stepped in, taking over ownership and he was able to complete the project just as he had envisioned in his mind.

Months later, Michael told me over dinner that he had faced many challenging and uncomfortable moments and he had nearly given up.

When that happened, he reminded himself to keep focusing on seeing the project finished and not allow himself to get caught up in the daily turmoil he faced prior to the new owners taking over the project.

'Yvonne, I hope you don't mind me asking about your gift. I am curious to know how you saw the image of the two men when you were treating me. How did you see that image?'

'Well, seeing clairvoyantly into a person's energy body first happened when I was treating a lady with a back issue a few months ago. I asked for guidance to help me understand how it happened. A couple of weeks later, The Voice said to me…

"Yvonne, you are seeing deeper into consciousness."

'Michael, I was excited when I grasped what my inner guidance was saying to me; I had expanded my awareness enough to see clairvoyantly deeper into consciousness via our spiritual third eye. When open, it allows us to see into a person's psyche because vibrational energy work can bridge a mental disturbance to the physical discomfort and when a client is willing, a door opens. I can sense or "see" through images the connecting memory threads between their physical discomfort and the mentally troubling issue. I love sharing this part of my work. I get so excited. It's wonderful to experience a depth of consciousness available to us.'

Our conversation stopped as the waiters placed down our final course along with our coffees. We had all ordered tiramisu and our conversation was delayed as we devoured our desserts.

Michael, who was keen to understand more, said, 'I am curious to know more about how you do what you do?'

'Many healers work using their senses to tune into a soul's multi-layered energy body. When a client experiences a shift of mental awareness, changes can automatically take place, resulting in an increase of energy flow circulating throughout their whole being, which you experienced for yourself.

'When we picture and focus on a desired end result as you did, we are attracting and drawing in energy to bring about our desired outcome. Some very apt sayings are "like attracts like", "as above so below and as within so without".'

'Can anyone learn to do this?' asked Michael.

'You were using this power,' I replied. 'It assisted you in getting the project finished.'

'I was, wasn't I! I hadn't realised that,' he said excitedly.

Michael called the waiter over to clear away our plates and requested more coffee, and the guys decided to include a liquor to finish off with. Michael's wife and I chose that moment to visit the powder room. Upon returning, I overheard Michael telling Graham that his asthma has cleared up and asked Graham how I saw these images.

Graham glanced over at me as I sat back down, saying, 'Over to you. This is beyond me.'

'Michael, I love talking about energy work. It's Spirit's attributes flowing into each person's awareness, and consciousness operates through mental pictures, that can assist us in healing or manifesting a desire.' I took a sip of my coffee before continuing. 'When we say "I" with an idea in mind, this potent power is paused and ready to be directed towards a purpose. When we follow on with the word "AM" with a clear intent, we activate the energy, directing it, coupled with our focused intention to fulfil a goal we choose for ourselves.'

I added, 'You came to see me with a specific purpose in mind and your inner guidance answered your desire. That's why I saw the image of the two men. We all see life through the "eye" of Consciousness, internally and externally at our level of understanding.'

We realised we were the last clientele left in the restaurant. We stood up and after Michael generously paid as a thank you for my support, we retreated outside. The glass doors closed behind us, shutting out the cool air and we were immediately reacquainted with the familiar busy hum of cars honking their horns and motorbikes roaring past as the warm muggy oppressive night air hit us. Our husbands requested the security guard to call for our drivers. After saying goodnight, we stepped into our cars, joining the other streams of vehicles on the road as we made our way home.

Refer to chapter 24 – Why We Ask Three Times for more detailed information on manifesting including a detailed student's personal experience.

We are multi-dimensional beings and our individual soul resides in a higher realm than our physical existence on earth.

All things in existence are made up of subatomic particles vibrating at differing frequencies and vibrations. These particles are vibrating so fast that they appear as a solid mass on Earth.

From my experience working with clients, Consciousness guides and manages our DNA structure and in some instances, it is not a fixed component – it is receptive to change. I read recently that some scientists now believe that aspects of our DNA are 'not' set in stone!

Our soul records significant happenings that can have a positive or negative effect on our outlook on life. Our energy is always shape-shifting.

We all have the ability to either retain, refine, add to or let go of anything residing in our soul. So often we hang onto traumatic experiences because they may have been too difficult to deal with the pain at that time. Hanging onto our trauma can affect our outlook on life and fragment our soul's consciousness restricting our ability to see life clearly, as in my situation.

Energy follows thought.

CHAPTER 16

A CHALLENGING YEAR

Queen Elizabeth II called 1968 an *annus horribilis* year (Latin for 'horrible year') due to the events that took place around her. Sadly, 1992 turned out to be our annus horribilis year.

Our first Christmas in Jakarta was just six weeks away and when stock arrived in the stores, the word spread rapidly and items quickly disappeared from the shelves. Along with many other expatriates, I went to the store to stock up for Christmas. I was pushing a shopping trolley down an aisle and without thinking I stopped and picked up a bottle of Moët champagne, placing it in the trolley. I continued browsing items until it registered in my mind what I'd done.

Oh, I thought, *that is expensive; we're still on a budget. I'd better put it back.* As I walked back to return the champagne, The Voice came through, surprising me, saying,

'Yvonne, this bottle is to celebrate Graham's new job.'

UH! What did The Voice just say? Logically, the words I heard clearly didn't make any sense. I stood in the aisle, staring at the bottle of champagne as a feeling of apprehension rose inside me as I attempted to make sense of what I had just heard. When doubts popped up in my head, I often ended up arguing with my own brain, yet I trusted The Voice.

What's going on? Surely that can't be right. Graham has a two-year contract. What's The Voice talking about? I remained standing in the aisle for a short time with a big frown on my face. My stomach churned over as the words slowly registered. I purchased the champagne, deciding not to mention it to Graham, and when I returned home, I placed it out of sight in one of the cupboards.

Two weeks later, after four hours in the car with our driver travelling to different supermarkets to get our fortnightly shop completed, we went to pick Graham up from work. I walked into the company's building and made my way to Graham's office. After I walked into his office, I froze on the spot. I sensed something was very wrong and my stomach immediately reacted and I felt uncomfortable. I looked at Graham; my eyes filled with tears and I quickly retreated back to our car. Graham came out after me with a confused look on his face.

'Yvonne, what's wrong? Are you okay? Why did you just walk out like that?'

'I don't understand what happened or what I felt in there. All I know is I will never be walking into your office building again. I don't have a good feeling. I sense something is very wrong.'

The following night when Graham arrived home from work, he walked into the kitchen asking Suti, our cook, to delay dinner for a short while. He poured us both a glass of wine before sitting down and informing me that his contract was being terminated at the end of December 1991. He told me he had raised suspicions to the expatriate manager about some disturbing practices going on between a couple of people in management and contractors. After voicing his concerns about the disturbing practices, Graham was informed a few days later that his job was going to be terminated at the end of the year.

One thing I know about my husband is that his morals and ethics are excellent – those are two of many traits I admire about him.

The hare is now racing ahead of the turtle a few years. In 1994, the Australian managing director overseeing the Indonesian branch came to Jakarta after the truth was uncovered. Graham's suspicions were confirmed and the people involved were sacked.

The little turtle is back again. We had saved some money, nevertheless, being unemployed in a foreign country was very different to being unemployed in Australia. With an election looming the following year, we were warned by expatriate friends to be careful about what we said in public and at home as we didn't know who an informer for the government could be. We nicknamed President Suharto 'Fred' (Graham's father's name) so we could talk freely.

Graham's green eyes creased with worry and his face was drawn. 'What are we going to do? Jakarta is known to become quite volatile at times, even more so at election time.'

I kissed him and walked over to the cupboard. 'I have something to show you, love.'

I retrieved the bottle of champagne and showed it to him. I proceeded to tell him what The Voice had said. 'We are being reassured by The Voice's message that all will work out for us.' I picked up a pen and wrote on the label of the bottle 'Graham's new job'.

'Yvonne, regardless of what The Voice you hear said, I still have to consider what the best pathway for us is to take. Let me think about it for a few days.'

Over the following days, Graham spoke with a few friends who had been residing in Jakarta for many years and all said the same thing. 'No new projects will be considered prior to and after an election until things have settled down.'

Hearing this didn't inspire confidence that a new job would turn up before we would have to leave.

The Suharto government banned large groups of people from meeting in homes until after the election which was to be held in early June. Any residents who had high front walls, which couldn't be seen over the top of, were told they had to create see-through openings, spaced evenly across their front wall. You could feel the tension starting to build up around Jakarta.

We mulled over what to do for many days and then finally we decided to stay. It was a very risky decision to make, which was partly based on the message from The Voice, and also we couldn't bear the thought of having to send our two beloved fur kids to England to be placed into quarantine. I reminded Graham that I felt extremely peaceful when we made the decision to bring the dogs with us to Jakarta. It was a decision we didn't make lightly. Little did we know the challenges that lay ahead of us and how my trust in The Voice would be sorely tested.

We vacated the company house at the end of January 1992 and we found a tiny house in a kampong (a local village) costing us US$500 a month, paid bi-monthly thank goodness. The two years' rent on the company house (US$2,000 a month) had been paid upfront in full. We could only afford to take one of our staff with us and fortunately, the house came with a cook as the kitchen's facilities were very limited.

We were the only expatriates living in the village. It was a real challenge. The local mosque was situated adjacent to our rental house. Five times a day from early morning until evening the call to prayer would go out over the loudspeakers. The house had no fly screens and the only air-conditioning unit was in our bedroom. It struggled to cope with the heat and humidity.

We had no car. We budgeted our money to last us until the end of August. Our plan was if Graham failed to find work in time, the dogs would be sent to England two weeks prior to our leaving. We would then fly home and sell our house to pay the costs for the dogs' quarantine. Back in 1992, Australia, along with some other countries, had very strict quarantine regulations – seven months in England followed by another two months in Australia.

Early April, I received two phone calls from two girlfriends, Liz and Ann, advising me that my mother had collapsed and was given four units of blood and was now in a stable condition in hospital. Liz was waiting on a call from the specialist and she'd call me back. She rang back informing us that the specialist had diagnosed my mother with an aggressive form of cancer – non-Hodgkin's lymphoma. We immediately flew to Perth.

Under the doctor's recommendation, we moved Mum from her self-contained unit in the Masonic retirement complex along with some of her furniture and sentimental items to a bedsitter within the same complex, which also housed a C-class hospital. Graham flew back to Jakarta to continue looking for work. This was made even more challenging due to demonstrations taking place prior to the upcoming election and all new projects were shelved indefinitely.

I stayed on looking after Mum. Every time I booked my flight back to Jakarta, Mum ended up back in the hospital. Many times my booking was cancelled.

At the beginning of June, Mum once again ended up in the hospital. The doctors called me aside one afternoon, informing me that her condition had not changed since her first diagnosis in April. In their professional opinion, they believed she could live to Christmas, if not longer. The doctors suggested I fly back to Jakarta as they were aware of our predicament. My ticket expired on the 16th of June, which happened to be the same day as our wedding anniversary.

Mum became extremely difficult and very troublesome as she didn't want to be in the bedsitter but due to her condition, she wasn't able to look after herself properly as before. The doctors thought it was best under the current circumstances to move her to the adjacent C-class hospital facility before I left, where she would receive a higher level of care and still be near friends. Unfortunately, the management of the complex refused to take her.

In their words... 'Your mother is too disruptive; we have to consider the other patients.'

The doctors found my mother another C-class hospital, which she hated. All her friends lived in the retirement village and at this hospital she didn't know anyone and she was too far away for friends to visit.

Mum said to me after I moved her to the hospital, 'Yvonne, what a fool I have been.'

I could see clearly where Mum was coming from; she realised for herself how her angry disruptive behaviour resulted in her ending up in this overcrowded busy government hospital. Mum was put into a small room, sharing it with another lady. It held two single beds, a side table and a wardrobe each. It was a depressing sight to walk in to and experience.

I went every day to the hospital and when she found out that I was leaving in two days, she said to me, 'I don't know what I have ever done to deserve such a selfish daughter as you.'

Although I had heard those words often in my life, they still felt like a stab to my heart. I also knew that she loved me and said those things because she didn't want me to leave. I felt torn in two. Both Graham and Mum needed my support.

The night before I was to leave, my girlfriend Liz drove me to the hospital. I said to my mother, 'I promise you whether Graham gets employment or not, I will fly back at the end of August and look after you for as long as you need me.'

As I bent over the bed to kiss her goodbye, I told her again that I loved her.

Her face contorted and her eyes hardened, repeating the words she had spoken to me the day before, adding, 'I hope I am not here when you return from Jakarta.'

She closed her eyes, shutting them tight, rolled over in bed and lay with her back to me before pulling the sheet up over her head, refusing to kiss me or say goodbye. I thought I was about to crumble into pieces onto the floor.

Liz came from a very loving family and was shocked at what she saw and heard. After we walked out of Mum's room, Liz put her arm around me and we walked to her car, both of us with tears in our eyes.

The following morning, with a heavy heart on the 16th of June, I flew back to Jakarta. I knew deep in my heart that under different circumstances, Mum would have understood why I had to return to

Jakarta. I knew she loved me but her cutting words still hurt me deeply.

Four days later the hospital rang, informing me Mum's kidneys were failing. I cried on the phone, pleading with the hospital staff to keep Mum alive until I arrived. My sister had been advised by the hospital and decided not to travel from her home, situated a few hundred kilometres from Perth. I understood my sister's response as we all handle pain differently. I think she could have felt it hypocritical to see Mum.

The next morning, suitcases in hand, we were about to step into a taxi to leave for the airport when our staff ran out, calling us back to take an urgent telephone call. Mum had gotten her wish. She died on the 21st of June 1992.

I was devastated; the guilt I felt for leaving her completely overwhelmed me. I felt angry and distraught. Although I was grateful a cousin was with Mum when she died, I wanted to be there also so Mum had someone of her very own to support and care for her until she passed over. The funeral home allowed Graham and me to have a private viewing of Mum after they had embalmed her. I had to physically see her to accept that she had died. The reality of the situation hit me and as soon as I saw her lying in the coffin, I vividly recalled how we had parted the last time I saw her.

Graham kept his arm around me in his attempt to comfort me. I was a blubbering mess, so many mixed-up emotions poured out. Even in death, the memory of her harsh words brought me to my knees as guilt and pain tore at my heart.

Graham looked down on Mum and said, 'Even in death your mum still doesn't look at peace.' He was right.

The days before and after Mum's funeral felt surreal. It was as if I was being carried along. I realised afterwards, even though I had been upset over what happened, Spirit had been there uplifting me the whole time.

The Minster who conducted the funeral knew the pain and guilt I felt and said 'Yvonne, you both gave each other a gift by not being present. Neither of you could bear to let each other go.' His words gave me comfort.

One lovely thing I remember happening at the funeral service – as I stepped down from the pulpit after sharing some happy memories about Mum, I walked over to the coffin touching it lightly before placing a kiss on top. At the exact moment I did that, the sun came out, sending forth its light pouring in through the small chapel windows and some of the rays landed directly on the coffin and me. Again, I was reminded no matter the situation, Spirit will always find a way of letting us know we are not alone.

Mum had very little money and what she did have was split between my sister and me. That gift of money enabled us to stay on in Jakarta one extra month, so instead of leaving at the end of August we could stay until the end of September.

Elections had been held in June and President Suharto was re-elected. The riots finally stopped and in August the economy slowly started picking up again.

Unfortunately, we discovered upon arriving back in Jakarta that all our furniture and goods, stored in a spare bedroom of the rental house, were infested and damaged beyond repair by white ants. Everything had to be destroyed, which included the video of our wedding and reception, except our glassware and crockery.

I became very anxious and stressed as the time came nearer for us to leave. I struggled to stay positive – the thought of having to send our precious fur children away especially pained my heart. Whenever one of us had a down moment, and we had plenty of those, one of us would go to the refrigerator, pull out the bottle of champagne and hold it up, saying out loud, 'Remember what The Voice said.'

Time was running out fast and I struggled to remain positive.

The first week of September, just two weeks before we had to send the dogs to England, Graham was interviewed for a job on a new high-rise project, which was still in the planning stages. Over nine months had passed since I had purchased the champagne. It had proved to be a wonderful support and encouragement in one way; however, I still battled to trust that The Voice's message would prove true. It definitely tested my faith and trust. I admit I failed miserably.

The second week of September, on a Friday, Graham signed the contract for the job. When he arrived home, he walked in, waving the contract in his hand. We didn't waste any time removing the champagne from the refrigerator. It was a most welcome sound to our ears to hear the cork pop off with a bang. Graham poured us both a glass and as I put the glass up to my mouth to take my first sip, the effervescent bubbles tickled my nose. I thought, *the bubbles are happy for us too*. After almost ten months we finally got to enjoy this long-awaited celebration. I'm sure if the dogs had known their very near fate, they may have insisted on having a drop too.

The Voice knew back in November 1991 what the immediate future held for us and it has been proved to me many times that timing is always perfect in our lives, even if we cannot see it at the time.

How did Spirit know? Because this unseen power is all-knowing and all-seeing. In death, Mum had given us a precious gift – the money I received enabled us to stay on an extra month in Jakarta. During that month, Graham continued working for the same company and living in Jakarta until we were transferred to Bangkok in 2002.

CHAPTER 17

THE DISCOVERY

As Power of Attorney, I had the job of finalising Mum's affairs. My sister Nancy, Graham and I were sorting through Mum's briefcase after the funeral. I was never allowed delve into Mum's briefcase and it was with great trepidation that I reached in and pulled out the first item. Sorting through, we discovered two passports belonging to my father. Both passports had different birth dates and different places of birth. We were mystified.

Nancy, who was nearly five years older than me, said, 'Can you remember all the presents we used to get at Christmas, then suddenly things changed?'

'I only have one memory of us all on holidays together one Christmas, and the pillowslip next to my bed was full of presents.'

'Yes. That was the last family holiday we had together. Dad stopped coming with us after that. That was just before you turned five. I wonder if these two passports are connected to the "secret" work that Dad used to do?'

I glanced quickly at Graham with my eyebrows raised before looking back to Nancy, asking, 'Secret work! What secret work?'

'Dad never forgave Mum for breaking a promise not to reveal the secret government work he did back in the early 1950s. It was at a time when the Australian Government and other countries were concerned about communist infiltration. I overheard Mum and Dad having a huge argument one evening. Dad used to go to certain gatherings at night and report back to the government.'

'What did Mum do that caused Dad to stop coming away with us?'

'Mum became angry at his going out some nights and accused him of having another woman on the side. Dad attempted to convince Mum to trust him and that her accusations were unfounded. Mum was relentless and he caved in, telling her about his secret work, making her promise not to tell anyone about it. Unfortunately, Mum had mentioned to her brother her concerns that Dad was perhaps having an affair, then later she repeated to her brother what Dad had told her.'

Nancy went on to say that one night, after having a few drinks following a Masonic lodge meeting, our uncle gossiped to some men at the bar about his brother-in-law's work. Within a couple of days, Dad was admonished and totally cut off from the work he loved to do.

'Oh no!' I said. 'What happened when Dad found out?'

'Mum totally destroyed Dad's trust and possibly his love for her by telling her brother about his extra work. He would have been extremely distressed by Mum's betrayal, because after that Dad changed. He withdrew into himself.'

Nancy and I both recalled a big argument between Mum and Dad one night. It was Dad's birthday. I would have been about maybe eleven at the time. We had started eating dinner when Dad walked in. I was keen to finish my dinner so I could have some chocolate cake that Mum had made for the occasion.

Dad sat down; Mum was dishing up his dinner when an argument broke out between them. I don't recall what transpired or the cause of Mum's angry eruption as I was too busy staring at the last two green objects on my plate – brussels sprouts! Oh, how I hated them! I knew from past experiences it wasn't any good sneaking them to Goldie, our cocker spaniel dog, as she didn't like them either. I had to eat them, otherwise no cake.

I was contemplating how I could swallow them without having to taste them when Mum, in a rage, picked up Dad's dinner and flung it at him. Fortunately, Dad ducked. The plate smashed against the wall, splattering Dad's food, including his brussels sprouts, all down the wall and spraying my father with gravy. We had never seen Mum do that before. We both sat in stunned silence.

In her rage, Mum blurted out something that shocked my sister and me. 'Well today isn't your "real" birthday, anyway!'

Nancy and I glanced up at each other with raised eyebrows to see if either of us already knew this. We both gave a slight shrug of our shoulders and quickly refocused on the food in front of us, pretending we didn't hear anything. That night, I was so distracted by what had taken place at the table that I ate my most hated vegetable in two big gulps. I didn't want to be on the receiving end of Mum's mood. I might get sent to bed with a red bottom or worse still, without any chocolate cake.

Those brief words registered deep in both our minds, yet with all the other turmoil going on in our house, we buried it. Dad quietly got up and walked out of the room.

The passports were put aside as we slowly continued working our way through the briefcase which was filled with memorabilia.

My husband lifted out a large empty brown envelope, which covered the bottom of the briefcase and resting underneath were two kettledrum sticks and a photo of my father dressed in a Scottish military band uniform playing the kettledrums. I froze. I sat staring down at what was sitting in the case. I felt lightheaded and my hands started to shake. There, in front of me, were what I believed to be the 'smooth sticks' I described during the re-birthing session. I felt sick. These were the objects used to try to abort me. My eyes welled up as I explained to Nancy in detail about the re-birthing session. I had only seen or spoken to Nancy maybe four times since my father's death in 1968. Nancy stopped coming to visit after Dad died. She had loved

Dad very much but had no respect or time for our mother, calling her a manipulative and destructive woman.

Explaining my re-birthing experience triggered Nancy's memory and she confirmed that a loud argument had taken place between Mum and Dad just prior to being told she was going to get a baby brother or sister. Nancy admitted she wasn't happy about it at all.

She sat quietly for a few minutes before asking me, 'Do you remember the elderly lady we called Nana Berry who lived on our street?'

I nodded.

'Nana had been a midwife who had worked in the outback of Western Australia many years ago and believed in using old remedies for certain ailments. Mum was very good friends with Nana Berry. I believe she may have helped Mum try to abort you because prior to my finding out Mum was pregnant, there were times when I came into the room and they would stop talking.'

I had received enough information to conclude all that I saw, heard and experienced during the re-birthing session was true.

Graham gently brought our attention back to the issue in front of us. 'The sticks.' He knew that I alone needed to deal with this issue.

Nancy said, 'Yvonne, why don't you take them and burn them? It may help you to find closure.'

I couldn't bring myself to touch them. Graham picked them up, wrapping them in newspaper before placing them in the boot of our hire car.

We were staying with friends before returning to Jakarta. Situated in a corner of their games room stood a huge combustion wood heater with a large glass door. Graham quietly spoke to Liz and David and the three of them left the room. A short time later, Graham returned, placing the kettledrum sticks by the fireside.

He looked at me and said, 'Love, I will leave these here for you to decide what you choose to do with them.'

I sat there looking at these two kettledrum sticks for some time, wondering what Mum had going on in her life that drove her to take such drastic measures. She must have been frightened of something. Was she scared that Dad would leave her? Mum often used to tell me that if she died tomorrow, Dad would return to England, leaving us behind. I feared being abandoned.

I knew what I had to do; I kept telling myself, *These sticks cannot hurt me now. Just pick them up and throw them in the fire.* It wasn't the kettledrum sticks I was afraid of; my mind was struggling with what my mother would say to me for taking such action. Even though she was dead, her voice still tormented my mind and that old familiar fearful feeling would rise up at the thought of disobeying her. Often arriving home from school, a feeling of apprehension would rise up as I reached out to open the front gate of our home. I dreaded walking inside.

As I stood in front of the wood heater, I battled with the two inner voices arguing with each other, my logical voice telling me to go ahead and burn them, whereas my critical voice condemned me for even considering such an act. Tears trickled down my face. I took a few deep breaths, hoping that would give me the courage to block out my mother's words I heard screaming out at me. 'Don't you dare disobey me. You will be punished, you bad girl. You are no good. You only think of yourself.'

After all the years of self-growth work, it was as if I had gone backwards. I was once again feeling crippled by her words. On and on harped the old familiar voice until I couldn't stand it any longer. I put my hands over my ears. I just wanted to block out the tormenting bombardment of negative thoughts. Anger built within me, acting as the motivation I needed to step forward. I yanked open the glass door to the fire and before I could change my mind, I picked up the two kettle drumsticks and with shaking hands, I threw them in. I couldn't bear to watch them burn. I walked away into Graham's arms.

As Graham consoled me, I turned my head, glancing up at the wall clock mounted in their kitchen, noting the time. It was 8.38 p.m. I wondered why I had purposely done that. I surmised at the time it was a meaningful moment.

Guilt overwhelmed me but at the same time, I knew by taking that action I had honoured myself and that felt empowering. I was so glad that I alone made the decision to burn them. That action presented a very positive picture to my mind. It is over. Finished. Enough is enough, I am now moving on. Sometimes we have to step back before taking a leap forward.

Approximately 700-plus kilometres away, a strange incident happened in my sister's house when I burnt the kettle drumsticks.

The next day I telephoned Nancy to tell her I had burnt them. We spoke about it and then she asked, 'Yvonne, do you know what time it was when you burnt them?'

I told her.

There was silence on the other end of the phone before she said, 'Last night around 8.30 p.m., after putting the children to bed, I sat down and switched on the TV to watch my favourite show, which started at 8.35 p.m. The glass door in my combustion heater blew out. It was fortunate that neither the children nor I were standing in front of it. My first thought was that Mum was letting me know how much I disappointed her as a daughter.'

Nancy went on to say that someone was coming to replace the glass today and sending the damaged glass back to the factory for analysing, as they had no record of this happening before.

Since my father's death, Nancy had rarely made contact. She handled her unhappiness in a very different way to me, by closing the door on the past.

When I rang Nancy a few days later, she informed me that the company couldn't find anything wrong with the glass. They had no answer. They were baffled; however, they were going to continue investigating the matter.

'I think it was Mum once again insisting on having the last say. I was the one who told you to burn the kettle drumsticks.'

We both had a laugh about it. I also informed her we were returning to Jakarta in a couple of days. Nancy didn't express any interest in keeping in touch. I wrote to her twice but never received a response.

I miss my sister. We haven't spoken since. Nancy had once again shut the door on her past.

The hare is back. In 1996, Graham and I went to England to meet my father's family and research Graham's family history. We had no idea we would uncover a buried family secret that left me in shock and at the same time elated. Wow, we had a ginormous skeleton in our spotlessly clean cupboard, which opened another door of understanding connected to the animosity that existed between my parents. They had both betrayed each other in different ways and destroyed whatever love, respect and trust they had for each other. Refer to chapter 30 – Discovering a Family Secret.

CHAPTER 18

HEALING FOR MY MOTHER AND ME

In November 1992, five months after Mum's funeral, I was still feeling sad that I hadn't seen her after she passed over. I sometimes naïvely thought, *Oh, she is so angry with me. She didn't even come to visit me after she died as other family members had done.* I needed closure.

During the early hours of the 23rd of December, I was awakened by The Voice saying,

'You are going to visit your mother.'

WHAT! I thought.

'Yvonne, your mother's vibration is not strong enough to come to you. You are going to visit her.'

I panicked and The Voice gently told me to take a deep breath and relax. I felt as if I was wrapped in a strong force. I was sinking very fast into myself through a tunnel of bluish-white energy. I panicked twice and came back. I remember opening my eyes briefly, thinking *this is a crazy dream,* although I knew deep in my heart it wasn't a dream; it was real. My heart was pounding so fast, I thought, *I'm going to die too.*

Once more, The Voice gently repeated the request, *'Yvonne, take one more deep breath and this time you will go through.'*

This time I kept control of my emotions and came out the other side and stood there dazed, calm and surprised. All I was thinking as I looked around was, *It's a city! I'm looking at a small city.* I remember thinking the sky looked different but I don't recall why I thought that. In my mind I asked, *How will I find my mother?*

The Voice answered, **'Your mother will find you. She needs to tell you something for her own healing and yours.'**

Glancing to my left, I saw my mother coming towards me. She appeared healthier. I turned to the left to walk towards her and my mother straight away put her hand up, indicating for me to stop. She was at my side in an instant and I'm not sure whether I sensed or heard her saying to me,

'You are to walk back the way you came.' (To my right!) Then she looked straight into my eyes, adding, 'My dear, be happy because I am happy.'

That was it! That's all. Just those few brief words. I was disappointed. Our conversation was so very brief. I know it was a very selfish thought of mine at the time. As I write this, I feel uncomfortable for thinking that instead of being grateful. Yet, I expected to hear more from her.

I felt a sudden jolt and I opened my eyes; I was back in bed and I rolled over, cuddling into Graham's strong body for comfort. Other incidents have frightened me, but none as frightening as this one. I couldn't sleep the rest of the night and kept wondering if I had dreamt it.

The next morning I repeatedly questioned myself. *Could I be mistaken? Had I dreamt this?* I knew in my heart something definitely happened and somehow I had communicated with my mother. Of course, logically I couldn't accept what had actually taken place. I prayed, asking for confirmation. Later that day I picked up a small book I had been given for Christmas from a friend two days prior and opened it at random to a page about astral travelling. One sentence written on the page caught my eye: *Heaven can appear as a city.*

Through that 'encounter' with my mother, I had at last found peace. I have never shared this experience before with anyone other than Graham because my mind found it difficult to accept. In saying that,

I have read that people believe we often go astral travelling at night when asleep. I cannot say exactly how this experience took place all I know is, it definitely happened. The beautiful gift from that experience was I finally had the closure I needed. Visiting my mother, however it transpired, helped me by clearing away the built-up pain I had harboured. Spirit knew it was necessary for me to be able to move forward.

I remembered a couple of years later while meditating in my bedroom, I left my body via my belly button and in an instant, I was on the other side of the room, looking back at myself. I panicked and then in the blink of an eye, I was back in my body. I admit I stopped meditating for a while because the experience frightened me.

On Christmas day an amusing thing happened. Whilst we had been in Perth sorting out Mum's things we came across her address book, important papers, along with some Christmas candles, serviettes and a few paper plates. I decided to take these back to Jakarta.

On Christmas eve, I placed all of Mum's Christmas items on the coffee table.

On Christmas morning we decided to have a glass of champagne and fresh fruit for breakfast, saving ourselves for a scrumptious lunch. I lit Mum's candles then handed Graham the top paper plate and proceeded to give myself one. Graham and I started laughing as we looked at the soiled paper plate I was holding. We also discovered some of the other plates were soiled too. Mum's eyesight was poorly and she didn't notice if any of them had been used. We used to smile whenever we went to her house to visit, as she occasionally reused a plate and didn't notice if it had already been used.

Instead of feeling sad about having our first Christmas without sharing it with Mum, Graham's family and our friends, we couldn't stop laughing each time we saw the soiled paper plates. I purposely left them on the coffee table all day as a fond reminder of Mum.

It wasn't until 2004 when we were living back in Perth that I saw my mother and father again. They had come to say goodbye.

We are all on an inner journey of unfolding our truths for us. It is an ongoing process.

Yvonne Fogarty

CHAPTER 19

INSIGHTFUL VISION

On the 21st of February 1993, I suddenly woke up out of a deep sleep. I rolled onto my back as I opened my eyes. Looking up at the ceiling, I saw a subtle mist moving around in the room and a faint pulsating light appeared mixing in with the mist. Again I experienced The Voice vibrating through my whole being, saying…

Yvonne, isn't it that the smallest impression from the universe is the beginning of understanding?

Yvonne, isn't understanding the seed of knowledge?

Yvonne, isn't knowledge* truth that embodies your life?

Cycles are events in our lifetimes. Lifetimes are forever.

As the vision ended, the pulsating light transformed into a circle and the mist turned into an arrow moving clockwise around the circle. From left to right.

* The Voice's meaning behind the word knowledge in the message above is explained further on in this chapter.

The words I heard penetrated my whole being, leaving my body buzzing. The way the vision played out and its related vibrations held a very powerful intention. The precise way the words were spoken and why The Voice kept repeating my name puzzled me. I quickly grabbed my pen and notebook from my bedside table and wrote everything down.

I described the vision to Graham later that morning. He pondered over the words and said, 'I think The Voice was attempting to jog your memory.'

'I do too. I wonder what the memory is connected to?' I admit I couldn't connect logically with the message nor what The Voice meant by the word 'impression'. I knew I already took note of inner niggles to help me, so what was The Voice implying? I pondered over it for a couple of weeks before the realisation suddenly came to me.

It was a very humid day; I was swimming in a friend's pool when the answer popped into my mind. Duh! Sometimes I can be slow on the uptake. I had been 'trying' too hard to find the answer, instead of allowing it to just flow in naturally. By trying, I blocked the answer from coming to me. When I was relaxed, the understanding popped in.

The message had finally sunk in...

The smallest impression means an incoming impulse/imprint, a seed of information, inner guidance from Spirit to our soul, and when embraced and nurtured, it will produce an insight, an 'aha' moment, allowing the insight and associated concept to reveal itself fully and our understanding takes on a deep inner knowing. We experience a positive shift in our conscious awareness as it becomes a truth for us and resonates in harmony with Spiritual truths.

I sensed The Voice was nudging me to venture deeper within. When we pay attention to the subtle inner impressions/impulses, we uncover a KEY that can unlock a door allowing us an opportunity to let go of distorted beliefs we have hung onto, beliefs that are holding us back from achieving our desires. For example, you would have read earlier that I used to react when someone said the word 'obey'. It triggered a disturbance within me until I discovered it was connected to an imbalance in my thinking. Refer to Chapter 3 – Stepping Out.

Many of us repeatedly experience fearful negative thoughts that may cause us to feel insecure. That kind of thinking can cause us to harbour fear and sadness, which at some stage during a disagreement with a loved one can cause our pent-up feelings to burst forth and we might say things we don't mean.

It is so important for our wellbeing to clear any belittling thoughts; otherwise, thoughts built upon can have a negative influence on our lives. If you decide to heal disturbing feelings and find it difficult to release a destructive pattern, seek out a psychologist or an energy practitioner to support you. Vibrational therapy can support us immensely as it works by gently releasing the blocked subconscious memory pattern from where it originated. A wonderful example is an experience in this book about a woman who was able to free herself from the deep-seated painful emotional memory she harboured. Refer to chapter 45 – The Healing.

This overall message from The Voice has supported others, including myself, to become more content and happier in life, through learning to 'listen to' and 'feel' deeply the impressions impressed on us by our inner guidance. These impressions give us the opportunity to tune into the associated feeling(s) connected to an issue with the aim of gaining understanding.

Understanding means becoming consciously aware through inner guidance of an untruth (imbalance in our thinking) held in our subconscious mind that stands in the way of moving forward. This is one-way inner guidance supports us by giving us an opportunity to investigate those niggling feelings which are a signal to us something is out of balance. When we grasp the understanding of what the misperception is, we have an 'aha' moment, when the impression reveals its meaning to our conscious mind. It's exciting when clarity flows in and we experience a shift in our awareness as we embrace the insight, knowing without any doubt we have embraced a truth for us.

The other word that accompanied understanding was the word **'seed'** – meaning when our inner guidance plants a more uplifting concept/possibility, opening a door in our mind for the new awareness to germinate and flourish, shifting our perspective to a more positive one with the intention of expanding our viewing platform to how we are seeing and experiencing life.

Isn't knowledge truth that embodies your life – In this context, it means our truth for us that harmonises with our innate frequencies and vibrations. The intention is to support us to think, speak and act in ways that will not harm our soul or hurt others. If our thinking is out of balance, it can cause an emotional blockage in our soul's energy body, hindering the natural flow of energy to support our overall wellbeing.

When we change a negative belief to a positive one, our soul automatically embraces this more uplifting frequency and vibration, embodying that truth throughout our whole being. There is a big difference energy-wise from knowing of something – head knowledge – to a heartfelt knowing. This new frequency is anchored in our soul, becoming a deep inner knowing within our heart, permeating every cell in our being and we naturally project this new vibration out into the world. We shine from the inside out. It's a joy to experience, we feel lighter as this new awareness settles down aligning with our authentic intrinsic nature.

Our whole being becomes more aware and our consciousness expands, allowing more spiritual wisdom to flow in, to guide and support us as we continue to evolve.

This vibrational support enables me to experience life with more awareness and insight, and express compassion towards the disowned aspects of myself, loving them instead of condemning them.

This power we all live off 'just is' and radiates pure unconditional love, e.g. love carries the highest frequency and vibration as does Joy. There are many varying degrees associated with a frequency, depending on our thoughts and attitudes at the time and the lowest vibration of love we can experience is fear, deep sadness and depression is the lowest vibration of joy.

Finally, the last part of The Voice's insightful message is a wonderful confirmation – **cycles are events in our lifetimes. Lifetimes are forever** and **the arrow moving around clockwise from 'left to right'** means our life continues moving forward, and there is 'no death'. We simply step out of our physical body and return to our original state as a spiritual being (Refer to chapter 47 – Roy's Passing). Our evolving soul carries on building upon itself through our many past, present and future life cycle experiences.

The last sentence spoken by The Voice is a precious gift to us all – our life truly does carry on.

Despite the questioning chatter and doubts that rise up, I knew I would never stop searching until I gained a deeper understanding of life and how I came to hear The Voice and have these experiences.

I had no idea what could still be in the way of freeing my self-expression. I still found so many things hard to accept. I wasted many years resisting letting go and accepting the existence of 'all' life seen and unseen. My analytical mind kept getting in the way, seeking logical solutions to the happenings. I know this supportive power doesn't operate to accommodate 'human logic'.

Although I had come a long way, I still had a way to go. I was still living a life shut away from feeling deeply and expressing myself freely. I was still protecting myself and fearful of what ugly things I might uncover within if I did delve too deeply.

However, that vision did open another door. I found the courage to pay more attention, sensing the subtle ways my inner guidance conversed with me, which is explained further on in the book. Refer to chapter 54 – A Soul's Associated Frequencies and Vibrations and chapter 55 – Our Sensing System.

If we can explore and nurture
that which resides deep within our soul,
immense potential can unfold.

Yvonne Fogarty

CHAPTER 20

STEPPING FORWARD

After receiving the first-degree Reiki training in 1991, I had taken to Reiki as a duck does to water. I attained my second-degree level in October 1992, opening another door for my inner gifts to expand. Then, following the insightful vision in early 1993, I gave myself permission to open up more to discern and learn, from the impressions and inner guidance I received as the vibrations flowed in, thus accelerating my growth.

I was at a stage in my life where I had been seeking guidance for my life purpose. I was happy giving Reiki treatments to others, serving on the social welfare committee, coordinating projects in the community and fundraising for the disadvantaged Indonesian people, yet my heart was yearning for something more. But what? I prayed, but no answer was forthcoming.

Frustrated and without inner guidance presenting itself, I decided to take matters into my own hands. Only in retrospect did it become clear to me that Spirit was waiting for me to do just that – take the initiative, by stepping forward in a direction and only after doing so could I receive the guidance I was seeking.

Why? Because we have freewill to choose our own direction. Sometimes we have to show initiative by becoming involved in our desire for a change to come into our lives, instead of just asking three times and blowing it away. In some situations, it is important to do things in support of moving towards our desire. All I had been doing was lazily sitting back, whining and continually asking to be shown my life purpose, like a squeaky old record player stuck in a groove.

I sent away for various distant learning courses and after receiving a pile of brochures and checking them out, nothing appealed to me. Although I felt disappointed, I continued going about my day believing that a door would open for me to step through into my life work.

One morning while showering, The Voice came through...

'Yvonne, you are to become a Reiki Master.' (Teaching degree)

'No, no, no!' I bellowed out loud.

'No way! Not that! That's not what I want to do.' I was confused. I knew I desired to use my gifts by running motivational self-growth workshops, spiritual healing and intuitive counselling, yet I didn't think I could work that way by becoming a Reiki Master. My desire was set on supporting others to experience a more fulfilling life.

I couldn't see at the time that I would be guided to utilise Reiki as a wonderful energy tool to accompany the inner gifts that were emerging to work in my own unique way, to support those who choose to commence a journey within to uncover their authentic self and inner gifts to share with the world.

The decision to follow The Voice's suggestion was mine alone to make. Even though I couldn't see the end result, I finally stepped forward in blind faith.

Why? The Voice always spoke the Truth. I trusted The Voice. It had never let me down.

After our financial setback in 1992, we were slowly rebuilding our bank account. I shared with Graham that The Voice suggested I do my Reiki Master's teaching degree and informed him of the cost. He was in the bathroom when I told him.

He stopped combing his wet hair and stood looking in the mirror, deep in thought for a few moments before turning to face me. 'Do you know how much money we have saved to date?'

'I've no idea,' I replied.

'We have that much in the bank, the money is yours.'

It was the exact amount I was to pay for my master's degree. What a man!

'But Graham, we've been living without any medical cover since 1992 because we couldn't afford it and if we have to be evacuated in an emergency to Singapore, the costs could easily exceed tens of thousands of dollars. It's too risky and in my opinion, it's being irresponsible.'

I pondered over what to do. I was fearful of not having enough money if we needed it.

A few days later, The Voice came through clearly stating,

'The Master will come to you.'

I had been considering going to Perth, Australia, knowing it was a short flight from Jakarta and I could stay with friends. The course was a lot cheaper there and we would still have enough money left over to pay for medical cover. I was so very tempted to go to Australia and ignore The Voice, yet I had no idea why I felt disturbed by that idea and I asked for clarity.

Early the next morning, The Voice spoke again, *'Yvonne, it is the "intent" behind your actions that colours your future pathway and experiences.'*

Oh, I thought. *The Voice is right. What was I thinking!* I had dedicated my life to supporting others in whatever way Spirit guided me. By considering going to Australia, my 'intention' would have inadvertently become 'conditional', instead of remaining 'unconditional'.

After experiencing what we went through in 1992, money represented security to me. The Voice desired for me to let go and that meant giving my all and trusting. I stepped forward and never looked back.

Within a couple of weeks, the same friend I had sat next to at a fundraising dinner, who had informed me originally about Reiki, rang telling me that a Reiki Master was coming to Jakarta from Holland.

I went through a very challenging time internally in preparation to do my master's. It felt as if I had a very large toothbrush inside me, scrubbing and cleaning out anything that was in the way of my stepping onto my chosen pathway. I admit it was an extremely uncomfortable time.

We emptied our bank account (US$10,000) and on the 3rd of October 1993, at precisely 10 a.m., I was initiated as a Reiki Master. The morning of my initiation I sat quietly on my own, meditating in my room at a friend's mountain retreat in Puncak, located in the hills approximately one-and-a-half hours' drive from Jakarta. Quietly praying, I reconfirmed my dedication to serving humanity when I suddenly experienced a very powerful vision. This vision was different to any other I had previously experienced. I couldn't stop the vision, whether my eyes were open or closed, and that unnerved me, so I kept my eyes closed as it felt more comfortable.

I watched as the vision played out as if I was watching a movie. I was observing myself in another time and place...

I was wearing a simple white robe, walking barefoot down stone steps into a very large underground room. The light-coloured sand on the floor felt fine yet gritty under my bare feet. I stood glancing around the huge room. Symbols were simply drawn in black individually embedded in large light-coloured stone blocks, which made up the inner walls of the building. Although I didn't see anyone else in the room, I felt a very strong presence around me and I inwardly knew it was a place of sacred knowledge.

The words that came to me were... 'Oh, my goodness, I am in awe at the spectacular knowledge before me.' Then I became aware of feeling the energy stirring up deep emotion in my heart.

The unseen presence then led me over to only one of the many symbols that were drawn on the walls all around me. I stood staring at this one symbol until the vision faded.

'Yvonne, it will all come back to you.'

When I opened my eyes, I was perspiring. The vision left me questioning once again why these visions were happening. I thought to myself, *don't go there. Just accept.* I quickly grabbed my notebook, drew the symbol and wrote down what I had experienced. It was the feeling I felt as I stood looking around at this ancient knowledge. This experience has never left me. I still carry the deep impression of that feeling of 'awe' within my psyche and I feel humbled by it.

The hare is back briefly. Many years later, I realised the vision I experienced prior to my initiation as a Reiki Master was also an 'initiation' opening another door for much deeper healing to take place.

The pathway I chose and my commitment to my future work commenced opening more doors within my mind, guiding me towards healing the pain held in my soul from eons ago connected to that room.

The insightful message I received in 1992 from The Voice – Impressions, Understanding and Knowledge (refer to chapter 19 – Insightful Vision) and the vision relating to the Room of Knowledge in this chapter are definitely interconnected.

The Master who initiated me donated some of the money I paid to the Australian and New Zealand Association and the social welfare committee was able to build a number of toilet blocks to service many villages around Jakarta.

In January 1994 after I completed writing the first-degree training manual, I began running Reiki self-growth training workshops. I see Reiki as a connector tool to our soul and a key to accessing more in-depth frequency of vibrational information to assist us in our lives to support our soul's individual journey. Reiki also aligns, fine-tunes and can enhance a person's ability to receive healing to support our self and other people. I see the Reiki initiations a student receives as a similar procedure to fine-tuning a radio station to receive a clearer reception.

For me, the healing that has taken place over the years has accelerated my spiritual growth and Consciousness operates in conjunction with my level of understanding and openness to receive.

During the first training class I held, one word was spoken to me in my heart: *'Memphis.'*

I automatically replied in my mind, *Oh, Memphis Tennessee?*

The Voice instantly replied, *'We didn't say that!'*

At the time, the use of the word 'we' surprised me. I know now that it is a 'unified' expression relating our individualised soul and our overall inter-connection with Consciousness.

Graham researched the word Memphis, discovering that the origin of the word Memphis comes from Greek and Coptic. The biblical name means 'Abode of the good'. Another version is 'Place of good abode'. Memphis, Egypt in ancient times was the capital of Lower Egypt and a regional centre for religion, commerce and trade.

At the time I had no idea why The Voice said this to me. I questioned Memphis as being the location of this library because the symbol I was shown was nothing like the symbols I have seen in my research on Memphis, Egypt.

I have never advertised my workshops. Instead, I set the dates for each class and Spirit brought the workshops together. At first, each class held approximately four students then slowly the numbers increased. The most I had in one class was ten students, along with past students sitting in free of charge. I preferred to keep the numbers down to eight and in some instances when it was necessary to support a student, I sensed to run a workshop for them alone.

As I grew in understanding and knowledge, so did the students. Spirit guided all the training sessions and the content varied slightly depending on the requirements of that group.

The first-degree initiations raise a student's vibrations. Training ran for two full days, in which I shared my understanding of energy flow and the students were taught how to work with the energy. After 21 days, the students returned for another full day where I focused on teaching them to tune into their senses, work with the energy and how to use their minds to think in ways in support of their own healing.

The second-degree initiation and training workshops ran for two full days initially and students returned twice more over a six-week period. This initiation connects them with three distinct frequencies and opens a door in their consciousness for accessing and utilising spiritual attributes to assist in working with energy. I shared with them different ways to create goals, to support family, to sense inner guidance and support others, using the three second-degree symbols a student receives during initiation.

Consciousness operates beyond time and space, just as we receive and send messages via an electronic device. Second-degree students can energetically do similar, sending healing vibrations anywhere in the world, connecting in with another person's energy body to support them as long as it is done with their permission.

Although I was a member of the Reiki Alliance, which stipulates you can only run a first-degree Reiki, second-degree Reiki and finally the level three master's teaching degree training workshops. I felt strongly that students could benefit greatly if they could do a master's degree without the teaching aspect to it. It was a huge jump financially from second degree to a teaching master's degree and many students didn't desire to become teachers. They desired a deeper connection purely for their own inner journey. I know the wonderful benefits that come from this deep commitment and the support this level of energy can bestow on us.

I was in a dilemma. I felt an inner pressure building in my heart, nudging me to step outside of the set rules. As a member, I continued to respect their guidelines, whereas my inner guidance had other ideas. The discomfort I was feeling in my heart increased.

The large healing room in our home held five treatment beds. During a healing day, a group of advanced students were giving each other treatments. After checking on lunch, I opened the door to walk back into the healing room. I watched them all focusing and working passionately. My heart desired to support them advance their growth. I remember gently shutting the door again and leaning back against it. I asked my inner guidance to tell how I may support them in their dedication and commitment to their inner growth.

A few nights later The Voice woke me saying, *'Yvonne, follow your heart.'*

Within a few days I had made my decision and the inner pressure dissipated. My intent and purpose for resigning from the Alliance came from my desire to support a student to advance without receiving Reiki Master teaching credentials. I named this level, '3A Advanced Spirituality Degree' and the cost was US$1,000. If they later decided to complete their master's training, it was deducted from the cost to do their master's.

After my resignation and through inner guidance, the 3A manual was completed within three short weeks. The workshops were much more advanced and we met for six full days spread out over six weeks. Students also had homework to do after each session prior to their two-day training attunement, after which follow-up sessions were held. The first group gave themselves a name – 'The Rascals'. It was very apt.

Prior to their attunement, it was very intense at times as each student prepared and cleared mental emotional blocks that sat in the way of them stepping out upon their chosen pathway of support and service to themselves and others.

For the master's 3B teaching degree, I met privately with the student for many weeks prior to the two of us going away alone into retreat for seven days. We worked from 9 a.m. until lunch. After resting for an hour, we continued until dinner. Then we worked until I sensed it was time to stop. Sometimes it was after midnight before we retired to bed. The techniques used to support each Master varied as the inner guidance guided both of us in preparation for their initiation.

All students received a free booster initiation after 21 days. All students were welcome to come back at no cost as often as they liked,

Opening Doors - The Enormity of Us

sitting in on any level they had been initiated into previously, except when running a master's 3B; that time was solely for the trainee and me. My door was always open to all and many of them came to the open and healing days.

I held a monthly get-together with all students. I also ran an open day every month for all students and friends where I gave a motivational talk on a subject and then we would discuss it.

I gave treatments to students and clients when requested and in turn, they gave a small donation which, along with a percentage of fees paid for from Reiki training courses, went towards supporting others and school students. Graham and I set up a medical sponsorship scheme in Jakarta to pay for hare lip operations and other facial deformities. I am happy to say that this program is still running through the Australia and New Zealand Association in Jakarta. We will continue supporting causes through book sales.

137

If you ask for guidance, expect an answer;
it will always come.
It may not be immediate or come in the way we expect.
All that is required of us is to remain open to how
the answer may present itself to us.

Yvonne Fogarty

CHAPTER 21

THE UNEXPECTED GUEST

My husband had arranged to meet with Mark, a fellow Australian expatriate and business associate, at our home. Mark arrived and was waiting patiently in our lounge room, enjoying a cold drink.

When Graham eventually arrived, he apologised for being late. Mark only laughed.

'I live in Jakarta too,' he said. 'I know the traffic is very unpredictable.'

I left them alone to talk business while I went to the kitchen to check on dinner. Our cook, Ngatmi, had a very concerned look on her face. 'The roast dinner is ready for serving, Madam.' Then she looked at me with anxious eyes as much as to say, *what do I do?*

I patted her on the shoulder and said, 'I'll be back in a minute.'

I walked back into the lounge room and I stopped abruptly. I was startled at what I was observing in front of my eyes. A third person was standing in the room.

Beside Mark, I could see a cheeky-looking little blond-haired boy holding on to Mark's left trouser leg. He was very wobbly on his feet and clung on tightly with his little hands, attempting to steady himself. Mark was well over six-foot tall and the small child stood no higher than his knee. As Graham and I did not have children, it was difficult for me to accurately estimate the child's age. I sensed the boy was around twelve months old. This gorgeous boy gave me a beautiful smile, then glanced back up at Mark again before disappearing. Both

Mark and Graham were oblivious to the child's presence. The vision was clear and vivid. If I hadn't known better, I could have sworn the child had a physical presence in the room.

I retreated, walking back towards the kitchen door, out of sight as my mind searched for answers. Had Mark and his wife lost a child? Was this child simply missing his dad? Or even worse, could something untoward have just happened to the child? I slowed my breathing down and expanded my energy, recalling the scene again. No answer came to me. I was still baffled when the kitchen door flew open and Ngatmi walked straight into me.

'Oops,' I said with a start.

Ngatmi stood, looking at me with her eyebrows raised slightly in anticipation of me telling her to serve dinner.

I gave her a questioning look and she politely said, 'Madam, what time are we eating?'

'Oh,' I stammered. 'I'll be right back.' I rushed back into the lounge room.

'Excuse me, Mark, is your wife in town?'

'No, she isn't.'

'Well, would you like to join us for dinner?' And before he could respond, I raised my voice and boisterously added, 'We are having... Australian roast lamb!'

'Roast lamb!' he said excitedly. 'Thank you. I would love to stay for dinner.'

I gave Ngatmi the thumbs up and she beamed with relief at being able to finally serve dinner. Whenever friends from Australia came to visit us, we always requested they bring a leg of lamb, bacon and sausages as these items were not available in Jakarta back then. During dinner, I casually asked Mark if he had any children. 'No, we don't unfortunately, but we would love to have a child. We have been trying for many years and we have both had tests; maybe it's not meant to be.'

Graham gave me one of his looks, which said *where are you heading with this?*

I smiled at him and proceeded to tell Mark what I had seen and explained this was the reason I had retreated so quickly from the room earlier. 'He is a strong little boy and so determined to be noticed. I could have reached out and touched him. I believe he is wanting you two to hurry up. He wants you to know he is ready and waiting. He gave you a glimpse of himself to encourage you both not to give up.'

Graham then explained my unusual gifts to Mark, who fortunately was very open-minded.

'I don't do readings, and I only "see" into consciousness when Spirit initiates it,' I said to Mark. 'If an incident like this happens it's for a very specific reason.'

He was so impressed he later rang his wife to tell her.

A few weeks later she returned to Jakarta and came to see me. We talked and I described the child to her in detail. I explained slowly what I was sensing around her.

'I have been told to tell you to give your husband a teaspoon of honey every day and you are to eat watermelon. I believe a door of opportunity is open to you both right now; otherwise, I would not have seen this eager little boy. It's up to you two to decide what you do with this information, I'm just the messenger.'

They heeded the message and commenced having honey and watermelon every day. Then six months later, Mark rang telling me his wife was pregnant. They were both very excited.

Eighteen months after first meeting Mark's wife, I met up with her again and was introduced to their little blond-haired boy.

I affectionately leaned over the pram and said, 'Hello again little one, remember me? You are definitely going to be tall, just like your dad.'

I believe the honey and watermelon may have only been a support mechanism, or possibly a distraction. This baby was meant to come to them. Spirit answered their desire by giving them an insight of their future child.

By focusing their attention on what they were to do every day, plus keeping the image of the child in their mind, they overcame whatever mental/emotional blockage was in the way of preventing them from having the baby they so much desired.

Energy follows thought.

Note: This experience was published in a book called 'Chicken Soup for the Soul – Miracles Happen' in 2014. Publisher Simon & Schuster USA.

When we are living with an open heart,
we offer no resistance to life and in turn,
Spirit is able to support us,
manifesting the desires of our hearts.

Yvonne Fogarty

CHAPTER 22

HOLIDAY IN SPAIN

In January 1994, a student, Maxine, and I were giving each other an energy treatment.

During the treatment, she placed her hands on my right knee, when all of a sudden she saw very clearly *a picture of a man who appeared to be tall, fair-haired with a slightly receding hairline, dressed in white and lying on an outdoor lounge on a terrace high up on top of a hill with views out to the ocean.*

As she was telling me, I also tuned into the energy picking up the same scene. *I sensed it was the Mediterranean Ocean. I also saw low stone walls on the left-hand side of the house that continued on down into the valley.* Maxine saw it too. Then the picture disappeared. Later, I documented and dated the experience.

In February, I experienced another vision *where I again saw the Mediterranean Ocean and this time, I saw a very clear picture of the same man. He was reclining on a patio lounge and his legs were hanging over the end. He was wearing glasses, reading a newspaper and was dressed in white.* I wondered what the connection was!

I could see that Graham needed a holiday. Every time I suggested somewhere to go he wasn't interested. He was too tired and grumpy; it was all too much of an effort to even think about. I prayed about it three times then blew it away, believing a door would open for us to have a restful holiday.

A week or so later, a lady by the name of Ingrid came to see me for support and in late March, she joined a first-degree Reiki workshop.

Ingrid began coming regularly to our group discussions, and one day we were sitting and chatting in general about our husbands and their work when I mentioned that Graham was very tired and in need of a holiday.

Ingrid quickly sat up, pushing her blonde shoulder-length hair behind her ear, and said, 'We own a villa in Spain and it needs someone to go there and give it an airing. It's been many months since we've been there and there's a car sitting in the garage available for your use. Are you interested?'

I thought *wow* as goosebumps popped up all over my body. I thanked her and said I would speak to Graham and let her know.

To my surprise, Graham immediately responded with a 'Yes! That sounds like a great holiday.'

Within a week the 'rascal' had organised a two-week break from work and we arranged to go to Ingrid's house the Sunday before we were to fly out to pick up the keys and gather information about the villa.

We knocked on their front door and when Ingrid's husband Bob opened it, I stood there staring at him with my mouth open. I couldn't talk. I was speechless. Surprisingly, true! My normal chirpy self was stunned to see the same man I had seen in the visions standing in front of me.

While enjoying a pre-luncheon drink I told Ingrid and Bob about seeing him and the villa in a vision and she went away and came back with photos taken from their hilltop home that overlooked the countryside and ocean. Included in one of the photos was Ingrid, leaning on the balcony railing looking slim, elegant and just as beautiful as she is now, except her hair appeared longer in the photo.

Bob said, 'I wondered why you had a strange look on your face when I opened the door. I actually discreetly checked that my fly was zipped up.'

We all laughed.

Then my smarty pants husband added, 'I think it was the first time I have ever seen Yvonne speechless.'

I simply glanced over at him giving him an eye roll. I went on to explain the visions in detail to them. 'Bob, I hope you don't mind me saying but you appeared to be a lot taller in the vision.'

I explained how I saw his legs hanging over a lounge settee on the terrace of the villa.

He laughed. 'The settee is a two-seater so when I lie on it, my legs hang over the armrest as it's usually hot when we are there and I wear a pair of white cotton trousers and a shirt.'

'And,' I added, 'you enjoy reading the paper out there and you wear reading glasses when you do.'

'You are right, I do. It's my favourite place to relax,' he said.

During lunch Ingrid took a deep breath, leaned forward and said to us in a quiet, serious voice, 'There is just one thing I need to warn you about in the house.'

We both stopped eating, looking up at her wondering what she was going to say. Then we too leaned forward.

She paused, lowering her voice before telling us, 'There is a Roman soldier who lives in the house as well.'

'Okaay,' we both said in unison.

Her piercing blue eyes looked at us intensely to ensure our attention and she purposely paused for effect before stating, 'He told me the land was given to him after winning a battle.'

'Okaay,' we both said again, giving her an encouraging nod to continue.

Ingrid took a sip of wine and took a big breath before telling us he was often mischievous and annoyed them quite a bit until she told him that he was welcome to stay on in the house but they were staying too. A few days after talking to him, she opened her front door and found a small Roman coin sitting on the front step. Ingrid told us the coin now sits on the kitchen ledge. She thinks it was his way of making peace with them.

The first thing we did upon arrival at the villa was to search out the Roman coin and it was sitting exactly where Ingrid said it would be. I then immediately walked out onto the long terrace to take in the wonderful view; it was exactly as I had seen it in the vision. Now I could also see a tiny village in the valley adjacent to the oceanfront.

I sat on the same settee that Bob had sat on and said, 'Spirit, you organised this holiday for us. Thank you.'

I never saw the Roman soldier. Nonetheless, we did experience a couple of incidents where we knew he was in the room with us. I asked Graham to share his experience with the spirit of the Roman soldier.

In his own words:

I was relaxing in the lounge reading the local newspaper, sitting at a 90-degree angle to the fireplace that was to my left. After reading for what seemed like a short while, I noticed white particles falling onto the paper. I wondered what it was and lowered the newspaper, only to see ash emanating from the fireplace in a small cloud-like formation. Then I noticed the speckled appearance of ash on the old black leather lounge, which set me wondering how it could have happened.

Being a fairly pragmatic person, I went to the fireplace to feel for a breeze coming through, but there wasn't any! What the heck caused the ash cloud to come out across the room when there was no wind? I needed to figure it out, so I decided to venture onto the flat roof that also served as a deck for the swimming pool. The top of the chimney was about two metres high, so I used a chair to inspect it. There was a flat concrete cover supported with evenly spaced bricks and gaps to allow smoke to vent into the atmosphere. This also meant that any breeze on the roof would merely travel through or over the chimney, being the least resistive path.

I concluded that it was nigh on impossible for the cloud-like ash from the fireplace to have been caused by an act of nature. Before leaving to travel to Spain, we were advised there was a spiritual being about the house.

Given past experiences with Yvonne, I merely accepted that the spiritual being was active and said, 'You're welcome to visit with us.' I then returned and continued reading the newspaper.

A few days later, Yvonne and I were again in the lounge area, reading, when I heard the unmistakable creaking of the old leather lounge. Without looking, I thought Yvonne was getting up. When I noticed she wasn't moving, I asked if she heard the same as I did, to which she said 'yes' and added that she thought it was me who was getting up.

We both acknowledged the presence of this spiritual being and I went back to reading my book. Yvonne, who was slowly becoming more accepting of a spiritual being, decided to say hello and chat with him, thanking him for allowing us to share the house with him.

We have travelled quite extensively; however, that holiday in Spain remains one of our most memorable.

Graham Fogarty

Our illusions feed our ego
but not our soul.

Yvonne Fogarty

CHAPTER 23

A LESSON IN LETTING GO

The lease on the house we were renting in Cipete was coming to an end in June and we needed to find a new place to live.

The international Japanese construction company my husband worked for supplied us with a budget of US$1300, which was paid to us monthly. House rents during that boom period in 1994 had skyrocketed up to US$4500 a month and above. Many owners requested the whole contract money – between 2–3 years – upfront. Many of the oil companies complied. Our company didn't. There was no way we could afford that, so we were limited to finding a house that met our budget.

Unfortunately, once some owners received the money, no further repairs were done and many expatriates moved every couple of years as the houses started having serious issues, mainly with white ants, which happened for the people renting on the lower end of the scale.

Knowing how difficult it was to find a good house, I started looking in early March. After inspecting a minimum of 70 houses and still not finding anything, I was getting very anxious. It was nearly the end of May and we had four weeks left to find something. I had a basic list of what we desired and kept putting it out to the universe many times a day in the form of a 'plea'. That was my first mistake.

My second mistake was that I still continued to worry about finding somewhere to live instead of letting go and trusting what I was asking for would happen (just as I had done for our holiday in Spain). But this situation was different.

Why? We were on a deadline. Then I remembered we had been on a deadline back in 1992 too and here I was doing the same thing yet again, showing a lack of trust by getting stressed and anxious for certainty!

My actions were saying, 'I am asking for guidance to help me, but I am lacking trust and I do not really believe in my heart it will happen.' I felt a discomfort building up in my heart, which wouldn't go away.

The next morning, The Voice came through and said, **'Yvonne, the house will come to you.'**

I thought, *we only have four weeks left. I have to keep looking.* Unfortunately, I couldn't let go. I ignored the discomfort and the message and continued searching. I was going everyday house hunting. Some days I was only able to see two houses in a day due to the extremely congested roads. I walked back into our house one afternoon after a frustrating day of searching. The staff looked at me inquiringly, I just shook my head in disappointment. The build-up of stress I was feeling became too much to bear and I finally let go.

I called out loud to The Voice, 'Okay, I promise to stop looking. You find the house, please.'

The next morning, I told Graham, 'There's no need to send the car back for me today or for the rest of the week as I won't need it.'

That comment quickly retracted his head from behind the Jakarta Post newspaper. 'Why not? Aren't you going to look for a place today?'

'No, not anymore. I promised The Voice I would stop looking. I am going to trust and wait. The Voice in the past has always answered our needs. Remember it didn't fail us in 1992, even though we had our doubts, so why would now be any different?' I replied in a voice that relayed more confidence than I felt.

'Yvonne,' he said, raising his voice. 'We have approximately three weeks left to find something.'

'I am aware of that,' I said as I quietly enjoyed the moment. 'It's up to The Voice now. I promised The Voice I would not look on the noticeboards at any shopping centres or in the daily newspaper for a property.'

It truly was a huge challenge for me not to peek at the rental page of the Jakarta Post newspaper each morning. Inwardly, I was feeling the best I had felt in months. The pressure in my heart had dissipated and I was feeling extremely peaceful and happy. It was now Graham who was getting anxious instead. Bless him, he didn't say a word.

One friend said to me when I told her, 'Isn't that being irresponsible?'

'No. I truly believe the house will present itself to us, and I'm being asked to trust.'

I went about my daily chores and voluntary social welfare activities. Every day I read through the basic requirements of our new home and instead of keeping on asking and putting it out there, I simply gave thanks to The Voice for providing us with our new home. (I spoke as if it had already happened.) Whenever I went shopping, I was sorely tempted to look at the noticeboards advertising properties for rent. As tempted as I was, I resisted and inwardly reaffirmed my trust. I admit to feeling quite uncomfortable at times.

With nine days left until our lease expired, I was shopping in an expatriate store called Kem Chicks. I walked out to the front of the store and requested security to place a call for my driver to come. Adjacent to the security desk stood a huge noticeboard full of advertisements, all flapping in the breeze as if they were taunting me to come over and take a look, as most advertisements were usually for houses for rent. I took a deep breath and resisted the temptation to peek, forcing myself to turn my back on the information board.

When our driver arrived, I stepped into the car just as a security guard came up to the car window and spoke with our driver. I thought, *what's going on? Something appears to be very well orchestrated between them both.*

'Madam, my friend has a house to show us. It's around the corner if you are interested. He gets off work in half an hour. Can you wait?' (Many Indonesians act as a go-between to earn extra income and have an arrangement with the house owners.)

'Yes, certainly. Thank you.' Goosebumps popped up all over my skin.

When we drove around to the house, which was in a great location, it was perfect for our requirements. It still needed some work done but the spacious layout would work for us. The house was bright and airy, which was important, and the back garden, although small, was beautifully laid out. The house guard told me that the owner wanted US$2000 per month and two years' rent money up front at a cost of US$48,000, which we couldn't afford.

I just nodded to the house guard but didn't say anything as I sensed the house was ours and it would all work out. I rang my husband excitedly, telling him about the house and that evening we returned and my husband did the usual inspection. Does it have enough electricity to run the appliances? Does it have a water tank with a pump? Is the area safe for expatriates? Does it have white ants? Graham had quite a list. We had resided in some challenging houses since living in Jakarta and we needed to make sure it was liveable.

Graham telephoned the owner of our new house and arranged to meet with her the next afternoon. When we walked into the house, the owner greeted us by saying, 'Hello Mr Graa-ham, do you remember me? We used to work together.'

I turned, wide-eyed, looking back and forth between both of them. I was astonished and amused watching the interaction going on between Graham and the owner Yanti. I shook my head and chuckled to myself, thinking, *Spirit you are always surprising me.*

I believe I was being encouraged to deepen my trust and confidence in the use of our internal power.

Yanti was a visa agent who represented the previous company Graham had worked for in 1991 (I suspect from her comments later that she had a little crush on him). We not only acquired the house for the price we could afford, but Yanti also agreed we could pay her three months in advance. My heart was filled with gratitude.

The day we moved in, Yanti called in and when I saw her, I couldn't contain my feelings regarding her kindness to us. I enthusiastically bounded over to her and embraced her with a huge hug, air-kissing her on both sides of her face, which was the custom in Asia. I thanked her with all the love and appreciation I felt. As I released my hold on her, she burst into tears. I quickly stepped back and looked at her apologetically, hoping my over-enthusiastic manner hadn't offended her.

She responded by saying, 'I felt so much love coming from you, it touched my heart.'

Many Indonesians do not show affection in public nor do they like being hugged by people they do not know very well.

The house was very peaceful even though it was behind a high brick wall, which had large rolls of barbed wire and broken glass on top of the walls surrounding it to stop intruders, along with 24-hour guards. It was our little sanctuary away from the hustle and bustle of busy Jakarta. The house was very comfortable; we even had an enormous glass atrium in the middle of the house and our houseboy 'acquired' two pigeons for it.

By the time we left the house five years later, the number of pigeons had grown to 24 (even though we lost some to the rats that occasionally got inside. Yikes!) and we were given a beautiful Moluccan cockatoo, which Graham named 'Bogey', after having a frustrating day at golf. The garden felt very serene, with squirrels living in one of the trees along with other wildlife. We loved the fruit our mango and rambutan trees produced, unfortunately so did the bats, mongoose and squirrels.

I believe the house was there waiting for us all along. It had a separate entry and bathroom adjacent to a beautiful large room with massive sliding glass doors that opened to a small fernery, perfect for running training workshops. Through another door was a large guest bedroom and separate bathroom – all were set away from the main living area of the house by a passageway. All I had to do was 'let go' and trust that what we required would present itself at the right time.

Why was it so hard for me to let go? I was 'anxious for certainty', along with a bucketload of self-doubt. I hoped that I would never again doubt this inner guidance. But of course, I did. Being in a human body at times isn't easy when asked to trust in this spiritual power. Although it's mostly unseen, I 'know' it exists.

With all the experiences I have encountered to date, people would say to me, 'You are so lucky to have this wonderful connection.'

I answered by telling them it's readily available for you too.

Even with this connection, I still had a destructive pattern of self-doubt, which often raised its head. When guidance came through me for others, I rarely questioned what I received, yet it was a different matter at times when it came for me personally, and the house hunt was a classic example.

I didn't believe I was worthy to receive as readily as others did. I held on to a false belief in my mind that for me to receive help, I had to struggle for it, proving to myself that I was worthy to receive it. This spiritual power can only support us if we give it a chance to do so by opening our hearts and minds to receive in appreciation and gratitude.

I continued to work on clearing my ingrained negative belief patterns as they popped up. Some were embedded so deeply in my psyche, it felt as if I was slowly peeling an onion layer by layer. It's an analogy that has been used often and it's a good example. Healing deep emotional wounds can be a slow process, yet very rewarding when the end result is achieved.

CHAPTER 24

WHY WE ASK THREE TIMES

I would like to explain this process in more detail and follow up with an example of a student's actual experience creating and manifesting his desire using the creative attributes of Consciousness.

The number three represents Spirit's natural doorway of creation. In some Indian philosophies, they call the number three a natural birth canal for creation to manifest. In many documented religions and philosophies, the number three is reflected in their beliefs and cultures.

The 'power of three' vibration is readily accessible and through our focused intention, we can direct Consciousness' creative forces into action. We have an (1) 'ideal' outcome (imagining the end result), (2) formalise our 'idea' utilising our five senses and finally (3) manifestation. 1 plus 2 = 3. The energy builds upon itself before manifesting.

An ideal outcome focused upon in our mind creates a thoughtform an idea (a seed), which begins to germinate. By reinforcing our desire daily, coupled with gratitude and appreciation, we can manifest our desires – ask and you can receive.

We are all on Earth learning to use our mental faculties in ways that are harmless to ourselves and others with the aim of overcoming any imbalance between our limiting beliefs (duality – being of two minds) and our inherent nature, bringing harmony and balance to the two opposites.

When we decide to create a desired goal, it is important that our intention is pure and our heart's desire and mind are in agreement, in order to be able to step over the emotional pull of our limiting beliefs. For example, if we ask for something yet we 'feel/sense' deep in our heart we don't really believe we will receive it, it's possible we won't!

When we ask three times with our heart and mind in agreement (key element), we automatically activate within us the creative forces to commence creating our desire. We have power over the 'elements' and this power is readily available to be of service – we all have this ability within us to manifest a desire. I liken it to making a cake, after mixing all the right ingredients together and following instructions, we see the end result of our effort. If our desire is focused negatively towards someone or something it could still manifest but down the track, we will experience the result of our actions whether in this life cycle or a future one.

Conviction of belief in our mind and with our heart in agreeance, coupled with trust and faith, can bring about our desired result. This power can only be experienced fully in the NOW moment when we are able to stop and rest our mind's busy-busy mode. If our conscious awareness is not fully NOW HERE present within us, it is NO WHERE, to be able to fully support us.

I had been running an advanced Reiki class one day back in 1997 and the above information popped into my head. I wrote it on the whiteboard and one of the students said,

'Yvonne, what about goal setting? Isn't that done looking into the future?'

'That's a good question,' I said. 'Any desire we choose to focus upon towards setting a new direction for ourselves or to attain a goal is achieved in the NOW moment. See, the reality you desire to manifest "accomplished" in your mind's eye NOW. Our point of power is always in the NOW moment.'

'The past is behind us. The future hasn't happened yet. We are asked to trust in the power behind this creative process. Our mind operates in pictures and that's how Consciousness operates. Energy follows thought. The instant you imagine your goal clearly in your mind, you have already created it mentally. It is just as alive and real as I can see you sitting in front of me now.'

Consciousness gives us the ability to be aware of life 'all' around us and we can use our mind's imaging tools to utilise the creative forces to create our desires for experiencing and learning.

Jason, an advanced level two Reiki student, came to me after the training session asking for help to create a goal, with three different aspects to it, which he saw as difficult to achieve in a one-pictured scene I recommended. The following example can be adapted to suit any desire you wish to manifest.

Paraphrasing Jason's words...

Yvonne, my wife is scared living here in Jakarta with the ongoing unrest around us. We would like to move to live somewhere where she feels safer. We have been hoping to have a baby but as yet it hasn't happened. I am not happy in my current job and I would like to move where I can work for a company using my creative skills in a more productive way. How can I achieve that goal in a one-pictured scene?

We talked about it and with the ideas he came up with, I asked him to write out the scene. When he had completed his almost 'full-page' description, I asked him to reduce it to three sentences, then reduce it again to just one sentence. He looked at me in stunned silence, then cast his eyes down at his lengthy description.

I smiled and added, 'Jason, you will feel very connected to the outcome by accomplishing this task yourself. End it with a simple one-line affirmation to repeat daily and start it with the words "I AM". Picture one scene only, bringing all your desires together using all your senses and do not go into detail, keep it simple. Most of all, do not change the scene once it's set in place – fill the scene with emotion. Emotion moves energy focused upon into action. Focus on the scene you created in your mind, then repeat the affirmation three times. Each time, encase it with your intent and really feel what you are saying. Don't rattle off the affirmation without feeling the words. Feeling each word you speak feeds the energy pattern to build upon your desire.'

Then say out loud, 'This or something better will manifest for me for the highest good of all concerned.' (Refer to Creative Visualization by Shakti Gawain). 'Then blow it away.'

Maintaining trust in this power is the KEY to accomplishing our desire. Continually doubting 'dilutes' the power to manifest as we desire. A few times daily, see the pictured goal in your mind and when able, repeat excitedly out loud your affirmation. Finally, with a grateful heart, thank Spirit and blow it away out of your thoughts.

In the scene Jason created, he pictured himself home from work, standing in his business attire with his briefcase in hand, his wife standing at the front door of their home with a baby in her arms, and he kisses and hugs them both. He can smell the aroma of food cooking. In that one scene, he had utilised his senses.

He says to his wife, 'I am so happy. I love my job and living in this safe environment.'

She replies, 'I AM happy too.'

The basic key element to achieving any goal is our 'intent'. It's so important to picture the same scene without changing a thing, including clothing, feelings and words spoken (otherwise energetically you are creating a new picture and starting all over again). Picturing the whole scenario is encasing desire, intent and feelings into a thought form, a mould for the energy pattern to build upon to bring to manifestation.

When we send out a request to Spirit we receive its frequency and vibrational response. Reiki students who have done second-degree Reiki can connect and draw upon distinct universal frequencies and vibrations to support their desire, thus enhancing their abilities to manifest them. You are receiving 'from' Spirit the focused upon frequencies and vibrations 'through' you 'to' manifest an outcome – in the same way I give an energy treatment to someone. The energy flows from Spirit through me to the client and they draw in the energy they are open to receiving.

Jason sat quietly a few times a day focusing, pouring his heartfelt feelings into his desire as he pictured the scene in his mind's eye. Finally repeating out loud his affirmation, he added, 'This or something better will manifest for us for the highest good of all concerned.' Then he blew it away out of his mind, saying thank you.

Many months later, Jason rang me distressed. 'It looks like the company is going to be taken over and I could lose my job.'

My impishness sometimes steps in and I replied in a raised, excited voice, 'Congratulations Jason, that's great news. It sounds like the energy is working to bring about your desire. Keep it up.'

There was dead silence on the other end of the telephone. That wasn't the response he was expecting until he grasped my meaning. Something was happening. There were changes taking place.

He rang me a few months later to say that an opposition company had heard about the takeover and had offered him a job. 'It's a higher paid position, a managerial role with freedom to be creative and we are moving to Singapore,' he said.

From the moment he set his intention, it took approximately eight-and-a-half months before it manifested. There is a big difference between building a small hut and building a solid house. Patience and trust are required.

After they moved, we kept in touch by email and some months later I contacted them letting them know I was going to be in Singapore on business for a couple of days and I would love to meet them both for lunch. We decided to meet close to his work at the Raffles Hotel.

When Jason walked into the restaurant with his wife Nena, I couldn't help noticing she was pregnant.

'Many times I nearly gave up focusing on the goal. I am glad I kept at it,' said Jason. He smiled and added, 'Well, the whole goal isn't quite complete, but it will be in a few months' time.' We all chuckled as Nena gently placed her hand protectively over her abdomen.

'The outcome is better than I imagined happening for us,' said Jason. 'I am now using what I learnt from you in my work projects and any other challenges I face.'

The key to achieving our desires is trust. For example, if you desire to move, clean out cupboards while waiting. Refer to chapter 48 – Manifesting a Heart's Desire.

You will have read that when I was deciding whether to become a Reiki Master, Spirit was more concerned with the 'purity of my intent' behind my decision. Our actions are not measured by the amount of money we donate, nor all the good things we do for others; only our 'intent' behind our actions as its crucial for our soul's growth, wellbeing and future outcomes. There is no hiding from the frequencies and vibrations we create and send forth through our intentions.

This spiritual power created the universe and everything we can see and touch in front of our eyes is energy. Whatever you look at – e.g. art, furniture or a house – it was once an idea, a thought held in someone's mind before it was created. No matter what we desire to create, nothing is impossible. Below is a quote by Mahatma Gandhi.

'Be the change that you wish to see in the world.'

A precious friend and student I trained, Lea Soebroto (dec), desired to move to Australia from Indonesia with her husband and have her adult children, who were living in other parts of the world, live there too. Lea set her intention and commenced seeing all the family in Australia sitting down to a Sunday dinner.

Then a couple of weeks later Lea said to me, 'I realised I don't need all my family around me. I now understand this need was coming from insecurity.'

We are utilising a power that 'just is'. It's not positive or negative: it's 'neutral'. It's a potent power that responds to our thoughts, intentions, words, choices and actions. We are all here to learn to utilise this power in ways that are harmless to others and ourselves.

Energy follows thought.

CHAPTER 25

SAIRA'S EXPERIENCE IN A COMA

Saira Jethnani is a lawyer, and friends with numerous Indian students I had initiated, many of whom I met up with monthly at the open days I held. Saira and I did not know of each other, nor did she know about Reiki when she was taken ill. Her friends asked me to help by sending her distant healing.

Saira is happy to share her experience from when she was in a coma in the hope it will give loved ones comfort to know that although physically unconscious, some coma patients can be very alert mentally to what is going on around them.

In Saira's own words:

I was in a coma in October 1996 in Jakarta. My memories while in the coma were that I could hear everybody talking to me or to each other around me. I remember initially feeling as if I was talking to them but they were not listening to me. I realised that I was mentally alert but physically I could not communicate. I was in the ICU of a hospital in a room that had eight beds, all separated by curtains.

While in a coma, I remember seeing a window and observing a lot of energy particles around me all the time. I instinctively felt somebody was sending me that energy. I don't know how I knew; I just knew. In fact, one day I went and stood near the window and I could see a beautiful lake with white swans drifting serenely on it. The sky looked pure and clear.

A voice asked me, 'Do you want to come over to this side of the window?'

I said, 'Wow, this is just beautiful and peaceful. This is what I am seeking in my life.'

Just as I was about to take a step through, I heard my nine-month-old daughter crying. I hesitated, then stopped myself from going any further and told the voice, 'My child is still very young; she needs her mother and I want to go back to her.'

After a day or two, I opened my eyes and I could literally see energy all around me. I asked my husband and other family members if they could see the energy in the room and the beautiful view from the window.

They looked at each other and my husband quietly said, 'Saira, there isn't a window in this room.'

I think they thought I had lost my mind. Since the coma, I had felt a connection to some energy, which I didn't understand. I started recovering and a month later I left the hospital and went back home to India to my family. I could still see the energy. My family back home also thought I was going through depression because of the things I was seeing and feeling.

During my time home I had become very quiet and wasn't talking too much to anyone, which was not like me. I am normally bubbly and laugh a lot. I had many visitors and one of the cousins mentioned Reiki to me, but nothing in detail, just a few things. Then another friend mentioned that her Master was sending me Reiki healing while I was in a coma.

I started questioning myself as to why this had happened to me. I started searching for answers. Four months later, even though I have always had a spiritual connection I was feeling a much stronger connection to the energy and universe but didn't know who or what it was that I had the connection with, or how I had come to have this connection.

In April 1996, when I was back in Jakarta, one of my friends mentioned to me about Reiki and Yvonne. She said that some of her

Indian friends had learnt Reiki from their Master Yvonne, who at their request had been sending support energy to me when I was in a coma.

When I heard that, it felt very familiar to me. I immediately obtained Yvonne's telephone number and called her, registering for a first-degree class.

When I went to Yvonne's house to meet her a few days before the class, I was sitting waiting in the front lounge of the house when Yvonne walked up behind me, gently placing her hands on my shoulders. For a moment I was shocked. It was the exact same energy I was feeling; the warmth, comfort and support that I experienced while I was in a coma.

I would like to emphasise here from my personal experience, in a coma people can feel, can hear, can sense, can even talk to themself, but cannot communicate with people around them. This is my own experience, which until today few people believe and understand yet my experience will always remain a fact. Today, even doctors believe that a person in a coma is mentally alive and active, only physically passive.

Saira Jethnani

I clearly remember receiving the request to send energy to Saira. My heart had gone out to her when I was told Saira was in a coma due to undiagnosed diabetes.

I commenced sending energy each day by focusing on her name and where she was, sending her light and love only (so as not to violate her own freewill). I often call this energy our 'lifeline'. This omniscient power knew the intended destination because energy follows our thoughts. Where our thoughts go, we are mentally instantly there too.

After sending energy to her for a few days, I sensed she had begun drawing in more energy through me and was quickly absorbing it. It felt to me as if she couldn't get enough. After a couple of days of experiencing her hunger for the energy, I began sending her energy twice a day. We don't have to be present with the person for the person to benefit from the energy. Each of us is interconnected to each other via Consciousness.

One evening I was sending energy to Saira when I experienced a shift in my awareness and the next minute I watched myself standing in a hospital room at the foot of a bed. Although we had never met, I knew intuitively the woman I was looking at was Saira. (Known as remote viewing). Her face was very clear to see and I too saw a window to the right of her bed and there were lots of people standing around in the room. My heart reached out to her as she lay there in a coma. I felt as if she could sense my presence and was reaching out to me too, drawing in strength through me and I instantly knew I had a heart connection with Saira. What I found interesting, when told later, was that there was no window in the room. The only conclusion I could come up with from that experience was that my whole awareness was present with her and I had connected in with her soul's awareness at that time. It was hovering at a crossroads (e.g. the window) between our physical reality and our spiritual home.

Saira came out of the coma and returned to India, staying with her family while she recovered. Whenever she popped into my mind and when able to, I sent her energy. I do not recall my conversation with Saira on the telephone prior to meeting her at our home. What I do vividly recall is seeing her for the first time at our house. I immediately recognised Saira from seeing her in the vision.

Saira was sitting, looking out the front lounge window where I ran my workshops. I walked up behind her, gently touching her shoulders and I quietly said, 'Hello Saira.' We embraced as if we had always known each other. Our close connection and friendship continue to this day.

Reaching out to connect with another soul, whether they are present in the room, on the other side of the world or have passed over, is only a thought away. Consciousness knows no boundaries and whoever we focus our thoughts on, energy follows and we are instantly mentally connected to them.

If a loved one is in a coma, I recommend that only positive conversations happen in their room. Talk to them, recall fond memories, take in a photo album, share, describe and recall fun memories. Read a favourite book of theirs to them or talk about what you have planned to do after they come out of the coma, because they could be as Saira was, aware of everything going on around them.

Energy follows thought.

CHAPTER 26

OVERPROTECTIVE MOTHER

Lisa was unable to have children. Fortunately, an opportunity arose for her to adopt a beautiful Asian baby. It was love at first sight.

I received a phone call from Lisa who had been recommended by a client. She was upset and distraught on the phone. She had been called to her daughter's school the previous day to collect Nicola, who was now six years old. She had suddenly developed asthma while playing at lunchtime and needed to see a doctor.

Lisa and Nicola came to our home and I gave Nicola a treatment without Lisa present in the room. We talked about school then I casually brought up the subject of how much her mother loved her. As I was talking, I could sense Nicola's energy change and her chest tightened.

I gently redirected our conversation to our dogs, telling her about their antics and continued treating her as I cleared away the built-up energy around her heart and lungs. A thought popped into my mind: *Her mother is over-loving and overprotective of her. She is unknowingly suffocating her daughter's ability to be herself and breathe freely.*

Afterwards, while Nicola entertained our two dogs (or was it the other way around?), I talked to Lisa about what I believed may be the cause. Lisa poured out her heart, telling me how precious Nicola was and talked about her constant fear of losing her. She knew she had become extremely protective of her. Lisa cried when she realised what she had been unknowingly doing out of her love for Nicola. I suggested they have a mother-and-daughter chat. Lisa stepped back from being an overzealous protective mother and within approximately six weeks, Nicola's asthma had completely disappeared.

I mentioned to Lisa we can all connect energetically with anyone at any time. 'Sit quietly, rub your hands together in front of you at chest level until they feel warm. Then, with your palms facing each other, keeping a slight gap between them, imagine Nicola in your mind's eye, and then see or feel that image between your hands, sending support and heartfelt love to her. When you decide to stop, simply blow between your hands three times and give a quick swipe of your hands to break the connection.'

I went on to explain to Lisa how love is a very powerful force, especially when sending it to a family member you have a very strong heart connection with, e.g. as she had with Nicola. Where the intended person is, that's where the energy will go instantly. There is no need to have done an energy course to send loving thoughts of support to a loved one. Sending love to them is not violating their freewill choice. You may even feel the palms of your hands grow warm, and/or a slight resistance builds up between your hands, or you may feel a tingling sensation as the energy flows out through you to them.

Anyone can energetically connect with another person no matter where they are. We all have this natural ability. This technique of sending light (support) and love (unconditional) can be used with a pure intention when you may feel concern for a friend or family member. For instance, they could be sitting for an examination and feeling nervous or any other activity where you sense they may require some extra support at that time.

Lisa looked at me, confused. I decided to demonstrate to her how consciousness operates to help her understand how she can connect with Nicola easily.

'Let me share a recent experience. Graham and I were sitting on our patio, enjoying a 'medicinal' gin and tonic and out from behind one of the pot plants jumped a large vivid red frog. We had not seen anything like it before. Over its back were bright purple spots. Its eyes were a brilliant green colour and it looked as if it had black eyeliner surrounding each eye.

'Lisa, did you happen to see the picture of the frog in your mind as I described it to you?'

'Yes. I did.'

'You just saw consciousness at work, instantly forming a picture energetically in your mind's eye. Our thoughts are a living entity and as soon as we picture something in our mind's eyes, it is real and alive because...'

Energy follows thought.

CHAPTER 27

PLEASE SHOW ME THE ENERGY

After being initiated with Reiki for the first time, most students feel the energy buzzing in their hands as it flows through them. It's wonderful to experience. So much so that they desire their family to understand and believe in this power too.

One of my American students, Deborah, asked me when we met up at an open day, 'Yvonne, I have a question. How can I show my husband John that the energy is real?'

'We can only show others this power is real by living it in our daily life. No matter what we seek, an answer to Spirit's power is unlimited and is always ready to support us. It's our personal inner guidance system. All we have to do is ask for assistance; it will not let you down. Simply send your request forth encased in a pure intent. Trust the energy to show you a way for John to see for himself this unseen spiritual power in action.'

In Deborah's own words:

I had completed my first-degree Reiki with Yvonne in March of 1995 in Jakarta and I was attempting to enlighten my husband, John, as to how the energy worked, but to no avail. John was very sceptical about what I was doing with my hands-on technique, although I could feel the energy pulsating out of my hands whenever I laid hands on others or myself.

I was a novice and I thought it would be more meaningful to physically show someone proof of how the energy came through me, my newest open vehicle for energy movement, than to merely tell.

Yvonne had taught my class that anything we ask the energy to do for the highest and purest good of all involved would not be denied. The energy would answer, even so, I wasn't sure what to ask of it. Then in April, one month later, an opportunity presented itself in a most curious way. I didn't recognise this opportunity for proof of energy until I had received a third message to pay attention.

John loves golf, second to breathing. He had played in many golf tournaments in Jakarta within the expatriate community. He was invited to attend a 'Calcutta' on a Thursday night in April 1995 before the upcoming SPE (Society of Petroleum Engineers) golf tournament on the following Saturday. A Calcutta is a pre-golf tournament event where gambling and much drinking of alcoholic beverages take place.

For this group, this event usually took place in a local bar owned by one of the expats. The golfing teams for the following Saturday tournament were organised into groups of four people, or five, depending on the particular tournament. For this format, they often teamed up one of the best golfers: an 'A' player, with a slightly less skilled player; a 'B', with another even less-skilled player; a 'C' – until they even pick from golfers who are in the 'D' and 'E' categories. So each team would have an A, B, C, D or E player on their roster. Then these teams were listed on a big board. I think for this tournament there were approximately 40 teams to buy.

Each team was then auctioned off to the highest bidder that night. You win the bid on a team; you pay and then you own that team for the tournament. If your team took a money place in the finish, then you as the owner made money. Big money. John asked me to accompany him to this Calcutta so we could both enjoy an evening out with other expats. I happily agreed.

I walked around the bar, having a drink and chatting with friends.

I watched them place the names of the players in their teams on a board on the wall and I asked questions as to how this auction was handled. During the course of my socialising, three different people at three different moments told me to buy a team that evening. I heard this message twice, dismissing the idea. When I heard the same message from a third person, I woke up to the meaning.

Then I began to ask myself well why would I buy a team in this Calcutta? What team would I buy? I didn't know what I was doing. The SPE tournament was played for the enjoyment of its members. It also served as a community fundraiser. The event gave twenty per cent of its proceeds to the Indonesian scholarship fund to send Indonesian students to college. I sat by myself for a moment, surveying the room.

What do you want me to do? I realised I was asking the power greater than myself what to do. A moment of clarity and calm came over me. An idea flowed into my mind and thoughts followed. Choose a team and buy it. Your team will make money. Give the money back to the Indonesian scholarship fund. Do not keep any money for yourself. Be The Vehicle. You will get proof that the energy works. John will see visible proof in a medium he can understand – 'golf and money' – that the energy works. Money is another form of energy; you can allow this energy to flow through your vehicle. You can plant a seed for others to follow on this same path.

It was very clear to me in my heart the thread of intention behind why I would buy a team, although I had no idea what I was doing. I asked for guidance from the energy.

'Show me which team to buy. Tell me how much to spend. I'll do it. Please guide me,' I asked.

The auction began. Some of the favourite teams went quickly and for high prices. I didn't have a chance of buying a team at that price. Every bid I made was outbid by some guy or a conglomerate of guys who had more money than I did. At times I was even bidding against my own husband. The room was charged with electricity; noise, laughter, smoke, glasses clinking, the auctioneer's voice booming, applause as teams were bought and the pot grew bigger. I was caught up in the excitement. I watched and waited and learned how to buy a team.

A team came up for auction, a team everyone light-heartedly made fun of. Apparently, they weren't the best group of golfers. They were the most unlikely players to make up a golf team in fact. They were the underdogs. My chance. No one wanted them. A few bids were made on this team, but nothing serious. I noticed the number of their team was 22. I had studied some numerology and I used this knowledge to recognise that this was a good sign, as 22 was a highly evolved spiritual number.

I decided this might be another message of guidance for me, so I kept bidding on this team. I won the bid for US$500. I bought the team that no one wanted. There was laughter and applause in the room as my name was listed as the owner of this team.

At the end of the Calcutta, some of the team players came up to me and asked why I bought them. All I could do was smile and say to them, 'I'll tell you when the tournament is over.'

That night at home I explained to John what I was doing and why. I told him that if my team won money, all the money, minus my investment to buy the team, was going into the scholarship fund as a donation. I made sure he knew that I would not keep the money, as I had promised any money won would go elsewhere. John just listened. I asked him not to judge me, just go along and play it out to the finish.

The tournament was to be held in two days on Saturday. John asked me to come out to the tournament and help out on some of the holes. We arrived early on Saturday morning at the Halim Golf Course near the military airport to begin the SPE Golf Tournament. I found out my duties for that day. I was to be a judge at one of the par threes for a 'closest to the hole' competition.

I saw my team members in the clubhouse before the tournament began and wished them good luck. I wished my husband good luck and left the clubhouse to go out to my position as a judge. While I was working, the par three hole my team passed through and I said hello to them and asked how they were playing. They answered they were playing so amazingly well and they didn't know why. I told them I thought I knew why they were playing so well and that I would tell them later. I hugged each of my players and told them to have a good time. I didn't want to tell my team the real reason why I had bought them until the tournament was over because I didn't want to place extra pressure on them. Maybe I was also afraid of being ridiculed.

Later that day when my assignment on the par three was finished, I went into the clubhouse to check on the teams. To my shock, I found out that my team was tied for first place and entered into a 'putt-off' to determine the winner. There was quite a bit of money for the first-, second- and third-place teams to split in the pot from the Calcutta. I only asked for the energy to make the outcome for the highest good of all involved in the tournament. I recommitted that the money that my team won would go to the students' fund.

I watched the 'putt-off' on the practice putting green with blood pounding in my ears. The ending for me was perfect. My team won second place that day! I ran inside the clubhouse and downstairs to the women's locker room and I cried tears of joy and excitement. I thanked Spirit for entrusting me to such a project of raising money (energy) in support of others.

I went back upstairs to find my team to congratulate them and hug them again. My guys asked me why I bought them and this time I told them what had motivated me to buy their team and what I would do with the money they had won. It seemed to me that the guys were teary-eyed as I told them what they really had been playing for that day. I told them they truly had been involved in a 'higher purpose'. We all had been vehicles that day for energy in the form of money.

I found my husband and caught his eye and he just shook his head at me and smiled, and I think that day even John believed in what I had tested.

I don't know if it's okay to test the energy or not. I don't know if it's okay to ask for proof if the energy exists or not. But I did ask, I did test and I received a beautiful answer. For me, Spirit will always guide me even if I don't always understand how it's flowing or working through me.

As soon as I got home, I rang Yvonne and shared my experience with her. For days after that SPE golf tournament, I walked or glided two feet off the ground. I was on such a high from the experience of dancing with the energy for being a willing player. No alcohol or drugs could leave me with such a wonderful feeling as I had inside of me from that golf tournament. I was given such a beautiful and calm sense of wellbeing. That was my reward.

In the end, my golf team, number 22 and I raised together a net of US$2500 to put back into the Indonesian College Fund. There would be no piece of jewellery or physical possession that I could have purchased with that money that would have left me feeling half as good as I did from visiting the office of the SPE President and turning the money over for the future students. I believe that the money went to a student, a future doctor, an engineer or a teacher who would use the money to get an education to help lead their country one day. I trusted the energy to guide the money to the right students. I trust the energy and I'm content to know that somewhere in a future existence I might get to know how that money helped people.

That day at the tournament during the awards ceremony and presentation of money purses to the team owners a friend of ours, a fellow American, Phil D, who was acting as MC and giving out the prizes, announced to the audience that I intended to funnel my winnings back into the scholarship fund and applause went up. I allowed that moment to happen, a moment of vain glory in front of a public audience, because I was hoping that a 'seed' might be planted that day in someone else's mind to channel the energy another time for a higher purpose.

As for me, well, what works once may work again. The very next year I was attending another golf tournament with my husband in Bali. I asked to be a player again, to be an energy vehicle and my desires were granted. At this tournament, I was able to channel another US$2,000 for an orphanage in Bali. Once again, I asked and I received from the energy. I had asked for proof and I received it. As I think back, I realise that the whole process was guided by a power so much more powerful than me.

Deborah Shucart

The week following the golf tournament, was my regular open day in our home and Deborah came along with a huge smile on her face. She shared her experience with a large group of about 40 students in my home. The joy and enthusiasm that Deborah's vibration sent forth inspired and touched every one of us.

Whatever we desire with a pure intent in our heart for the highest good of all concerned Spirit will always respond.

Why? Because…

Energy follows thought.

CHAPTER 28

KIDNEY FAILURE

An Indonesian man by the name of Budi came to me for help. He was extremely ill. Budi was on a dialysis machine twice weekly because his kidneys were failing. He wanted desperately to be healed from this illness.

He joined a first-degree Reiki training class. On the evening of the second day after completing the training, I was saying goodbye to him at the door when I suddenly saw a picture of his kidneys and a picture of a woman standing next to his right kidney.

'Do you mind me asking if you have been married before?'

'Yes, I have. Why?' He responded without hesitation.

I asked him to sit down and I talked to him about what I had seen and how issues of letting go of the past, especially personal relationships with others or with ourselves can affect our kidneys. In some cases, I have seen where kidney issues can be connected to self-criticism and self-loathing and/or anger and resentment towards other people, which can in time affect the functioning of their kidneys that hinders the energy flowing freely through that area of the body. He told me the break-up of his first marriage was very painful for him and that he still loved her very much, even though he had remarried.

I explained the vision suggesting it could be the cause of his illness. His prayer had been answered, giving him an opportunity to heal his kidneys. The choice was up to him what he chose to do with the information; I was only the messenger.

He talked at length about his first wife and his deep feelings for her. I sensed he had been struggling for a long time to let her go. I explained that failed relationships we are unable to move on from can hinder our health, putting a strain on our energy, causing an emotional energy blockage in our body, e.g. kidneys. Living in the past and continuing to hold onto the disappointment of his failed marriage eventually affected his physical health. He was living daily with regrets regarding his first marriage and continually thought about 'what if' scenarios. His feeding energy back into the past denied his body of the energy he required to sustain it.

We both sat quietly as he mulled over what we had discussed. A short time later, I looked up and above his head, I saw a picture of an open door and a heart encased in light and at the same time, I saw his eyes light up as thoughts poured into his brain.

Budi had an 'aha' moment and saw his situation clearly and understood the root cause of his kidney problems for himself. To heal himself he needed to let go of his deep emotional connection to his first wife.

Budi's insightfulness helped him to see with clarity the root cause of his current illness. When this happens, a person's illness can change for the better, depending on how deeply layered the issue is – in those situations the process for healing to happen can be slow.

Within a month he was off the dialysis machine and stayed off the machine for many months. All his friends said he was a walking miracle; he had a spring in his step and was looking so well. He came to a few open days and shared with other students his astounding recovery.

Then sadly his first wife died and overnight he fell apart emotionally. A month after her death, Budi was back on the dialysis machine and died a short time later. Sadly, Budi hadn't completed the process of letting go of his deep emotional attachment to his first wife.

I went to see him a couple of days before he died and I sensed that his heart was already with his first wife. His love for her was as strong as when they first married and by dying, he could be with her again. Life brings us choices; it's up to us which road we choose to take.

When we have what I call an 'aha' moment, a realisation, an insight into a possible cause of a disturbing issue, we can experience healing, as in Budi's case. Unfortunately, Budi's first wife dying rekindled his heart's desire and yearning to be with her and this desire became his focus.

When insights come to us, it is our inner guidance offering us an opportunity for a shift of perception, opening a door for healing to take place. When we follow through focusing on following a thread of insight, we gain 'understanding' transforming our previous mistaken belief into a deep-seated knowing, embodying a more uplifting truth for us. Refer to chapter 19 – Insightful Vision.

With patience, wonderful lasting results can be achieved. We not only sense it, but we also know without any doubt when we have achieved the desired outcome. We are no longer inclined to entertain the old belief pattern and if it does pop up, we can easily dismiss it from our mind. We don't think about the issue any longer because we know deep within our hearts, we have pulled out the root cause – it has no substance.

Why? Because...

Energy follows thought.

It doesn't matter where a loved one may be;
they are only a thought away.
All beings are interconnected through Spirit's consciousness.
Consciousness knows no boundaries.

Yvonne Fogarty

CHAPTER 29

FATHER-IN-LAW'S PASSING

In 1995 my husband Graham was transferred to Singapore to work on the design elements of a project on Bintan Island (Indonesia). The dogs and I remained in our rental home in Jakarta while Graham shared an apartment with the Japanese director. I visited Graham whenever I could.

With his work completed in mid-December, Graham returned to Jakarta. A week later we flew to Perth, Western Australia, to spend Christmas and New Year with Graham's family. His father had been ill for many years and was not expected to celebrate another Christmas with us. All the family came together, sharing Christmas brunch at their parents' home as his father was too ill to leave the house.

Before flying back to Jakarta, we called in to say goodbye to his parents on our way to the airport. As we left their home, Graham turned to me and said, 'I think that will be the last time we see Dad alive.' I took hold of Graham's hand and squeezed it as we walked towards the hire car. We returned to Jakarta the first week of January 1996.

There were many problems on another project at Batam Island (Indonesia), which was being managed by the Japanese director with whom Graham had shared the apartment in Singapore. He rang and asked Graham to assist him on the project, which was halfway through completion.

After some discussion between us, considering the long-term career benefits for Graham by being on the project, it was agreed that we would live apart for a further six months. However, Graham insisted on one condition that they fly him back to Jakarta every Friday evening, returning to site Monday mornings, to which the company agreed. Unfortunately, that didn't always happen.

Graham shared a house in Batam with three Japanese managers who were also involved in the project. There were many issues to overcome on the project that required high-level meetings and strategic planning, due to the complex nature of the project Graham had to meet up regularly with the owner's representatives located in Indonesia, Singapore and Malaysia.

Over a twelve-month period, our time together was reduced to approximately 71 days. It was a very challenging time for both of us. The times he was able to fly back, he was so exhausted he slept most of the time. I felt that we were drifting apart and I desperately longed for the connection and closeness we had always enjoyed.

A few days after Graham had left for Batam, early morning on the 15th of January, I woke up with a jolt and sat up in bed as a vision appeared...

I saw a Qantas plane landing at a busy airport with an enormous #12 stamped on the body of the plane. I relaxed and expanded my awareness into the vision and sensed the plane was landing at Jakarta International Airport. No more information was forthcoming.

Then as quickly as the vision appeared, it was gone. I recorded the vision and after a few days, it was forgotten.

On the 22nd of February, the day before I was to leave on a girls'-only holiday to India with four other expatriate friends, Graham arrived back from Batam Island and asked me to come into the lounge and sit down. I thought, *he's looking very serious. What's going on?*

He took hold of both my hands, squeezing them tightly between his, and taking a deep breath, he said, 'Yvonne, I want you to listen very carefully to me. If Dad happens to die while you are away, you're not to come home.'

I objected strongly as he continued to keep hold of my hands. I like to use my hands a lot when I talk and I couldn't get them out of his grip. Damn it. We had quite a discussion about it. In the end, Graham made me look at him and promise not to come home in the event of his father's death. I reluctantly agreed, whilst all the time I was convinced it wouldn't happen anyway, because Spirit knew that I wanted to be there with Graham and his family at the funeral.

We were enjoying some exciting adventures on this holiday as we didn't have husbands pulling us out of all the shops we visited or counting the money we spent. One day in the desert, not far from the Pakistan/Rajasthan border, the five of us decided to have a camel ride. I was on the back of the camel with my girlfriend Jill Oakes sitting in front of me. We were laughing and joking when suddenly I saw my father-in-law appear a few metres in front and to the 'right' of me. He stood there smiling at me until I acknowledged his presence and then he vanished. I looked at my watch; it was 3.55 p.m. on the 5th of March 1996. I was stunned. I replayed it in my mind before I spoke to Jill.

After taking a deep breath, I blurted out, 'I've just seen my father-in-law.'

Her head rotated back and forth 180 degrees, looking around for my father-in-law, causing her to almost fall off the camel.

Pushing her glasses back up on her nose, she said, 'Where is he? I don't see him.'

'I think he may have just died,' I replied quietly.

Graham's sister Denise told us later that Dad had been in a deep coma all afternoon and she had been with him at the hospital when he died.

By the time I was able to finally make contact with Graham, he was in the process of packing his bag to fly to Perth. He told me that his father had died at 6.50 p.m. Perth time. The time difference between

Perth and New Delhi was two and a half hours.

After doing the calculations on my fingers, I said to Graham, 'Oh. I saw your dad before he passed over.'

Once again, I talked about flying straight to Perth to be with him. Graham reminded me of the promise I had made. I was sad that his father had died, yet at the same time, I knew his dad was at last free from the poor quality of life his ill health had imposed upon him for quite a long time.

My emotions were in turmoil. One minute I was angry that my desire to be with Graham was not answered, then the sadness I felt for his mother and all the family (especially his sister Denise who was close to her father) would take over and dispel my anger.

Jill came into my room, listening quietly as I paced the floor pouring out my heart, sharing my emotional roller coaster of thoughts until finally I was able to settle my agitated feelings and relax.

Later, as I sat quietly meditating, I realised my anger was due to the fact that I was missing the close connection Graham and I had always enjoyed. I sat up straight as I gasped at seeing the whole picture clearly – I desired to be with Graham at the funeral for all the wrong reasons.

I opened my heart and forgave myself for my selfish attitude. My heart released its pain and the heaviness I felt in my heart lifted. I then focused on sending love and strength to all the family to support them. I connected with Graham's dad mentally and chatted with him in my heart, thanking him for coming to say goodbye to me.

I arrived back from India the day before Graham flew back into Jakarta from Perth. The next evening, our driver drove me to the airport to meet him. Graham arrived on a Qantas flight on the 12th of March. Graham scanned the crowd for me and walked over. He turned towards me, put his arm around me and gently kissed me. I was surprised as showing affection in public in Indonesia was frowned upon back then. He shook hands with our driver, who then left to bring the car around to the pickup area.

Leaving his arm around me, he quickly kissed me again before rubbing his lips against my ear, whispering the words I had been longing to hear. 'I love you.'

We didn't go straight home; instead, we went to our favourite place: the Fountain Lounge in the Grand Hyatt Hotel. We sat close together and I was once again aware of that wonderful warmth and closeness between us I thought was missing.

Graham talked in-depth about the funeral then turned to me and said, 'You know the one thing I missed most of all at the funeral… was you!'

I was so moved to hear his words that my eyes welled up. I explained to him I had wanted to be there for all the wrong reasons at one level and for all the right reasons at another.

'Yvonne, if you had been there, I wouldn't have realised just how much I love you and how much you mean to me.'

I realised Spirit had answered the desire I held in my heart; however, not in the way I had envisaged it happening. I realised once again that if we have a pure desire for something, there is no way it is not going to be fulfilled. I had mixed reasons behind my intent yet at the same time, my heart's desire was pure. We ask. We will receive. We just have to let go, trust and keep an open mind as to how the desire will manifest. More importantly, that our desire is not harmful to self or others and is beneficial and supportive to all people affected by the desire. (Refer to chapter 21 – The Unexpected Guest.)

Energy follows thought.

CHAPTER 30

DISCOVERING A FAMILY SECRET

Three months after returning from India, the project Graham was working on in Batam was nearing completion and we decided to go on an adventure to Ireland and England to research both our families' histories. It had been three years since my mother's death, which had left some unanswered questions, and Graham's family were researching their ancestry.

From the time we left our home in Jakarta to arriving at Shannon Airport in Ireland, which was not far from the bed & breakfast place we booked, 27 hours of real-time had elapsed. Although we were blessed to be flying business class (thanks to Graham's contractual agreements with the company), we collapsed on the bed at around 4 p.m., intending to rest for a couple of hours before having dinner.

Sometime later I woke up with a jolt. I could hear voices coming from outside our room and the sun's rays were shining brightly into our room. I glanced at my watch. It was 8.45 and my tummy was grumbling. I quickly woke Graham, informing him we had slept through the night and we had better get cleaned up quickly and go to breakfast before everything gets cleared away. We rushed out of our room, apologising to the host, hoping that we could still get some breakfast.

The host looked at us quizzically, before replying in her delightful Irish accent and a smile on her face, 'You are a bit early for your breakfast but you have definitely missed out on dinner.'

It was only nine at night! We all had a laugh; it was the first time we had experienced the sun remaining bright in the sky well into the night. We were then directed to a pub ten kilometres away where the owner kindly reopened the kitchen, satisfying our hunger.

The following day we set off on our journey and made our way slowly through the beautiful countryside, passing some lovely towns until we reached the county of Tipperary. Of course, we sang at the top of our voices the words we could remember of the well-known song, 'It's a long way to Tipperary,' which locals affectionately call 'Tip Town'.

We arrived at the town of Roscrae, where we soon discovered the Fogarty surname was very common with the name appearing on many storefronts.

I said to Graham, 'Gosh, the Fogarty name is everywhere we look. They must have bred like rabbits.'

It was from this area that Graham's family members had lived before they departed Ireland during the potato famine, bound for Australia. The devastating results of the famine took place between 1845-1849 – approximately one million people died.

The next stage of our journey was to fly to England to meet Uncle Jack, my father's brother. When we arrived at his home in Nottinghamshire, I was nervous and asked Graham to knock on the door while I waited in the car. When I saw him come out of the house, I gasped. It could have been my dad standing there. They were the spitting image of each other.

After general chit-chat, I asked him what he knew about my dad's past, prior to him leaving England for Australia. He told me a little about their childhood and added that their mother had given all the children the same second name, which he thought amusing. What he said next really surprised us.

'Before leaving England, your Dad was married when quite young.'

My mouth fell open in surprise and I'm sure my eyes were the size of saucers. I had no idea that Dad had been married before. When he told me her name, I recalled having seen initials tattooed on Dad's right arm in the shape of a heart. They were the initials of his first wife 'R.H.' I remembered asking Dad what those initials stood for and he just said he had been very foolish once and they didn't have any real meaning.

I asked Uncle Jack what happened. Now here is where it gets very interesting.

Version one: Uncle Jack told me that after the marriage ceremony, Dad's bride and the bridesmaid ran away together and their mother took him back the next day to the parish to have the wedding annulled. Wow!

The next day we drove to another part of England to meet Dad's sister.

Version two: (I love this version, which I believe is the whole truth after speaking later to other family members.) Dad's sister, who was the baby of the family and thirteen years of age when Dad got married at 21 years of age, told us after the wedding ceremony, his bride and the bridesmaid left the local pub and went on ahead to Dad's house. When he arrived home, he found them both in bed together! Double WOW! They then ran away, leaving Dad alone in the house!

I could hear Graham attempting to stifle a laugh and that set me off. I clapped my hands together and started laughing. I couldn't stop. I thought it was hilarious. Graham and my aunty, who had Dad's blue eyes, started laughing too. Aunty told me it was the truth and that her brother Jack was embarrassed by it all and had given us a gentler version.

Although I saw the funny side of the situation, I also felt for Dad. I said to Aunty, 'It must have been a terrible shock for Dad as he was a very conservative man, especially that happening back in 1925.'

Aunty said, 'I idolised your dad. He was devastated and Mum had taken him back to the church parish the next day to get the wedding annulled.'

From there we went to stay with my cousin, who lived in London with his family and he confirmed everything my aunty had told us. He'd heard the same information from his mother (dec). We rang the parish where Dad had married and requested a copy of the wedding certificate along with a copy of the annulment. A few days later, we received a phone call from the parish saying they were faxing a copy of the wedding certificate but couldn't find any annulment! *What!* They said the procedure they followed back then was the annulment would have been noted on the wedding certificate record if it had been annulled.

HUH! Again, I was stunned. I said to Graham and my cousin, 'That's not possible. I'm sure it would have been annulled. Dad was too prim and proper for that to have happened.'

My cousin, with whom we were staying, suggested we go to Somerset House in London. The following morning, after a restless night's sleep, we walked into Somerset House where the public records are held. We were directed to a counter and requested a search of ten years on either side of Mum and Dad's wedding date (believing I was being thorough), hoping to find the annulment notice.

In the meantime, we went to a nice restaurant for a leisurely lunch. I kept reassuring Graham that it was only a formality and that when we returned in a couple of hours, they would hand over a copy of the annulment or a copy of the divorce. Dad was always a real gentleman and very proper. He would never have married again without an annulment. Graham simply smiled and continued eating and nodding his head.

On our return three hours later, the same clerk served us again and said, 'I'm sorry, we checked twice and couldn't find where the wedding had been annulled or that a divorce had gone through.'

'What!' I said in a raised voice. 'Please, check the records again. It must be a mistake.'

The clerk looked over at Graham as if pleading for help before looking back at me, saying, 'We have checked the records thoroughly and there is no mistake.'

I stumbled out of there in a state of shock, shaking my head back and forth, I kept repeating to Graham, 'I don't believe it. I don't believe it.'

We sat down on the well-trodden front steps of Somerset House. I was oblivious to anyone else around us; I was like a parrot, mumbling over and over the same four words. To someone looking at me, they might have thought I was on drugs with my blank eyes and rambling voice. Unbeknown to me, Graham had cheekily been recording my shocked reaction on our video recorder.

Graham has a dry sense of humour and knows just when to say something in a witty way. He turned to me, leaning in so close our heads were almost touching and I'm thinking, *Ohhh, he's going to say something sweet to comfort me and/or give me a kiss.*

Instead, he whispered, 'Yvonne,' then he paused long enough for effect, waiting for me to look into his eyes before adding in a mischievous voice, 'You little bastard! You're a little bastard!'

We both burst out laughing.

'Wow,' I said excitedly as this realisation occurred to me. 'We have a ginormous skeleton in our closet. We always appeared so squeaky clean and Mum always worried what other people thought. Perhaps now I understand why.'

I truly felt ecstatic and elated at this new discovery; the rascals had been probably living in sin all these years in the eyes of the church.

An old memory stirred in my mind and I remembered the doorbell ringing one evening when I was maybe six years old. Mum opened the door to find the Red Cross standing there. Dad's family in England had been searching for him as they feared he might have been killed in the war. They had no idea where he was.

After they left, I remember Mum saying to Dad in front of us kids, 'Why didn't you ever mention that you had half a dozen brothers and sisters?' I don't remember Dad's response. The Red Cross gave Mum

Dad's sister's address and she started writing to his family.

In 1963 they travelled by ship to England and again in 1966 when Dad was ill. I can only surmise that Dad had told Mum about his first marriage years earlier because she knew he had changed his birth date.

Meanwhile, back in London I was still sitting on the steps of Somerset House in shock and still repeating the same four words. I suddenly stood up. I just had to get away. As soon as a bus stopped out front of Somerset House, without thinking, I jumped on and Graham had to run to catch it. We had no idea where we were going.

Every time I mentioned those same four words, Graham piped up and whispered cheekily in a singsong voice, 'Youuuuuu little bastard!'

That night my cousin suggested we go back into London and search for a death certificate for Dad's first wife from the date of their wedding until after the date Mum and Dad married. Again, there was nothing.

So I cannot say for sure whether the marriage was annulled and the paperwork was lost, or whether in fact I am what they used to call children of unwed parents, 'a little bastard'. Thank goodness that era has passed long ago. What's important is that all children are loved and cherished unconditionally however they come into the world.

Later I realised that Dad's first marriage was in 1925 and he left for Australia soon afterwards. His second marriage was in 1939, which left a four-year span not researched. Our search was only for a ten-year span. When I told Graham this, he reminded me that neither the church nor Somerset House had an annulment on record.

I get excited to think that my parents possibly weren't legally married as Mum had continually drummed it into me to be a 'very' good girl! I was too scared not to be. What a darn shame!

In some ways, it may answer one query. I don't believe the passports we found were connected to the government work he undertook. Instead, the two passports may have been to cover his tracks with a slight change of his second name, change of his birth date and where he was born. He left England in 1926; back then Australia was so far away and records weren't easily available to trace people's background. An unanswerable question remains: why would he do that if he believed the wedding had been annulled?

I now understand why Mum treated Dad so rudely at times. The tables had turned. It was now Mum who had the upper hand, she had something over Dad. Knowing Mum, I can only imagine the huge shame she carried around, especially with her upbringing and the strict religious rules, which she and her family had lived by.

As for me, I am overjoyed that we may or may not be the 'squeaky-clean' family we were led to believe. If it's true and I have no doubt that it's not, it's exciting to have a huge skeleton in the closet. It does answer a lot of questions regarding their relationship, e.g. the abortion attempts and Mum's outbursts and unhappiness we encountered in the home a lot of the time. One day I may decide to do further research, although I don't believe it really matters in the big scheme of things.

*The power of love can be experienced when we carry
a deep love within our hearts for another being.
The boundaries of our physical reality have no hold over those
whose hearts and souls are connected by the power of love.
The nature of this power is such that it is impossible to be
confined to an existence that knows only limitations.
Our soul's interconnection to Consciousness is unlimited,
boundless and free.*

Yvonne Fogarty

CHAPTER 31

THE POWER OF LOVE

In mid-1997 Graham and I decided to return to England again for three weeks. We loved having staff yet we were in need of some quiet time alone together and away from a crowded city. A few days before we were to leave, our thirteen-year-old Lhasa Apso dog Kouchi appeared unwell.

We had the local vet around who said, 'It's just her age.'

The day we were to depart, I felt quite concerned about Kouchi as her eyes were looking very glazed. I again called the vet, who promptly came to our home and reassured me Kouchi was okay. The vet promised to come twice weekly and check on Kouchi and our younger Lhasa Apso dog Sharza until our return. The vet spoke to our Indonesian staff and told them if either of the dogs appeared unwell, they were to contact her immediately.

Despite the vet's reassurance, I still had an uneasy feeling. I rang a friend, Lyn Kearney (dec), who kindly offered to also keep an eye on the dogs. We informed our staff to ring Lyn if any problems arose. About an hour before we were to leave for the airport, I rang Lyn again, instructing her that if the unthinkable happened to Kouchi, she was to empty our deep freezer and place her in it.

When we leave on a trip the usual routine plays out: Sharza continues to jump around whether we have suitcases surrounding us or not. We called him our little 'slow thinker', except, that is, when it came to food. Kouchi was quite the opposite. Whenever she saw a suitcase, she would become very moody and miserable. She could really use her eyes to relay her emotions and her whole facial expression would clearly show her disapproval. We always felt guilty at the thought of leaving them, so much so that we would delay packing our suitcases until the very last minute.

Our driver came in and collected our luggage, giving my husband an anxious look that indicated we should have left by now. We missed a flight once due to the heavily congested roads. When travelling around Jakarta, if asked how far it is to a place, we would never give an answer in distance. The answer is given by the length of time it could take to get somewhere and that varied greatly even if it was only a few kilometres away.

Graham told to me to hurry up or we might miss the flight.

I walked out of one of the guest rooms in a panic, declaring, 'No. Just wait a minute, please. I am not leaving until I have kissed Kouchi goodbye but I can't find her.'

Graham walked back into the dining room glancing around. 'What are you talking about? She is right here, sitting by your hand luggage.'

'Oh! That's unusual,' I said.

In the past, I would usually have to search for her and then pull her out gently from under a bed by her little legs.

I picked her up, smothering her in lots of kisses and hugs and said, 'Now remember, we will only be away for twenty-one sleeps.' I purposely left a lipstick imprint on top of her head before putting her down. Then I quickly gave Sharza another lipstick kiss.

As I collected my hand luggage, Kouchi walked to the entrance of our bedroom and then stopped in the doorway glancing back at me. Our eyes met and my uneasiness returned. I watched Kouchi walk to our bed and instead of jumping up as usual, she slid under my side of the bed and lay down.

During the flight, I managed to doze off for a while before waking up suddenly. I sat up, opening my eyes, and all I could see in front of me was an oversized image of Kouchi's face smiling at me, with her little moist pink tongue hanging out and her eyes looking bright and clear.

I started to cry and woke Graham, saying, 'Graham, Kouchi is dead.'

Graham tried to console me. 'Oh, Yvonne, don't be silly. You know how attached she is to you; she is just missing you.'

'Graham, something is wrong, I know it.'

Graham took my hand, reassuring me she was okay.

When we arrived in London, I immediately wanted to ring home. Graham kept reassuring me there was no need. Kouchi was okay.

At five o'clock that morning in Jakarta, one of our staff telephoned the home of Lyn and Peter Kearney. Lyn's husband Peter answered the phone and before he could say anything, he heard a distressed woman's voice say, 'Mister, Mister. Anjing meninggal.'

Peter turned to Lyn and said, 'I know that meninggal means dead, but what does anjing mean?'

Lyn quickly sat up in bed and said, 'Oh no, Kouchi must have died.'

Lyn and Peter quickly drove to our house and cleared out our chest freezer before wrapping her in plastic and placing her back into the freezer.

The staff had found her under my side of the bed. My friends back in Jakarta banded together and decided that if I rang to check on Kouchi, they would tell me everything was okay.

I felt extremely unsettled and I just wanted to scream. I told Graham that I needed to get out of London to a place where I could be quiet, but where? That night I prayed and asked three times for guidance to find us a place where I could settle myself down. I blew my desire away, trusting an answer would come.

The next morning, I woke up early with The Voice saying to me, **_'Yvonne, go to Harrogate.'_**

I shook Graham. 'Graham, Graham, wake up. We have to go to Harrogate.'

'Oh, Yvonne, what are you rambling on about?' He looked at his watch and then added, 'It's only five a.m.'

'We have to go to Harrogate today.'

Graham, still half-asleep, responded, 'Harrogate? Where the heck is Harrogate?' (His actual words were not that polite – I toned them down.)

'I don't know. The Voice suggested we go there.'

Thank goodness I have a husband who accepts my messages, even though he says he still doesn't understand how I receive them. Nor did I back then. We looked up our tourist map and found Harrogate was only a few hours away by train.

When we arrived, we hired a car and were directed to a tourist office. I explained to the lady behind the counter what I required. It was as if she was an angel in disguise; she straightaway seemed to sense exactly what my needs were. We ended up in a picturesque bed and breakfast farmhouse perched on a hill that overlooked a tiny village surrounded by rolling hills at a place called Pateley Bridge, situated about 22 kilometres northwest of Harrogate in North Yorkshire. It was the perfect location.

During the night, I woke up as a vision started playing out in front of my eyes.

I saw Kouchi sitting with her old boyfriend Rusty, a golden retriever who had died a few years earlier. They were both sitting close together on a green-grassed hill with a perfect blue sky behind them. Both were looking very happy and content.

Then the vision changed and I saw Graham and I returning to our home in Jakarta and our staff welcoming us. When we walked into the house, Sharza ran up to greet us. Kouchi was nowhere to be seen.

I started sobbing. There were other guest bedrooms on either side of us and once again my husband was consoling me. Although I felt washed out the next day, I noticed that the disturbed energy that had built up in my heart over the past few days had dissipated. Graham again talked me out of ringing home. I can only assume that was his way of protecting me from more pain.

Upon arriving back at Jakarta International Airport our driver Sofari was waiting for us.

My first words to him were 'Sofari, is Kouchi okay?'

'Yes, Madam.' He turned away without looking at me. He quickly left to fetch our car.

While we were waiting for the car to arrive, I started to cry and said, 'No, she isn't. She's dead.'

When we got into the car, Sofari reached back, handing me a letter. I looked at him quizzically. His eyes welled up and tears started rolling down his face. The letter was from Lyn, telling me Kouchi had died while we were on the plane to London. The pain was almost unbearable. When we arrived home, we greeted Sharza before taking Kouchi out of the freezer and I kissed her before placing her back.

A few days later we went out to the Chinese crematorium as that was the only place in Jakarta we knew of where cremations were done. Unfortunately, the manager told us they definitely did not cremate animals. Their facilities were only for human cremations. I heard their words yet my heart was clearly telling me otherwise.

Driving back home, I said to Graham, 'I don't want to bury her in Indonesia. I prefer to take her ashes back to our hometown.'

For three weeks I struggled inwardly until I finally let go and accepted the reality of the situation. Later that same morning while lying down, I felt the impression of dog's paws on the side of the bed where I was laying. I opened my eyes as I reached over to lift Sharza up as I usually did but he wasn't there. I sat up and saw him lying over by the window. I lay back down and thought, *did I just imagine that or is Kouchi around?* I closed my eyes and thought of her and my heart filled with joy. I gave thanks for having had the pleasure of her in my life and for leaving me with so many happy memories. When I got up, I felt lighter; a heavy weight had been lifted off me. I realised that through my pain I had lowered my vibrations and had shut myself away from being able to see her.

Later that day I was sitting with my feet up on the lounge room couch, reading. Once again, I felt the familiar impression of dog paws just before they spring up onto the couch.

I looked over towards my feet where I had felt the impression and there, sitting looking at me, was Kouchi. Our eyes locked onto each other. It was as if time stood still. I smiled at her and I could see that her eyes were bright and sparkling once again and her little pink moist tongue was hanging out like it used to do when she was happy. No words were necessary, our eyes and hearts spoke for us and then she jumped off the lounge and walked out through the open sliding doors towards our back garden and turned to the right before vanishing from sight.

She had been waiting for me to raise my vibrations enough for me to see her so we could say goodbye.

A month after she died, our precious little Kouchi was still wrapped in plastic in the freezer. Graham was getting to the end of his patience. I guess he had his own vision of Kouchi staying in our freezer forever.

'Yvonne, you can't continue to keep her in the freezer. What are you going to do with her?'

'Trust me, I believe it's all going to work out,' I replied.

Six weeks later Graham raised the subject yet again, this time in a frustrated impatient manner.

'Graham, I will be told when she will be able to be cremated.'

'But they have already said no,' he replied.

'That doesn't mean anything to Spirit. I truly believe that despite what we have been told, it will somehow work out.'

I admit I was getting a little anxious myself but of course, I didn't let him know that. I knew deep in my heart I wouldn't have felt that strong reassuring feeling to wait if it wasn't going to happen somehow.

Whenever guests came and only saw Sharza wagging his tail and wriggling his bottom excitedly around them, they would ask, 'Where's Kouchi?'

'Oh, she's in the freezer!' I would answer in a casual manner as if it was quite normal to have your dog in a freezer. Once I let go of the pain of loss, I still experienced some sadness yet at the same time, I could laugh again because my heart had embraced the treasured memories of our loved one.

Seven weeks later I was awakened in the early hours by The Voice saying, *'Go back today.'*

I requested Graham get a taxi to work as I wanted our driver to return to the crematorium early that morning.

When our driver arrived back, he said excitedly, 'Madam, they will cremate her tomorrow morning. You are to make a coffin and put her in it. Do not seal it as they need to inspect it before cremating her.'

'Well done. Thank you Sofari.'

He lowered his eyes giving me a sheepish look and grinned, adding, 'Well, Madam, I spoke to the "new" manager in charge and I told him you would like to give a donation.'

'Thank you, Sofari. That was a very good idea.' I smiled.

Sofari advised us against going as well as it would incur quite a bit of attention, which the new man in charge wanted to avoid. Our day guard made the coffin himself.

I wrapped her in one of my well-loved caftans, which had its hem chewed and torn. She used to play hide and seek under it when I was standing still and she often grabbed onto the hem with the intent of taking me for a walk around the house or garden.

Early the next morning, Graham, our staff, Sharza and I all stood around the coffin and we had a little ceremony and said goodbye to Kouchi.

Lightness fills my heart whenever I think of this precious little soul who brought so much joy into our lives. Through my pain I had unknowingly lowered my vibrations, closing off my heart's connection to Kouchi. It felt like I had shut myself away into a cold dark place where no one could reach me. I realised that reconnecting with her and experiencing her presence was only a thought away.

I know from personal experience when we love someone, whether it is an animal or human, and they have ceased living in their physical body, their soul lives on and can remain connected to ours through the power of love, resonating within our soul's vibration.

In that brief moment, I saw Kouchi, I was once again reminded that our life is eternal just as The Voice said to me when I received the Insightful Vision message in 1992… 'Lifetimes are forever.'

That experience taught me a big lesson and that experience has since supported others, like a friend Carol Burgess who courageously confronted her buried pain. When I first met her, I sensed she carried a lot of sadness. One afternoon she came to me and talked about her young grandson who had been killed in an accident. The next time I saw her, I handed her a copy of 'The Power of Love' experience as I sensed it may support her in some way to accept her grandchild's tragic death, which had occurred a few years earlier.

Carol came to see me a week later, clutching the story in both hands, holding it close to her chest with a big smile on her face, telling me how much my experience had helped her and could she keep the story. She hadn't realised how closed off she had been towards life, adding, 'I can now dust my grandson's photo without feeling bitter and angry. I feel very close to him again.'

A neighbour, Margot, and I were enjoying a coffee, getting to know each other. I shared Carol's healing experience after telling her my experience when Kouchi died. I watched Margot's energy expand, as her thoughts took her to another place.

In Margot's own words:

I had only just met my new neighbour, Yvonne; she was warm and openly friendly. I liked her instinctively. Yvonne was relating a story to me about a woman she had met who had lost a much-loved grandchild. The death of her grandchild had caused the woman great pain and bitterness. She couldn't bear to look at the photograph of her grandchild on display because of her unresolved sorrow.

As Yvonne talked, the woman's story suddenly became mine. I found myself in 'another realm' as I was flung back in time to more than 40 years ago when my sister's first-born son had died. Simon never left the hospital. He lived for 26 long days and nights. I hadn't been supportive; I wasn't there for my sister and I hadn't been a comfort to her. Unlike now, my sister and I were not close. I was young, self-centred and working full-time. I was too busy to think too long about her distress.

Time catches up though and eventually, my thoughts processed the reality of Simon's death and I became aware of the loneliness and all-engulfing sadness my sister had endured, going home to an empty house without her baby. She was so alone. I have always felt guilty and such a failure for not realising at the time, the true extent of my sister's grief over the dreadful loss of her precious son.

Suddenly, I was aware of Yvonne speaking to me again. I had never spoken to anyone about Simon, my sister or my feelings and here I was telling Yvonne my story.

Yvonne's words, which I can only describe as a 'power', somehow conveyed light, which allowed me to release the guilty feelings I had carried for so many years. I felt extremely emotional, happy and a little lightheaded as I walked home. Yvonne was able to help me, along with the woman who had lost her grandchild.

Margot Storer

Just as Carol and Margot experienced, connecting with another person's experience can bring about a healing. When I am giving someone an intuitive energy treatment, spiritual counselling, or sharing how changing my thinking changed my outlook on life for the better, I sometimes receive the comment 'It's so easy for you to say – you are a positive person.'

That comment fills me with joy and I say thank you, then I explain to them that I haven't always been this way; in fact, I used to be quite the opposite.

I have paraphrased a wonderful Louise Hay quote: 'I can assure you the key to unlocking the door for change is simply by having the willingness to listen to what the Spirit of Truth impresses upon us.'

It was up to me whether I used the challenges I encountered as stepping-stones to improving my life or continue seeing my challenges as stumbling blocks. Chapter 40 – Journey From Misery To Contentment is a wonderful example of a brave woman who did just that.

I have spent many years on personal development and have come a long way towards understanding myself and letting go of survival patterns I no longer required. I used to cling onto these old structures, even though I had outgrown them. It was as if my life depended on them. They were mine. I owned them and I wasn't going to let them go even though they were a big hindrance to my growth.

Why? I had clung onto what was 'familiar' to me. I hung onto what felt comfortable and safe, even if it was detrimental to my wellbeing, because they gave me a false sense of security. I liken my old survival patterns to continuously trying to squeeze myself back into a much smaller dress size, one that I had worn when I was a very young girl. It just didn't fit anymore. Throw them out! Get rid of them. Shoo!

All I had to do was let go of my 'self-depleting' belief patterns and open my heart to allow the inner guidance to show me 'my' truths for me, not someone else's. I know from my own experience that holding onto self-depleting beliefs (some I was not even fully aware of) affected my physical wellbeing as they slowly ate away at my inner core's strength, which can bring about a serious illness.

CHAPTER 32

JAKARTA RIOTS 1998

In the early hours of 20 March 1998, I woke up with an uneasy feeling stirring in my heart. I immediately sat up and opened my eyes as a vision spread out across our bedroom and beyond.

I saw what appeared to be a small fire flaring up close to our bed, but not touching it. Further across the room, I saw two more fires flaring up. In the distance, there appeared a much bigger fire and then other fires started to flare up. Instead of suddenly disappearing as other visions have done, this vision slowly disappeared.

The vision left me feeling deeply disturbed. I sensed there was serious trouble coming to Indonesia and it would escalate coming close to our home. I attempted to go back to sleep; however, I was unable to. As I lay there, words started tumbling into my head. I quickly got up, grabbed my notebook and headed out to the dining room table and started to write. When my husband surfaced around 6 a.m. he found me sitting at the dining table staring out the window at the squirrels running up and down the trees, collecting their breakfast.

After giving each other a kiss and hug, I said, 'Graham, I experienced a very disturbing vision early this morning. The pain and sadness I felt in my heart from the vision poured out in the form of a poem, if you can call it that. I've never written or ever received anything like this before and I couldn't stop the words from flowing, they just kept coming. This precognitive vision I received is warning us that serious trouble is coming to Jakarta, and before you say anything, I sense this time it's going to be much more serious than all the other riots we have encountered since living here. I feel a deep sadness for the Indonesian people.'

I explained the vision to Graham and said, 'I sense the separate fires I saw represent different parts of Indonesia.'

Graham sat, listening without saying a word. When I finished, I could see that he was pondering over what I had told him then he looked at me intently before quietly asking, 'Show me what you've written?'

He looked at my scrawl and then said, 'Why don't you read it to me?'

THE CRY OF A TROUBLED NATION

A poem by Yvonne Fogarty. March 1998

I'm travelling along this dusty old road looking for a place to hide.
I'm tired and worn, my heart's crying out,
why do such atrocities go on?
With each step I take in my old dusty shoes,
I hear the rhythm of a beating drum.
Let's live in peace – let there be peace – may peace return to our land.
They say our world is highly developed,
yet still peace eludes us – why?
These thoughts constantly harp at me as I look for a place to hide.
I have ragged clothes, and stars for a bed,
yet I have one thing to call my own.
It's my dusty old shoes, as they carry me along
looking for a place to hide.
I have come so far, though many have died,
may my journey not be in vain.
Why don't we strive for a peaceful solution, instead of raging war?

Will the world take note of our sadness and loss
that others will not have to endure,
the struggle of being different, only by birth, religion or law?
They say we're advanced as a human race and
technology has bettered our world.
But with men at the helm with only power in mind,
its ego-fed bullets destroying innocent lives.
I've travelled far in my old dusty shoes seeking answers to my plea.
I hear the voice of the beating drum; it's coming nearer
with its message loud and clear,
What if we sowed love and embraced all mankind,
despite our colour or class?
Is the answer too simple? I hear myself ask.
Am I too simple-minded to hope that love could unite us all?
Yes, I'd like to believe it's possible. Yes. It really can I thought.
If all men listened to the voice of the drum,
located deep within their hearts,
which talks of love, saying, come on all, let's unite and live as One.
If we can show love to all mankind from deep within our hearts
Just maybe peace will come again and our world will be free at last.
I sigh heavily at my simplistic thoughts as I walk along the road,
listening to the rhythm of the beating drum,
Let's live in peace – let there be peace – may peace return to our land.

'Yvonne, your messages are always for a purpose. You will understand in time.' Graham gently rubbed my back.

'Are you concerned about this message Graham? Because I am. We are being forewarned by Spirit.'

'Of course, I am,' Graham said. 'Let's just hope that whatever is brewing can be resolved quickly.'

It wasn't long until the trouble became visible. On the 4th of May, we heard the price of fuel was going up by about 70%, and the cost of electricity was going to be increased. We knew this meant trouble; it was too much for the many struggling Indonesians.

Medan (the capital of North Sumatra) had already been having student riots for a month and the news created more havoc. The crowds had to be dispersed with tear gas.

By the 8th of May, the unrest had quickly spread to Solo (a city in Java) and that day later became known as 'Bloody Friday'. The unrest around Indonesia created a domino effect and quickly spread to other cities.

A few days later on the 12th of May, four students were killed outside a university campus in Jakarta and many were injured.

The following day was my fortnightly healing day in our home. There were about twenty local and expatriate women from many different nationalities present. We were all sitting around enjoying morning tea when suddenly mobile phones started ringing. Women rushed to their handbags, delving inside to retrieve their phones. It was their husbands advising them to go home immediately.

Almost simultaneously, a number of drivers came running frantically into the house, waving their arms and telling everyone they needed to leave now before the roads became blocked. Bedlam broke out.

Graham rang me to say all offices were advised to close and he was coming home. He told me Sofari was checking on the safest route home and reminded me not to go outside our home and to make sure our day guard kept the gates locked.

As each lady left, I hugged them quickly, reminding them to surround themselves, their driver and their car with the white light of protection. I asked each of the ladies to let me know when they had arrived home. Refer to chapter 33 – The White Light (including instructions).

All arrived home safely although for some, the trip took many hours compared to the normal hour or so, as some roads were already blocked with debris.

I went into our bedroom and sought out the notebook where I had recorded the vision. I sat re-reading my notes. Although one of the fires was close, it definitely was 'not' touching our bed and that was very relevant. I sensed strongly the vision was showing me we would be safe from harm. I prayed I was right. (Often, it's the small details in my visions that have proven to be significant).

I sent my cook to ask all the staff to come into the house. I could clearly see our younger staff were scared. I spoke in simple English and my cook translated for me.

'I am sure we are all going to be safe here. Our house is in a small quiet street and Allah will protect us.' (As they were of the Islamic faith, I used words they could relate to.) I suggested if any of their immediate family felt they were in danger in their kampong (village), they were welcome to take shelter in our home. Within two days we had some of our staff's family staying on our property. Three of our six staff lived on our property each had their own living quarters, sharing a small kitchen and bathroom all separate from our house.

As I sat waiting for Graham and Sofari to arrive home, I pictured the car in my mind, encircling it with light. I prayed for Indonesia as a nation and asked for guidance. A sense of calm eventually came over me as I once again reviewed the vision in my mind. I again sensed in my heart we would be safe.

A day later, a department store was torched and it was estimated at least 1,000 people died inside the store and surrounding buildings during the fires. All embassies advised expatriates to leave the country. The Australian Embassy was extremely helpful and supportive during this troubling time. Most expatriate companies evacuated their staff either back to their home country or to Singapore and Malaysia. Graham's company had recently given us open airline tickets to return to Perth to be used in an emergency. With the rioting widespread on the streets, it was virtually impossible to get to the airport unless you had an army escort.

We heard that many wealthy Chinese-Indonesians were stopped

close to the airport and after handing over a hefty amount of money, they were allowed through a roadblock, driving their cars to the airport and abandoning them. (Sadly, whenever there is trouble in Indonesia, those of Chinese origin were often targeted.) The Australian Embassy rang, advising us to leave. We sat down and discussed the situation. We decided to stay.

Many friends from around the globe rang telling us to leave and some thought we were very foolish for staying. The decision to stay was not made lightly. Friends and family did not understand that I sensed in my heart it was safe for us to stay. I guess if I hadn't had the vision and the feeling of calm and peace deep in my heart, we may have made a different decision; still, I don't believe so, as we would not have left without our remaining fur kid Sharza coming with us.

Within 24 hours we had set up a small network with those who chose to stay and others who couldn't afford to leave as Indonesia has been their home from birth. We spoke often on the phone and were fortunate the electricity didn't go off. We had television continually broadcasting updates on the situation. Although the best way to get the news of what was happening in our area came from our staff.

Many friends lived close by to where the riots were taking place, especially our Chinese-Indonesian and Indian friends, and some homes were being vandalised around them. Whenever they felt frightened, they would call and we talked until they felt peaceful again, and I reminded them to keep the white light around their home and give thanks for the protection that was surrounding them. It was also a reminder to me, as I too had my moments of inner panic when we heard from our staff that the trouble was creeping closer towards us.

I often thought of the vision I received and reminded myself to focus only on the reality I chose to see transpire, not on what I didn't want to see happen. It was a challenging time. I was battling with the fearful thoughts that rose up in my head against the deep calm in my heart. I reminded myself often not to go left or right with my thinking – to keep it focused straight ahead on the desired goal of seeing Indonesia peaceful again.

The Australian Embassy phoned again, this time advising us the last Qantas flight evacuating expatriates was leaving the next day and there would not be another. They strongly recommended that we be on it and a bus with a military escort would pick us up and take us to the airport. They couldn't guarantee our safety if we stayed. Graham had the phone on speaker and he looked over at me, raising his eyebrows. I shook my head.

Graham advised them, 'No, we are both staying.'

Graham hung up the phone and for a few moments I felt physically sick.

The riots appeared to be intensifying as the trouble came closer to our home so I decided to remove our money and important documents from our safe and hide them out of sight, ready to grab them and leave quickly if we had to. It was just on dusk when I called Graham into the bedroom.

With a smug look on my face, I said, 'I bet you won't be able to find where I hid our cash and documents?'

He narrowed his eyes as he looked at me thoughtfully, turned, walked back to the entrance to our bedroom and switched on the light so he could have a good hunt. He stood there, casually scanning the room then, darn it, he looked up. He turned, looking back at me, shaking his head from side to side, then with a smirk on his face, said, 'Y.' (This was his nickname for me.) 'You are so naïve at times!'

'Damn,' I replied in a disgruntled voice. 'I thought the large overhead light fitting was a good place to hide everything, but I didn't count on someone switching on the light.'

'Well,' I added loudly as he walked away, 'if the power to the house had been switched off, it would have been a good hiding place.'

Unbeknown to Graham, the following night the guard had placed a ladder by the side of the house and helped me climb up onto the roof. We heard a car explode and saw flames and smoke, heard people yelling and saw a building on fire about half a kilometre away from our home. We could also see what appeared to be looting on the main thoroughfare lined with local shops many owned by Chinese-Indonesians two streets over.

Every morning and night I encircled our house with the white light of protection. We stayed behind the high brick walls that surrounded our home with our gates locked for ten days. Most houses in Jakarta have bars at the windows, broken glass and barbed wire on top of high brick walls as we also had, except our windows were without bars. The end result of the devastating riots that shook Indonesia to its core triggered the downfall of President Suharto on the 21st of May. We were both watching the news as was delivered on television.

Graham turned to me and said, 'We are witnessing history in the making right now.' It was a surreal moment.

A week later many of the army tanks and barricades had disappeared from some streets, leaving a small military presence and a few army tanks dotted around Jakarta. Most of the debris had been cleaned up. It was as if, in some ways, the frightening events had never happened. The only remaining evidence was the burnt-out buildings and the heavily armed military posted at some of the main shopping centres, embassies and hotels.

A few days later, Graham and I were once again sitting in the Fountain Lounge of our favourite hotel, The Grand Hyatt, listening to the resident Philippine band. We glanced through the expansive floor-to-ceiling windows looking down at the large roundabout outside. It still felt surreal. One week earlier, there were tanks and barricades protecting this area where some large hotels and an embassy are located. Now it was quiet and peaceful.

Expatriates living in foreign countries have different stress levels to deal with. Some postings were much more challenging than others. Friends thought we were lucky, having staff that took care of everything and a driver to drive us around, yet the situations we faced daily could be very challenging and we occasionally experienced some very scary moments.

I remember one such incident (post-Jakarta riots) when I was out with an Australian expatriate friend at a fabric shop and we were in her Mercedes car when a student riot broke out 60 metres up the road from us. The owner of the shop quickly moved rolled fabrics out of the way and her driver backed the car into the shop where the staff then quickly placed large rolls of fabrics in front of her car, hiding it from being seen and vandalised. (In times of trouble, expensive cars were often targeted.) Some companies had changed their company cars after the riots to less conspicuous ones.

I believe the poem and the intensity of my vision embraced not only the imminent heartfelt pain of the nation but also the centuries of struggle the Indonesian people endured under different rulers.

My desire is that all humanity will open their hearts to live in peace with one another, despite their colour, nationality or religion.

I often organised Reiki refresher sessions where students could come together, sharing their insights and growth. One Saturday, there were sixteen people – five men and eleven women – present in our house.

We were about to resume after lunch when I felt my awareness heighten. I glanced around the room, wondering what my senses had been alerted to. As I looked at each of the students, it suddenly dawned on me: many of us were of differing nationalities.

I said, 'We all come from different cultures and beliefs and we may each refer to this Spiritual power by a different name. Whatever name we use, the fact is, it exists. It is a "neutral" energy anyone can "tune" into and utilise. In fact, we breathe in this power every time we take a breath.

'We are all aware of the troubles in the world at the moment, especially the ongoing unrest in Indonesia, Israel and Palestine, and the genocide that took place in Rwanda in 1994 where approximately

800,000 people lost their lives. Some nations share the same motto as Indonesia does: "Unity in Diversity". Let's imagine a globe of the world in front of us right now and send forth light and love to the whole world.'

Without saying a word, we all stood, joining hands. We quietly sent out thoughts of light and love. The energy filling the room was felt by all. The interconnection we all sensed between us in that moment is something I have never forgotten. Though we differed in cultures and beliefs, we were standing together, sharing a common thread of love and unity in diversity.

Due to Covid delays, I was given an opportunity to re-edit this manuscript in early 2022 and I am saddened to see on the news, much unrest is still happening around the world.

CHAPTER 33

THE WHITE LIGHT

The white light is there for anyone to call upon for protection. When you do so, you are calling forth Spirit's frequency of light. This frequency is readily available to us all; it instantly forms a vibrational protective shield around us, heightening our awareness of possible outside negative influences.

Negative energy can be experienced all around us and our body can easily absorb these vibrations without realising it, especially in times of trouble, facing a hostile environment or another person's anger, resulting in our vibrations lowering through absorbing negativity around us.

When I call forth the white light, I visualise it as a bright wide white ribbon of light in my mind. I visualise 'I am' wrapping it around wherever I have intentionally focused the energy to go.

Reiki students who have been initiated in the second-degree training can utilise the 'power symbol's' frequency and vibration imprinted in their soul's energy body thus enhancing the white light, drawing in a higher sensitivity of awareness to their outside environment.

One of my students said to me one day, 'I cannot get the white ribbon of light to stay encircled around what I am attempting to envision. The light keeps coming apart.'

I smiled. 'I used to experience the same problem. When you encircle the light, tie a knot in it so it won't be able to come apart. It doesn't matter how we envision it; we just have to trust in this power to follow our directive and I assure you it will. Why? Because we as spiritual beings have power over the "elements". Our focused intention behind our action directs the power to fulfil our instruction.'

That worked for her.

'Remember,' I added. 'The only thing that can dilute the power to fulfil our desire is our negative thoughts and beliefs.' E.g. Desiring it to work for you but at the same time doubting it will.

During my sessions with students and clients, I always remind them our thoughts are 'living entities'; they are real and can powerfully influence our lives. We all need to be aware of what we intentionally focus our thoughts upon repeatedly as one day we may end up experiencing them because…

Energy follows thought.

CHAPTER 34

MY COMMITMENT

The Voice awakened me one morning in March 1999…

'Yvonne, write.'

Those two simple words spoken subsequently turned my contented existence upside-down.

I asked The Voice for confirmation as I still had a big issue expressing myself and the thought of writing a book terrified me. Writing any type of manual was easy. In my mind, it wasn't a book, no matter how many pages a manual held! Back then I believed writing a book was way beyond my capabilities.

That same day I received a telephone call from a client, Mr Harish Chandra Dubey, who had returned back home to India some months earlier. As soon as I said 'hello', Mr Dubey spoke…

'Yvonne,' he said. 'I felt strongly upon awaking this morning I had to ring and tell you to stop teaching and to write a book.'

I chuckled to myself and thanked him for his wonderful insight and told him his words were the confirmation I was seeking. I am indebted to Mr Dubey for listening to his inner guidance that morning and acting upon it.

The little hare is racing ahead again… I rang Mr Dubey in India in April 2021, advising him my book had been accepted by a publisher and may I mention his name in the book. He said he felt honoured and very happy for me to do that.

I admit I was terrified when I decided to follow the inner guidance by expanding my support towards others through writing. Although, somewhere in the recesses of my mind, I doubted it would ever come to fruition.

Why? Because I lacked confidence in myself and I had never finished high school. That was my logical excuse until later years, the real reason behind my fear of writing was slowly revealed to me.

I followed The Voice's recommendation and closed the door on accepting new students. I suggested names of other teaching Masters whilst still leaving my door open to support existing students and those who asked for vibrational healing or guidance.

I started thinking about how to approach writing, as one of my greatest desires in life has been to free my self-expression and write freely from the depths of my heart without fear sitting in the way.

As you may have read in the introduction, Graham gave me an essay to write on something I enjoyed doing – playing golf. After writing the golfing essay, I felt confident I could write this book. I spent many weeks attempting to write before fear took over. Unfortunately, my mind would go blank and I couldn't seem to find the right words, then slowly after many years of being free of panic attacks and anxiety, they rose up once again overwhelming me.

Yet, deep in my heart, I believed that behind my fear of expressing myself lay a wonderful gift of uncovering my authentic voice. To achieve the desired outcome, I knew I had to persevere and overcome this emotional hurdle as I couldn't write freely until I had cleared whatever was in the way. I guess that's what kept me plodding on. Or was it my tenacity? Graham still calls it my stubbornness!

I continued writing spasmodically, willingly accepting any distractions that came my way. I occasionally thought back to 1986 when I was working as a manager of information systems for a large and diverse organisation. The managing director had arrived back from attending a motivational seminar. He walked into my office and plonked one sheet of paper on my desk in front of me.

'Yvonne, have you read anything by Abraham Maslow?'

I had never heard of him but of course, I didn't tell him that.

'Not as yet,' I politely replied, 'but I think I am about to.'

We both smiled. As he walked out of my office, he glanced back at me and added, 'It's an interesting theory.'

I looked at the article titled 'Maslow's Hierarchy of Needs'. The five needs were layered within the shape of a pyramid. The article stated that people are motivated to achieve certain needs: physiological, safety, love/belonging, esteem and self-actualisation. My eyes went straight to the top of the pyramid. Upon reading those words, I spontaneously jumped up out of my chair, stabbing my pen with a determined forcefulness onto where the words were written: 'Self-Actualisation'.

I said enthusiastically to myself, 'I am going to achieve that. I am going to reach the top of the pyramid.'

I don't know why I reacted the way I did as it equally surprised and excited me. Back then, I had no idea what my reaction meant or if I would actually attain it.

After photocopying the article, I popped my head into my boss's office, saying, 'Thanks for the article. I've decided I am going to reach the top of that pyramid.'

He laughed and replied, 'Knowing you and your determination not to give up on a challenging task, I wouldn't be surprised.' It was the only article my boss ever gave me.

I had set a long-term goal to reach the top. These days I call Maslow's Self-Actualisation as uncovering our authentic self.

Little did I know when The Voice suggested I write my first book in 1999, the journey required by me to achieve my desires would take over twenty years to complete. Although it was a shrouded journey, doors slowly opened until the memory threads and visions connected to my past came together revealing their buried secrets. Fears from eons ago rose to the surface of my awareness requiring acknowledgment and healing before my authentic voice found the freedom to express itself freely.

CHAPTER 35

A TIMELY COINCIDENCE

My biggest challenge living in a foreign country had been learning the language; my brain and tongue seemed to get tangled up, especially when I had been out of Jakarta for a few weeks. At the best of times, I struggled, often getting my words jumbled. My husband would shake his head in confusion when he heard me speaking Bahasa Indonesian.

Graham, along with my expatriate girlfriends, some of whom were married to Indonesians and living permanently in Indonesia (they called their group 'The Loonies'), named my version of the Indonesian language 'Bahasa Yvonne'.

I once mixed up two similar words and instead of requesting my cook to feed Sharza, I accidentally told her to cook the dog. Our cook looked at me with a puzzled expression on her face before realising what I had intended to say and she proceeded to demonstrate what I had asked her to do. Then we both collapsed in laughter. When our cook carried in beef rendang for dinner that evening, she jokingly said, 'Mr Graa-ham, Beef Sharza tonight.' Then proceeded to tell him what I had said.

Some years earlier we were flying back from Perth to Jakarta when Graham needed a toothpick and couldn't think of the Indonesian word for it. He knew the word 'pohon' meant tree and 'gigi' meant tooth, so he asked the air hostess for a 'pohon gigi' – a 'tree tooth'! She laughed and went away and we both sat there wondering what he might receive. She returned, smiling, carrying a tray with a few toothpicks sitting on a plate.

Life was never dull in Indonesia. Our friends and staff became our extended family and we all needed each other's support. At times, the pain and suffering we saw or heard about touched us deeply. Our hearts ached at times for the Indonesian people.

In May 1999, Indonesia and Portugal signed an agreement to allow the people of East Timor to finally have their say on their future in a referendum. The referendum was held on the 30th of August and the East Timorese people voted for independence from Indonesia. I read in the local newspaper the result of the people's vote totalled 78.5 per cent of the population.

On 4 September 1999, we arrived back in Jakarta after a four-week world trip, catching up with friends scattered around the world. We were excited to be home again and see our staff and dog Sharza. He sat on my lap, put his head against my chest and whimpered. We had organised friends to pop in and give him lots of love as it was the first time we had left him alone for any length of time since his big sister Kouchi had died. Our long-term staff had been marvellous and we showered them with gifts from Canada, being our last stop before flying home.

Within a week of the referendum, thousands of East Timorese were forced to leave their homes as bloodshed followed carnage. We read that over 1500 Timorese lost their lives on or around the 7th of September 1999 at the hands of the Indonesian Military. Despite Indonesia declaring martial law in the territory, the Military continued to create havoc. We were saddened and shocked to see on the news the extent of the destruction still taking place following the referendum to separate East Timor from Indonesia. It was a tragic and confusing time for the East Timorese people.

A decision was made by the United Nations: Australia would lead an International Force for East Timor (INTERFET). When we heard that Australia was the lead nation, helping to restore peace, many Australian expatriates living in Jakarta were very concerned about the potential repercussions we might encounter. Security was added to areas where expatriates were known to visit.

The first Australian troops arrived in East Timor on 20 September 1999, led by General Cosgrove. The same day the Australian troops arrived in East Timor, Graham, with me tagging along at the invitation of the managing director, arrived in Tokyo Japan to assist the company with the tender for a major project, knowing if they won the tender we would transfer there.

My time in Tokyo was limited due to prior commitments, and I returned to Jakarta alone on Monday 4 October. My gifts of insight had rapidly unfolded since 1991. After closing the door on new students in 1999, I focused my attention spasmodically on writing, working with existing students and anyone who required support for an issue. Just prior to my return, tensions had heightened in Jakarta and we were being warned by our embassy to avoid certain areas.

The presence of Australian troops in East Timor caused much disharmony and unrest in and around Jakarta. Students were demonstrating and Australians were targeted. Police stopped cars and passengers were asked to show their residency permits and when it was evident Australians were in the car, some received on-the-spot fines. During our travels around Jakarta, we were fortunate not to be stopped by the police. Our hearts went out to the Indonesian people; it was a very confusing and sad time for all nationals. Most did not understand and some were caught up with minority groups who supported the Indonesian Military.

After the 1998 riots, we had moved to a new house, residing in a beautiful suburb called Pondok Indah. We were blessed to be living in an extremely large palatial house, owned by a former Governor of East Java and situated on a main road. (Thanks to an oil company that had evacuated all families during the 1998 Jakarta riots and had over

50 houses, they desperately wanted to sub-lease at a greatly reduced price.)

On Wednesday 6 October, I received a phone call from a lady by the name of Janice. My name had been given to her by a colleague who thought I may be able to assist her with an issue she was experiencing at the time. I confess I was disgruntled after the hectic past couple of months. I planned to spend a nice quiet weekend with Sharza doing nothing and had no desire to see anyone. My head had willed me to say *NO* very strongly; however, my heart had other ideas. I could feel the inner pressure building in my heart urging me to say *YES*. I hesitated over the phone. My heart won and I answered 'yes'.

Janice and I arranged to meet the following Saturday 9th of October at my home. When she arrived, she told me she had been transferred to Jakarta six months earlier and was with the Canadian Embassy. We chatted for an hour, which can often shift a mental block thus giving the client insight as to a possible cause of their disturbing issue. A light goes on in their mind and there is a shift of perception and they see the situation in a totally different light. With further hands-on treatment, an energy shift can occur and healing can sometimes happen spontaneously. Most times after a session a person feels very light in the body and experiences a sense of inner peace.

My staff knew not to disturb me when I was working with a client. We had just finished the session when we heard a pounding on the door and before I could open it, my two female staff burst into the treatment room upstairs, speaking so quickly in Indonesian that I couldn't understand a single word they were saying. My head swivelled between Janice and the staff as I tried to comprehend what was going on. My cook saw my rotating head and, grabbing my arm, pulled me over to the window, which overlooked the main road.

As I peeked out cautiously from behind the curtain, I saw a large group of young people with sticks and two of the men were waving machetes. They were standing on the brick ledge and hanging over the wrought iron fencing yelling at our three male staff, including the Canadian Embassy driver. I saw the embassy driver and my driver step forward, speaking to them whilst pointing to the embassy car, which was parked inside our locked gates.

In Jakarta it only needs one person to incite a crowd, thus scratching the surface of festering anger and resentment. Trouble can quickly erupt and get out of hand.

Janice, who spoke excellent Indonesian, translated for me and said the group were asking if we were Australians living in the house. If the answer was yes, they were going to attack the house. 'Coincidentally' all our staff were wearing their new tee shirts and caps, which had Canada clearly printed on their clothing. They kept telling the group we were not Australians.

Our driver Sofari, along with the embassy driver (both spoke perfect English), entered the treatment room. The embassy driver spoke with Janice, saying 'I spoke to the crowd asking them to please stop and look at the car; it has Canadian Embassy plates. There are no Australians living in this house. Madam, the mob are university students and were dispersing for now but will return.'

Sofari added, 'Madam, the neighbours had told them you are Australians.'

I believe the presence of the Canadian Embassy car created doubt in their minds.

Janice said, 'Yvonne, I am returning to the Embassy now and I will send my driver back with a large flag to hang up in your garage along with some smaller ones.' Her face showed her concern.

I assured her, 'I'm sure we will be all right.'

Her driver returned with a number of small flags and one huge Canadian flag, which the staff quickly hung on the partially open garage door and smaller flags were placed on a couple of the front windows of our house. Our driver quickly claimed four of the small flags, attaching two to the side mirrors and placing one at the front of our car and one in the back window. All our staff voluntarily chose not to have their designated Sunday off.

The next morning Sharza and I were both enjoying breakfast in bed when I heard loud voices coming from outside. I quickly got up, shutting Sharza safely away in our ensuite bathroom and I sneaked a peek out of the library window. The group was back. Only this time there were more of them and again some were waving machetes. It is always better in situations like this for an expatriate not to make an appearance.

Our maids came into the bedroom, scared, and I put my arms around them, telling them it would be all right. I believed strongly in my heart (even though it was pounding) that we were being protected. I again circled our house a few times with white light. I guess I felt better by encircling multiple ribbons of light around the house. I was concerned too.

All windows in our house had bars on the outside of them and the garage door was open just enough for the group to see the very large Canadian flag hanging at the entrance. Again, the staff wore their Canadian clothing. After what seemed like ages, our male staff convinced the group that we were definitely not Australians. They retreated down the street, giving anything in sight a frustrating bang. They never returned to our home again.

Janice rang me the following morning to check on us. I told her all was okay – the embassy car and flags had done the trick.

'Yvonne, I feel wonderful – thank you. It was perfect timing, my coming to see you on Saturday, wasn't it?'

'Yes. We both received the support we needed at that time.'

Janice coming that day was not a coincidence. The embassy Janice worked for was 'coincidentally' the last country we visited on our holiday where we had purchased the clothing for our staff.

Graham arrived home from Tokyo on the 18th of October. There was still unrest on the streets so Graham decided to leave the Canadian flags on the car for another week.

On our way out to dinner the following night, I had draped a chiffon scarf around my head, which was suggested by Indonesian friends as there were still disturbances happening on some streets around Jakarta. We were both sitting in the back seat and I gazed out the window, noticing the flags flapping in the breeze.

I reached over and took Graham's hand. 'I feel so disloyal in my heart towards our own country by having Canadian flags on our car and at home.'

Graham looked over at me. 'I can understand how you feel; however, with my being away I was so glad Janice turned up when she did.'

'And furthermore,' I added thoughtfully, 'the embassy car parked in our driveway gave more credence, which created doubt in their minds.'

Mulling over the conversation, Graham mindfully added, 'Don't forget the tee shirts. That was a lucky coincidence, wasn't it?'

'Graham, I don't believe in coincidences.' After some thought, I said quietly, 'I wonder what may have happened if I hadn't bothered to listen to my heart that day Janice rang!'

Graham squeezed my hand as we both sat quietly, pondering over my comment.

When I was still learning to pay attention to Spirit's inner guidance on this journey, I was often challenged as to which voice to listen to. Do I listen to the gentle voice speaking to me in my heart or to the loud voice in my head telling me what I 'should' or 'must' do? I learnt to recognise the voice I heard in my head often had a very self-centred intention and a narrow view regarding a decision I was about to make. Whereas Spirit's softly spoken words in my heart only suggested a direction to take; it was never loud or demanding. The voice in my heart always comes from a much broader viewing platform and the intended outcome is always for the highest good for everyone.

I remember reading a native American folktale...

One evening, an old Cherokee told his grandson about a battle that goes on inside people.

He said, 'My son, the battle is between two wolves inside us all. One is Evil – it is anger, envy, jealousy, sorrow, regret, greed, arrogance, self-pity, guilt, resentment, inferiority, lies, false pride, superiority and ego. The other is Good – it is joy, peace, love, hope, serenity, humility, kindness, benevolence, empathy, generosity, truth, compassion and faith.'

The grandson thought about it for a minute and then asked his grandfather, 'Which wolf wins?'

The old Cherokee simply replied, 'The one you feed.'

Energy follows thought.

*The quality of our life is determined by
the quality of our awareness.
Our input equals our output in life.*

Yvonne Fogarty

CHAPTER 36

KUNDALINI AWAKENING

In 2001, Graham and I believed our time in Jakarta was coming to an end. A sister company in Thailand had tendered on a new major airport project just outside Bangkok, which required Graham's involvement. There was a possibility we could be transferred there if the company was awarded the work.

Unsure how much longer we would remain in Jakarta, I decided to take two of the Reiki Masters that I had trained away for five days from the 7th to the 11th of July to support them in their desire to advance their spiritual growth. One Master was an Australian, Marilyn Ardipradja, and the other was of Indian heritage, Sangeeta Jaggia.

The week prior to us going away, I experienced a series of three small visions over a few days, portraying a different image each time, all centred around the base of my spine. I drew the images in my notebook. I sensed something was happening within me; I had no idea what the images could be related to.

On the afternoon of the 9th of July, whilst away in retreat, Marilyn and Sangeeta offered to give me an energy treatment. During the treatment, I experienced a series of visions...

The first was once again of a man being stoned to death. Following that vision, I felt strong sensations of energy around my coccyx bone. The vision changed and I was looking at the top part of a small container with a gold lid, inscribed with three snakes (which was one of the three visions I had seen the previous week), then the gold lid burst open and I saw and felt a powerful force of yellow-orange fiery-coloured energy, starting at the base of my spine, spreading rapidly down to my feet and up my spine to my head and down my arms moving into each of my fingers and filling every crevice in my body.

The Masters treating me felt the force as my energy body expanded rapidly and they backed away from the table. I had no idea what was happening at the time. I automatically rolled over onto my stomach; the energy stretched my legs, arching my spine backwards and my arms were raised above my head. I remember having to lie down afterwards as I felt quite nauseous and dizzy, along with a painful headache. As I lay there, I could still see in my mind's eye the fiery energy.

Over dinner, we talked about what we thought may have happened during my treatment. They both believed my Kundalini energy had opened. I had heard of Kundalini energy but I had never investigated it. I showed them my notebook of the images I had drawn and explained the visions.

I could still sense the fiery energy around me when I went to bed and it unsettled me so again, I confess I slept with the light on all night.

The next morning the headache was gone and my energy had settled down, becoming very quiet. I did not feel any different and I eventually forgot all about it.

It was confirmed a week later when Sangeeta walked into my home, waving a book in her hand and with a huge smile on her face. Her husband had purchased a book on Kundalini energy for her while on an overseas business trip to America. She quickly opened the book and pointed to one simple diagram in the book on page 14. It was one of the drawings I had drawn and shown her from one of the visions. (Refer to 'Kundalini: The Arousal of Inner Cosmic Energy' by Ajit Mookerjee.)

In the book, Kundalini energy refers to a form of primal energy located at the base of the spine. When awakened, it rises up to the crown chakra and begins a journey of raising spiritual perception. I was told later by an Indian friend that the Kundalini energy gets awakened naturally when our energy reaches a certain vibrational level.

It still surprises me that I have these experiences. One thing I did notice over time was that my clairvoyance slowly became stronger; whether that was a coincidence, I have no idea.

Spirit continued supporting my journey towards freeing my self-expression as I continued refining my soul's frequency and vibrations. The more I grew in understanding, I expanded my awareness and the easier it became to clear my low vibrational energy patterns.

CHAPTER 37

SHARZA'S GIFT TO US

Early February 2002, Graham had just finished his contract with the Jakarta company and we were in the process of organising the pack-out back to Perth, Western Australia when Graham was informed there was a possibility of being transferred to Thailand. I commenced investigating getting Sharza to either Thailand or back home permanently to Perth if they were not awarded the contract. Fortunately, the quarantine laws in Australia had changed in our favour, requiring only a couple of months of quarantine back in Australia.

Sharza had just celebrated his fifteenth birthday when we were awakened one morning by him whimpering in pain. Our neighbour, who was a vet, ran some tests and informed us his kidneys were full of toxins and failing. She connected him to a drip and he rested in our bedroom. The vet came daily. The staff, Graham and I took turns watching him 24 hours a day, making sure he didn't pull the drip out. After a few days, the drip was removed and Sharza rallied. We were delighted as we watched him happily eating and running around. Sadly, the following morning he became extremely distressed. We carried him down the road to our vet, who gave him a lethal injection while we held him. It was a very sad time for us both. Sharza was our precious second-born fur child.

We wrapped him in one of my caftans, then into plastic before placing him in our freezer. (We hoped it wouldn't take too long for him to be cremated.) Graham telephoned the Chinese crematorium and the same man who had assisted us in getting Kouchi cremated was 'most' willing to help us once again.

A few days later at the crematorium, the manager politely requested I return to the car. He asked Graham to wait in his office with Sharza nestled under his chair in a small wooden coffin our day guard had made. When told to, Graham was to 'sneak' Sharza in-between services to be cremated.

Graham walked out a while later, attempting to look inconspicuous (how can a white-skinned expatriate not attract attention at a Chinese crematorium!) with a little container tucked under his jacket and his wallet a 'lot' lighter.

Sharza had imparted a painful yet loving gift to us. He gave us the opportunity to return home to Perth while awaiting our posting to Thailand.

We combined Kouchi's and Sharza's ashes together and with our pack-out completed, we flew back to the home we had built years earlier. I declared the ashes to Australian Customs, telling them, 'We are going to scatter them in the park behind our property where they used to love frolicking.'

The guy just nodded his head in an appeasing manner as he continued to inspect the tiny little pieces of bone.

For a couple of years, their ashes travelled back and forth many times and on each occasion, Graham patiently waited while Customs inspected them. What a wonderful husband I have. I chuckled to myself as I wrote that and then thought... *Well... most of the time!*

Yes, their ashes are still with us. Now I have a new plan. I would like all our ashes combined together, which will amount to a large quantity – Kouchi; Sharza; our fur babies Karza and Zoet (acquired after returning to Australia, who died in 2020); our new baby, a little Shih-Tzu called Roxie, who arrived from Sydney in November 2021; and finally, Graham and me.

I have informed our niece Ardathia that she has the task of scattering all the ashes into the Tasman Sea without getting into trouble for littering and to make sure she is not downwind when she does it.

CHAPTER 38

MIMI'S BOOK

Some years earlier I had met a remarkably gifted artist who came to me seeking guidance. Mimi was writing a fascinating book about the mystical puppeteers of Indonesia. She joined a Reiki class and had some startling experiences, which surprised her. We talked often and Mimi conscientiously continued to research and write her book.

Mimi's husband's contract with the United Nations ended in 1995 and they returned to Washington, D.C. (We kept in contact and visited them in 1999.) Mimi felt disheartened when her efforts to get the book published were unsuccessful. Due to the many coloured photographs, it was going to be a very expensive book to produce so she put it aside for a while.

One morning in 2001, I woke up, opening my eyes as a vision formed...

I saw a book, hanging in the air in front of me. The vision became clearer and I could see a colourful dust cover. As I watched, Mimi's face popped up next to the book and then the book floated down and placed itself on our cane coffee table.

I was hesitant about sharing the vision. I sometimes still doubted myself and I didn't want to get Mimi's hopes up. I pondered over what to do. A couple of days later I woke up with Mimi and the vision again on my mind. I took that as a sign and I rang Mimi, telling her about the vision. During our conversation, another vision popped up and I saw *an open doorway filled with light* appear in front of my eyes.

'Oh, Mimi,' I said. 'I believe a door of opportunity is open to you now.'
Mimi began working on the book again.

In February 2002 when preparing to leave Indonesia, we decided not to take our large cane suite, which included the cane coffee table (seen in the vision), back to Perth because we thought there wouldn't be enough room in the container. We sold the suite on the condition we could continue using it until we left at the beginning of March.

After organising the rooms ready for the packers who were coming the next day, I sat down to take a break, placing a cup of coffee onto the cane table. Looking down at the table, I thought *Oh, I must have been mistaken about that part of the vision.*

When the movers arrived later that day, the team leader advised us that 'there is enough room for the cane lounge suite.'

We were delighted. I rang the people we had sold the suite to and explained the situation and fortunately, they were very obliging.

The men were still in the process of packing when Mimi rang from Washington, asking if I would be free to meet her in a few days' time in Hong Kong where the book was going to print. The timing was not right. I was unable to share the joy with her of seeing the book being printed. I thanked Spirit for supporting Mimi to fulfil her desire to publish her book.

We returned to Perth in March 2002. Mimi Herbert's book 'Voices of the Puppet Masters: The Wayang Golek Theater of Indonesia' was published and a friend, Liz Murt, came to visit from Jakarta, bringing with her a copy of the book. When she handed it to me, I told her about the vision and then placed it on the cane coffee table. The vision had fully materialised.

Mimi's book sits proudly in my office. If I look over my shoulder, I can see it. It has been an inspiration, reminding me of what can be achieved through faith and perseverance.

CHAPTER 39

BANGKOK, THAILAND

With all that had been happening over the past twelve months, I had again shelved my attempt at writing. Looking back now, I know my decision came from the deep-seated fears I avoided facing.

Avoiding facing my issues only caused me more pain until I found the courage to open the door and face them, thus setting the painful memories free. I realised that pain isn't our enemy; it's there to tell us something is out of balance.

Graham was already in Bangkok when our shipment arrived back in Perth. He flew back to help me unpack everything because the insurance company wouldn't payout if we simply forwarded on the boxed items without removing everything, checking for breakages. Graham then flew back to Bangkok and by July I had almost completed the process of organising items for Thailand, ready for the company to come the following week to start another pack-out, when The Voice came through with its now familiar vibration…

'Yvonne, step forward, release your fears. The very breath you breathe is life itself sustaining you. Free your soul, allow Spirit to flow unrestricted and you will uncover your voice.'

I already have a voice and it's very loud at times! I stopped what I was doing and sat down, pondering over The Voice's words. I knew I had honoured The Voice in 1999 by not taking on new students but sadly I found it extremely stressful and difficult to engage easily with the writing. Whenever I sat at my desk to write, I activated a subconscious pattern and my inbuilt mechanical response would automatically remind me I wasn't good enough, it was too dangerous or it was not safe. Writing aroused intense feelings of anxiety and occasionally brought on a panic attack. I hadn't experienced any more anxiety attacks after the re-birthing session and I believed they had completely gone until they started happening again when I started writing this book.

Why were these feelings coming up strongly again? I had no idea. I was excited about writing I believed it was the direction I was to take, yet the reaction I experienced when attempting to write was not logical – it was irrational!

I made a promise to The Voice that once we were settled in Bangkok, I would write again and face whatever was sitting in the way of fulfilling this intense driving force residing in my heart to write. Even though I spoke the words out loud, I knew in my heart they were without substance.

I have never hidden the fact from students that I was continuing to clear issues, just as they were. I know from personal experience that once an issue is cleared, the outcome is wonderful to experience.

As I glance back at my years of inner struggle, I can see that my fear of writing had been a wonderful catalyst to keep me plodding on, not only to understand how I came to hear The Voice but also to free my self-expression and heal my soul. I knew in my heart whatever was still lingering was something I had to uncover and clear myself in order to reap the rewards and depth of satisfaction that comes from letting something go.

Not long after arriving in Bangkok, we moved into a spacious apartment, which suited both of us. It was situated 35 km outside of Bangkok, close to the new international airport project Graham was assigned to. We were living on the grounds of the picturesque Thana City golf course, away from the smog of the city. The eighteen-hole golf course had a number of lakes with a view as far as the weather allowed and we spent the odd weekend playing golf.

Graham and the caddies tried many times to help me overcome the dilemma I had hitting the ball. One day Graham suggested I bite hold of the collar of my golf shirt to stop me from looking up as I hit the ball so I wouldn't miss hitting that damn tiny thing. Unfortunately, I am still a 'yoyo' playing golf.

Bangkok was a much easier location to live in – drivers were much more orderly on the road, the majority of the Thai people spoke English, they had a wonderful train service around the city and surrounding suburbs and the Thai food was delicious.

One of my Masters, Sangeeta Jaggia, who had been with me when my Kundalini energy awakened in 2001, flew in from Jakarta in September 2003 to spend ten days with us. On our last day together, she was giving me a treatment when a vision suddenly appeared in front of my eyes and I saw myself back in the Room of Knowledge again after almost ten years since the previous vision.

I vividly recalled the vision the morning of my Reiki Masters initiation where I had walked down steps into this room and all the walls were covered in simple plain symbols. (Refer to chapter 20 – Stepping Forward.) Previously, I sensed a presence guiding me around the room; however, this time, I saw a man standing next to the symbol I had been shown in 1993…

The man said, *'It's important this information is preserved. This symbol represents the manifestation of life.'*

I documented the vision and information in my notebook, knowing the inner guidance would reveal more to me when the timing was right.

It was exciting meeting up again with friends we had met while living in Jakarta. One of my Jakarta friends, Barbara McHerron, had started up a 'Foot and Mouth Club' and invited me along. We would meet every Friday morning in Bangkok to have a foot reflexology treatment or a Thai massage and then off we would go for a long lunch and that's where I met Mary.

Hanging onto our past painful experiences
can become a stumbling block,
holding us back from moving forward.
Or we can heal our pain and use the experience as
a stepping-stone to a more rewarding and fulfilling life.
Every moment of our day we make choices
and the choices we make affect our tomorrow.

Yvonne Fogarty

CHAPTER 40

JOURNEY FROM MISERY TO CONTENTMENT

During one of our Friday Foot and Mouth Club luncheons, I met Mary, who later contacted me asking if she could come and talk to me.

The following week, Mary, who worked as a private tutor teaching English, arrived nervous and apprehensive at the door of our apartment. Although Mary was a very petite and pretty girl – her hair was pulled back tightly in a bun at the base of her neck – her shoulders sagged. Her clothing was inconspicuous to the eye and her whole demeanour had me wondering what she might be attempting to hide.

I opened up my arms and said, 'Mary, this is a hug house.' I put my arms around her, giving her a warm hug and I felt her body tense up slightly. I chatted, ignoring her reaction and lead her out to our balcony, talking about the view from our apartment to ease her tension.

Mary slowly opened up, explaining she had been in a relationship for two years and since becoming engaged to John, she suddenly found herself continually attempting to sabotage their relationship. She added that whenever John approached the question about setting a wedding date, she found herself avoiding the subject.

She quietly looked up at me with tears in her eyes. 'I am hesitant to get married and it has nothing to do with my not loving John – it's me. I have become very moody, argumentative and withdrawn, and I have put on quite a bit of weight since our engagement a few months ago.'

I listened quietly as she continued to share her feelings, telling me she had been on anti-depressant medications for some time to help her cope with the rollercoaster of feelings that tormented her. During our conversation, alarm bells were already ringing in my head. I wondered what deep-rooted trauma Mary held within. Her physical body was not handling the emotional load any longer. My heart went out to her. I prayed that Mary would have the strength to open up so Spirit's vibrations could touch her heart, guiding her to let go of her pain and heal whatever was causing her so much distress.

Mary went on to tell me, with tears in her eyes, that John had become frustrated with her avoiding him and brought things to a head last week, asking her if she was having second thoughts about marrying him.

'I do love John.' She cried. 'But I'm afraid. John told me no matter what has happened in my past, he loves me and is not going to let me go as he is certain I am experiencing an emotional issue that has nothing to do with him.' After much anguish, she had told him about her traumatic past.

Mary let out a deep breath and sighed. 'I am here because I have had enough of my past tormenting me. I truly desire to let it go and move on but I don't know how to do that.'

'I have been there myself,' I told her, 'and when the pain of hanging on to our issues becomes unbearable to hang on to any longer, we will release that pain. Thank you for sharing your feelings. I believe you are ready to work on healing your past.'

I explained to Mary that I had formal training as a Reiki Master, I was also an intuitive spiritual healer/counsellor and I trusted the insights and guidance I received to support a client.

Mary lay down on my treatment table. At first, I was unable to make direct contact with her body at all. As soon as my hands got anywhere near her body, she would stiffen up and start coughing. Nothing could penetrate; not even a burglar could get past her security system. I focused on working above her physical body in her energy body.

When a person is ready, their energy body will often provide me with an insight, which can support the person to open a door to heal the root cause. I myself 'do not' heal anyone; they heal themselves. I am an instrument, a messenger between Spirit and the client. Our soul's expressive nature operates through dynamic pictures. Memories are living entities and can only survive if we are subconsciously feeding them energy to keep a memory alive, or if we hold a strong emotional connection to them. E.g. sadness, guilt, resentment, regret, anger, etc. Every time I treated her, I repeatedly saw an image of a man. I sensed not to mention what I was seeing and to wait.

In our sessions over the following weeks, as I talked with Mary, a bond of trust developed and she slowly let go, allowing the energy to gently penetrate the tight web of protection surrounding her.

During one of our sessions, she opened up, telling me she was a victim of incest and had been abused by her father until she was approximately twelve years old.

Mary said, 'I hated myself and I left home a couple of years later to live with a distant relative. I was full of guilt for leaving my family as my dad always told me he loved me, especially when he came to my room during the night.'

She also felt betrayed by her mother, who she believed knew what was happening in their home and was too afraid to do anything about it. Mary said, 'I think Mum was scared of what the consequence may entail.'

Mary had struggled on her own for many years and carried so much guilt, anger and confusion inside her and the emotional turmoil she felt had manifested as acne on her face, overflowing to areas on her back. Slowly, Mary opened up drawing in more energy through me to allow the healing vibrations to support, comfort and strengthen her. Mary bravely let go, brick-by-brick, her protective barrier.

During one of our sessions, Mary had her first 'aha' moment. She realised she had been blaming herself for the abuse that had taken place. She opened her eyes and looked up at me. 'I have just realised it was not my fault at all what my father did. It was my father who was at fault, not me.'

That realisation opened a huge door for her and a shift of perspective took place, enabling her to let go of the guilt she carried, thinking what had happened was her fault. Mary was now on the road to reclaiming her power back.

When Mary arrived at my door a few weeks later, she was wearing a pretty sun dress and her wavy blonde hair was falling freely past her shoulders. It was the first time I had seen her wearing something other than plain clothing and her hair pulled back tightly. She spun around excitedly in front of me, exposing her back. We both shed a tear – the pimples on her back had completely disappeared and her weight had reduced. I thanked Spirit for the validation of our sessions together. Mary's self-loathing and feelings of powerlessness were dissolving and her self-worth was starting to shine through. It was on that day that Mary had a major breakthrough.

During the treatment, her body started shaking as waves of energy surged through her, causing her body to shudder involuntarily. After some time, her body relaxed. I helped her stand up and she cried and cried. I sat her on a chair, resting my hands on her shoulders until the crying subsided.

She then looked at me and took a deep breath before saying, with a smile on her face, 'WOW! I feel wonderful, washed out and empty all at the same time. My being able to verbally express my feelings over the past few weeks has helped me to see clearly that what happened to me when I was young was not my fault.' She added excitedly, 'That sudden realisation has helped me to let go of all the built-up emotional pain. A whole weight has lifted off my shoulders. I feel so light inside. Thank you.'

'You are a very courageous lady. It was you yourself who allowed the energy to slowly loosen the layers of pain that had accumulated and festered for the past twenty-five years, to slowly rise to the surface for releasing. I am just the middle person, so to speak.'

We hugged again and walked from my treatment room out onto the balcony where the maid brought us afternoon tea.

'Mary, I am so happy for you; many go through life unable to face their past. You, on the other hand, totally embraced it and "let go" of all the pain, guilt and anger you had accumulated.'

We increased our sessions together over the next month. Mary forgave her parents and during those sessions, her facial pimples disappeared and our time together was coming to an end. I knew in my heart that the timing was perfect to ask Mary a question Spirit had suggested.

I asked her gently, 'Mary, can you see a "gift"? A positive move forward from your past traumatic experience that could possibly be of benefit to others in some way?'

She pondered over the question for quite a while, nibbling the inside of her mouth before looking up at me through teary eyes and saying thoughtfully, 'Yes, Yvonne. Yes. I believe I can.'

This wonderful brave woman turned her life around. She married John and after his contract finished, they both returned to their home country. Mary went back to study and later specialised in working with abused children. She was able to assist others who had been traumatised by their past, giving them the support they required to move on with their lives as she had done.

Mary may or may not share with clients that she too had been abused. Her energy naturally sends forth a deep sense of compassion and understanding that uplifts others and a bond of trust can easily develop between them. A truth vibration can penetrate and touch another soul's essence and they know deep in their heart that what they are sensing is the truth.

Sadly, as a victim of incest, Mary had carried a load of conflicting emotions into adulthood, e.g. guilt, betrayal, feeling powerless, self-blame and confusion, to name a few. Any traumatic incident a person experiences, whether it happened in a past life cycle or in their present life cycle, can live on in every part of their being until cleared.

Mary turned her life around by having the willingness to face her trauma, emerging a happy confident woman who is no longer hiding from life; instead, she is embracing all that life has to offer.

CHAPTER 41

THE MESSENGER

I avoided writing for as long as I could before guilt gnawed at my conscience. I had promised The Voice I would write as soon as we had settled in, but regrettably I didn't go back to it until early 2003, then stopped again because I couldn't understand the information flowing in. It spoke of frequencies and vibrations. The information I received was too much for me to comprehend. I wondered if what I had written was rubbish. So I stopped writing once again. I know now it was fear and self-doubt stopping me.

On the 1ˢᵗ of April 2003, on a return flight from Dubai where we had taken a brief holiday, I 'saw' what I can only describe as a gold being wearing a simple loose-fitting gold robe appear in front of me. The being looked like an angel except this angel was gold, minus wings. The sight of this being truly surprised me. I sat, looking at it as it stood a few feet in front of me in the aisle of the plane's cabin, smiling at me. It was the first time I had ever seen a gold being so I smiled back. Then, in a blink of an eye, it popped into me through my crown chakra. I sat, stunned, staring at the now empty aisle, attempting to comprehend what had just taken place and then I closed my eyes. *Oh s—what just happened? Is it a good energy?* I asked myself. *Yes, it must be. It's gold!* I had been so distracted by what had happened, before I knew it the cabin crew were preparing the plane for landing at Bangkok airport. That was the quickest six-hour flight ever!

The gold being stayed connected to me until June. I would wake up some nights with a different image forming in front of my eyes, or I'd briefly hear a snippet of information being spoken to me. Without any in-depth knowledge, I documented the variety of information – from symbols and dates to Galileo, Isaac Newton and Abraham Lincoln, to a physicist named Paul Dirac, whom I had never heard of before, to a vision of a pinecone! I naïvely assumed I was being shown a tree's pinecone.

I discovered later the pinecone is known as a symbol for the pineal gland, which resides in the centre of our head. Some call the pineal gland the 'eye of God' and Descartes called the pineal gland the 'seat of the soul'. Buddhists believe the pineal gland is a symbol of spiritual awakening. Taoists believe it's the mind's eye. In Hinduism, it is seen as the seat of intuition or the third eye. Many believe it is the eye of God and it is the receiving centre of psychic awareness, e.g. visions.

In the Vatican there is a sculpture of a very large pinecone and other sculptures of pinecones can also be found in other countries' artefacts. In fact, before leaving Perth in 2010 to live in Tasmania, I was given a large Buddha statue by a friend, Jenny, and sitting on top of his head is the configuration of a pinecone.

I researched the information I received and some clarity came to me, while other information still remains a mystery at this time. This information lies in an A4 file untouched since 2003.

Timidly, I commenced writing again, although I felt quite uneasy when some of the information I received was about sub-atomic particles and frequencies. This again caused anxiety to rise up so I stopped writing before the anxiety turned into a panic attack.

I always pray for clear guidance and confirmation of what I hear or see when working with clients and students. So why didn't I ask for clear guidance when writing back in 2003? I simply didn't think to, or maybe I was too afraid to ask! Did I fear what I would hear if I did? Instead, I shut the door when the fear overwhelmed me.

I purchased a couple of books on physics and began researching until I stopped in frustration in December. I would re-read the same page a number of times, attempting to comprehend what was written. It was all beyond me and I finally gave up.

Although I had done much work on raising my self-esteem and clearing many distorted beliefs, I still felt I was missing a 'key' element to opening the door to uncovering the fullness of my expression. The key continued to elude me.

CHAPTER 42

MESSAGE FOR LORAINE

We were still based in Bangkok and I remember this incident so clearly because it was the first time I saw someone I didn't know or have a family connection to who had passed over, giving me a message for a loved one.

Upon waking, I had my friend Loraine on my mind who had some months earlier returned home to Queensland from Bangkok. I sensed to email her to ask if everything was okay. I received a quick reply telling me her mother had died earlier that day.

The next morning, Loraine was again on my mind, knowing she would have been feeling the pain of losing a loved one. Later in the day, a woman appeared in front of me a number of times whom I did not know. I sensed strongly the woman was Loraine's mother. Below is a copy of the email I sent her.

Dear Loraine,

I sense this is your mum in front of me right now. She has been very persistent that I contact you. I must say she is a character. She's keen to tell you she feels so free and able to move in ways she couldn't before. She loves being so flexible again. Does this make sense? She is dancing around and is so wiry and alive with movement. I don't know what it means, yet that's what I keep seeing in front of me. It's her aliveness she wants you to see and how happy she is having it again. She says she has the best of both worlds now. She wants you to know how free she feels because you will know how much that means to her. Does this make any sense to you? I hope so. Your mother wouldn't leave me in peace; she kept up a jiggling dance in front of me until I wrote you this email. I hope you find this a comfort and support, dear friend.

In Loraine's words...

The day after Mum's death, I received the above-mentioned email from my friend Yvonne in Bangkok. She had never met my mother and only knew her from my conversations in which I may have mentioned her. Nor did she know the circumstances surrounding my mother's death.

Yvonne's description of my mother, being so wiry and always on the go was spot on. Her determination to keep at something, like getting Yvonne to send me the email, was something I could see her doing. She was always a live wire but life slowed her down after her hip problems and her recent heart attack. Yvonne's description of her moving with agility and free of pain was an invaluable help to my family and me as we worked our way together through the grieving process.

Loraine C. Queensland.

CHAPTER 43

RETURNING HOME

We left Bangkok, returning to Perth, Western Australia, in 2004. I continued my inner journey with a very cute and mischievous distraction. It came in the form of a six-week-old 850-gram tiny white bundle of fluff: a Bichon Frise Shih-Tzu puppy. We named her Karza (K from Kouchi and arza from Sharza's name, our past two fur kids). We sprinkled her with a few drops of champagne, which we were drinking at the time, christening her Karza Fogarty. Karza ignored her little dog bed at first; instead, she claimed one of Graham's sneakers, snuggling into it for a snooze as she sucked on one of the laces before falling asleep.

I enjoyed catching up with friends and a group of us ex-Jakarta ladies formed a 'Stitch and Bitch' group. No! We didn't bitch… instead, we all definitely 'whined and wined' whilst reminiscing about the days when we had staff to do everything! We used to meet monthly, which was a blessing as we all struggled to adjust to living back in our home country.

We were told upon our arrival in Jakarta, 'You will go through culture shock; it won't be easy adjusting to a third-world country's way of life. It is very different from what you came from as living here can be challenging and things are not so easily attainable.' That was true; however, we all experienced reverse culture shock returning home to Australia. After living with staff for over thirteen years it was difficult to adjust.

Graham and I had changed, in a good way, from insular thinking people whose only focus was our own little world around us. After living overseas, we returned with a much broader outlook on life and a much deeper empathy towards others. We had taken for granted so many things before moving to Asia. We now delighted in being able to walk the foreshore of South Perth, looking out over pristine waters, clean buildings and parks. I even got excited going into our local supermarket; the shelves were packed with so many different choices. In fact, when we lived in Jakarta, whenever we returned to Perth, visiting family and friends, I always went to a supermarket to drool over the many different foods available and returned to Jakarta with extremely overweight suitcases.

Shopping in Jakarta would often take me all day as I attempted to get all the items on my shopping list with my driver slowly manoeuvring his way through the heavy traffic going to different shops spread out around Jakarta to get the food we enjoyed eating.

Now my food shop only takes me an hour at most with everything usually readily available and when I open my pantry cupboard, I even have a choice of so many different assortments of Gravox. I still smile whenever I see Gravox because it brings back fond memories. Memories can be wonderful; they can be reminders of so many things to be grateful for, even Gravox! Refer to chapter 13 – Jakarta, Indonesia.

Living back in Perth, we appreciated the simple things from healthy vegetables and fresh meats to paved sidewalks. Free libraries for all, feeling safe walking around the streets during the day, generally without the fear of being robbed. Beautiful pristine beaches, orderly traffic flow and 99 per cent of the time, the cars stayed within the white lines on the road. I definitely did not miss seeing the rats that sometimes found their way into a couple of the homes we rented in Jakarta.

Out of habit, I still go to the toilet before leaving home, even if it is just a quick trip down the road, in case I get caught up in a major traffic jam.

I recalled an incident in Jakarta, reminding us of how blessed we are to live in Australia. It happened one morning when Graham walked out the front of our Jakarta home to pick up the newspaper. A neighbour from further down the road came up to our locked gates, calling out to him. Graham could see he was extremely upset. He asked Graham if he could contribute something towards paying for his four-year-old's funeral; she had died during the night. We willingly contributed. Muslim custom is to bury their loved ones within 24 hours of death.

After returning to Australia, we were seeing life through new eyes, realising we have so much to be grateful for and we certainly appreciated the extensive freedom Australia offers us and felt so blessed to have so much support on hand.

Giving some thought to how much I have grown since starting my inner journey, I began jotting down and consolidating my past experiences and learnings to date with the intention of gaining more understanding of how this power operates through us. I realised I had been 'trying' too hard to connect to receive. These days I stop myself from using the words 'try' or 'trying' because that frequency and vibration causes confusion in my heart. The energy doesn't know whether my intent is to go left or right, thus blocking my ability to keep an open mind and heart, making it much more difficult for me to receive the guidance I seek. When I am simply 'being', my heart and my connection are open and it's easier to receive guidance.

Clearing emotional issues unlocks a door for experiencing greater awareness and clarity as to who we are and what each of us are capable of achieving.

Yvonne Fogarty

CHAPTER 44

BACK IN MY OFFICE

I had set up my office and a meditation room in two of the four upstairs bedrooms in our South Perth apartment and once again I turned my attention back to writing. I was meditating twice daily, walking little Karza and enjoying the freedom associated with being home again. I had come a long way since leaving Perth in 1991. My inner gifts and connection to Spirit had strengthened. At different times, students would fly in to work with me to advance their growth.

If a friend contacted me for lunch or for support, I eagerly jumped at the chance to avoid the internal battle I still faced whenever I attempted to write. Sometimes the feelings that rose up were too much to handle. My stomach would start churning and I would become light-headed, which resulted in anxiety and was sometimes followed by a panic attack. At that time, the issue was too deep to connect with easily to uncover the cause, thus blocking my ability to simply observe it and not be drawn into the discomfort as I had successfully done in the past in order to heal an issue.

When I injured my right shoulder in 2004, I realised I was avoiding moving forward in the direction I knew I was meant to go. A person's subconscious mind is very powerful and I probably created/manifested the shoulder injury to avoid writing. It was my way of escaping from facing my fears, blocking inner guidance and my injury gave me a valid excuse for delaying the inevitable.

I laughed as I wrote this because now I couldn't imagine myself not writing. I find it an exciting, fulfilling journey but up until I finally cleared my issues, I had lost count of the many times I stopped and started this book. Each time these feelings showed themselves I continued to suppress them. Avoiding doesn't help – it can harm our health and wellbeing, as in my case and in the case of my friend Kylie...

Her marriage was fast approaching and just prior to her wedding she had a water-skiing accident, severely fracturing her leg and was hospitalised, leaving her with two choices: to either get married in the hospital or postpone the wedding. As she thought about her options, she became aware of how relieved she felt at the thought of postponing the wedding.

We talked about her feelings and she realised she loved her fiancé but not enough to marry him and had been avoiding the issue because she didn't wish to hurt him.

Kylie asked me if it was possible she had brought this accident on herself. I told her about how I subconsciously avoided writing by getting a shoulder injury.

'I do not believe in coincidences. Only you know the answer to that question. Listen to your heart. After what you just told me, you may be right.'

A few weeks later, Kylie rang me saying she felt relieved and at peace after talking to her fiancé about her feelings. They both decided to take a step back and they eventually parted ways.

My friend Ann had a different experience in avoiding facing her bottled-up pain, as you will read about in the following chapter...

CHAPTER 45

THE HEALING

Another nice thing about being home was catching up with friends from the past. Ann Thompson and I have been friends for 30-plus years since being employed by the same company early in our working lives. Not long after returning to Perth, Ann called in on her way home from work one evening.

I was sitting opposite her, enjoying a coffee and a chat in our lounge room, when my energy went very still and I focused in on her energy. I sensed something was wrong but I was unaware of what it could be and because I love her, instead of suggesting she go to a doctor, I spoke bluntly to her.

'Ann, go and see a doctor, please; I have a feeling something isn't quite right with your health.' I believe the only reason I sensed strongly that something was wrong was because there was an unspoken trust between us. Ann felt comfortable and relaxed in my presence as I did with her.

A couple of weeks later, Ann rang me with the news that she had just been diagnosed with lung cancer in the lower left lobe. I suggested she come around the following night after work and I would give her a treatment.

As I was treating her, intuitively, my right hand tuned in to her energy body, causing my hand to rise up, hovering above her lung area. My own thoughts stilled; my mind went blank as my focus became very intense; I felt a slight tingling in my hand as an image appeared in front of my eyes – it was of a London landmark: the Big Ben clock tower. The image I saw was connecting me to a memory thread.

I sensed to ask Ann how she had felt about leaving England with her husband to live permanently in Australia. Her body tensed and tears filled her eyes as she recalled the inner torment she felt at leaving her parents.

In Ann's words...

I wanted the opportunity to start a new life in Australia. I didn't want to be the daughter who ended up looking after her parents in old age. I know that sounds selfish but I was young and I grasped the opportunity and didn't allow myself to think about it. I was looking forward to a new adventure in another country with my husband.

Even though I knew Yvonne's background and the sadness she experienced through her mother, I found it hard to comprehend the mentally abusive behaviour she endured. She never gave up on her mother.

I was so fortunate to have such loving parents and they did everything possible to support me. They loved my sister and me unconditionally and only wanted the best for us. Not once did they try to discourage me from going. I know it was very painful for them to see me leave but they never let it show, no matter how upset they must have been.

When we arrived in Perth and had settled, the guilt of leaving them started to build up inside me. I ignored it by pushing it down deep into the recesses of my mind. We were struggling to adjust; money was limited and neither my mother nor I had the money to call each other. We wrote regularly but it was not the same as being able to speak to each other.

My sister told me years later that Dad had offered to pay for Mum to come out and see us but she couldn't do it. Evidently, my leaving had been extremely painful for her and she felt she couldn't go through that again. Just the thought of having to say goodbye again would have been even more painful and too difficult for her, to have to leave me for a second time.

I never got to see my parents again. My mother died five years later and my father joined her a short time later. I never got the chance to return to England to visit them. Over the years, my guilt has continued to eat away at me, especially since they both died. The struggle to suppress the pain has been difficult to ignore.

Ann Thompson

My heart went out to Ann; I said a silent prayer of thanks to Spirit for supporting us both with this insight. I felt confident Spirit had shown us the mental-emotional blockage that had contributed to her disease. A mental emotional blockage can hinder the life force energy flowing freely throughout a person's body.

Ann used to be a smoker and it's possible the reason the cancer showed up in her lung area was because smoking probably created a weakness in that area of her body. It is also an area where unresolved heart issues can fester and eat away undetected until it has done some major damage to our physical body.

'Ann, I suggest when you get home, write a letter to both your parents pouring out your feelings, sharing and expressing everything you weren't able to tell them. When ready, feel each word you wrote as you read the letter out loud, imagining both your parents sitting in front of you, sharing your heartfelt feelings with them. Then light a fire and watch the flames engulf the pages you wrote until they slowly become ashes, then throw them away. Taking that action can be healing for your mind and body, relaying a mental message – the issue had been dealt with.'

Ann rang me a few days later to say she had done it. It was extremely emotional for her and she was now finally feeling peaceful. I suggested she come back for another treatment the next night.

When I connected with her energy, instead of the heaviness and pain I felt in my hands during the previous treatment, the energy felt lighter and I could feel her drawing in loads of energy through me (not from me), absorbing the energy into her body.

The root of Ann's cancer was guilt. Guilt can have a strong negative influence on the soul-mind-body connection, which can eat away at our body if not dealt with.

As I continued treating Ann, I sensed to open my eyes and as I turned my head to the left, a vision appeared of a large hand. In the hand was a beautifully formed red rose for Ann.

I said to Ann with tears in my eyes, 'You are being handed a red rose by Spirit. I sense you will be fine after they remove the cancer.'

I paused, waiting for the words I sensed were coming.

'Oh, Annabelle.' This was my nickname for her. 'Guess what, my friend?'

Ann opened her eyes and looked up at me inquiringly as my voice had become loud and excited.

I smiled down at her and with a cheeky grin on my face, 'Kiddo, I believe you are "over the hill" and it's all "downhill" for you now! You're going to be fine. You have been touched and blessed.'

Spirit's guidance continually flows into us carrying the frequency of light-intelligence and the vibration of unconditional love – a high-frequency healing vibration.

Two days later, Ann was admitted to the hospital and had the operation the following day. The day after her operation I went to our local florist and purchased a long-stemmed red rose and rummaged through their box full of messaged balloons until I was thrilled to find the perfect inscription.

I quietly walked into her room with the helium balloon floating in the air on the end of a long piece of white ribbon. Attached to the ribbon was a red rose and imprinted on the balloon in big letters were the words 'Over the Hill'. I found a vase and placed the rose on the ledge directly opposite her bed in easy view. I gently held her ankles giving her energy. Although Ann was high on drugs, she told me later she remembered me being in the room.

I visited Ann again two days later and we both laughed as she told me one of her work associates had come to see her and noticed the balloon, frowned at it and said to Ann, 'Who sent that balloon to you with the awful message on it?'

Ann related to me what she had said to him. 'No, no, it doesn't mean what you're thinking. It means the exact opposite. It's a confirmation that I'm going to be fine.'

We both laughed. Every time she looked at the balloon it made her laugh 'awkwardly', reminding herself of how sore she was and also how blessed.

The doctors confirmed the cancer was contained to one small area and no other follow-up treatment was necessary. It could have been a different ending for Ann if she hadn't been able to open her heart and act on the spiritual guidance she received.

From my own past experience when I had a shoulder injury, I came to understand to look again at my life if I injure myself or if I end up in a difficult situation. Or if plans to go in a certain direction suddenly go haywire, or whichever way I turn, there seems to be a roadblock in my way. I see it as an opportunity to step back and look again at a decision I had made or was about to make.

My challenges (which I call my 'gifts' for learning) are an opportunity for growth and expanding my awareness. My body's reaction isn't intended to cause me pain, nor is it my enemy; my body's reaction is showing me that something is energetically out of balance. From my own personal experiences, I do not believe illnesses happen by chance. I believe there is an underlying cause behind all illnesses. For example, a disease could be passed on through an ancestral gene or an illness could develop through burying a traumatic experience as in Ann's situation.

Listening to inner guidance may mean facing an issue we have avoided acting upon. In my case, removing the inner wall of protection

I had built around myself was frightening for me. If we genuinely seek to gain understanding by opening our hearts to receive and listen for an answer, the clarity will come to us. Sometimes we subconsciously block out receiving because we don't want to 'hear' or 'see' the truth. In my case, I blocked investigating my reaction to writing because I feared facing my buried fears.

Our deep inner desires can find a way to manifest – for example, uncovering my self-expression – even if they lie hidden away for a long time. I truly recommend, if something is causing a discomfort within, feel it and write about it. It can relieve the inner discomfort building up within and writing can open a door, giving us an insight regarding an issue we are having difficulty facing or a decision we are considering.

Did expressing my feelings in writing help me with some of my issues? It certainly did by allowing my feelings a voice. Yet, when attempting to write my feelings regarding my fear of writing this book, didn't help. Because subconsciously I wasn't mentally ready to connect with the memory threads to clear the issue(s). What helped was walking Karza along the South Perth foreshore. It calmed me when I directed my focus outwards to the beautiful surroundings and activities happening around me.

A key to opening the door for my memory threads to come together for gaining an understanding of my fear of expressing myself had been given to me back in 1996. Back then I couldn't see the connection because I wasn't mentally ready to go there. Refer to chapter 64 – Paris, France, Late 1700s – Past Life Regression Session. It wasn't until I was in Paris in 2016 (refer to chapter 65 – Paris, France, 2016) that the past and present memory threads came together for a brief moment in a very surprising way.

CHAPTER 46

MY PARENTS' GOODBYE MESSAGE

Upon waking one morning, on an impulse I picked up the 1992 notebook from my office where I had written down the happenings before, during and after Mum's death, then went downstairs. After making myself a coffee I settled myself down comfortably in our lounge area. I opened the notebook at random and started reading about the kettledrum sticks we'd found in Mum's case.

The pain and associated feelings from that memory suddenly rose up from deep within my abdomen, moving quickly through my solar plexus into my heart and throat, alarming me. My throat closed up and I felt as if couldn't breathe properly. I was gasping for breath. Graham quickly walked out of his office and tried to get me to drink water. I couldn't swallow, spraying the water onto the floor of our lounge area. He held me and attempted to force air into my lungs by squeezing below my rib cage to remove any blockage that he thought might be sitting there.

Graham said afterwards his main concern was getting me to breathe as my eyes had started to bulge. The difficulty with my breathing lasted for only a few seconds yet my throat remained uncomfortable for about half an hour. It felt tight and sore as though it had been scratched. I felt dizzy and spaced out. I retreated upstairs to my meditation room, sitting quietly on the meditation mat.

Karza wriggled her way onto the mat, snuggling her tiny body up against mine. She looked up at me with her big brown eyes as if to say, 'Are you okay, Mum?' She then laid her head down, resting it on my thigh whilst keeping her eyes on me. Dogs are so sensitive to our moods and are such a precious joy and comfort.

I sat connecting within and quietly saying thank you. I had no idea another layer of trauma still remained after all the work I'd done on myself regarding the abortion attempts. But Spirit did! The impulse to pick up the notebook came from Spirit.

I thought of my parents and all I could feel for them was unconditional love. It thrilled me to know I truly loved them both unconditionally without any remaining remnants of resentment, guilt or sadness. I felt extremely peaceful.

As the realisation touched me deeply, my energy changed. I relaxed deep into myself and I saw a brilliant white five-pointed star hovering above my head. At the time I had no idea why the star appeared. Although I was feeling physically drained, I was feeling joyful.

I am so appreciative for my life because without all these experiences I wouldn't be the contented person I am today; instead, I may have ended up a very bitter and angry woman.

The following afternoon I was lying on our bed and drifted off to sleep with Karza snuggled up next to me. I suddenly came out of my slumber, sat up, opened my eyes and there, standing at the foot of our bed looking at me, were my parents…

A very faint light surrounded them and I sensed them say to me, 'You are all right now; we can leave you.'

I was not only surprised at seeing them but their message also surprised me. I then watched as Dad took hold of Mum's hand and they both smiled at me again before disappearing. I thought, *Have I just imagined this? Of course, I haven't. They had come to say goodbye.* I lay back, wondering if both my parents had stayed around me all these years since the earlier encounters without my knowing.

I remembered Mum's vibration hadn't been strong enough to come to me back in 1992. *That's interesting,* I thought. *Her vibrations have improved and she has healed her pain.* Refer to chapter 18 – Healing for My Mother and Me.

Their appearance definitely wasn't a coincidence; their timing was perfect and I felt very encouraged seeing them after my experience the day before.

When we know without any doubt that we have forgiven another person, our realised truth carries a very powerful vibration. A truth vibration not only frees us from mental bondage but also sends forth a rippling effect throughout the universe, offering other souls the opportunity to also heal their pain. When we experience a deep heartfelt healing, it can not only change the DNA imprint in our body but also have a positive effect on our loved ones. It makes no difference whether the person we're forgiving is physically alive or if they have passed over because our loved ones live on in their spiritual body and Consciousness knows no boundaries.

I do believe a family unit plays a major role by giving each other opportunities to heal our soul's challenges in this current life cycle. We choose our parents for our growth and development.

Please note: I researched the five-pointed star where I read on Ananda Australia's website: 'It's a doorway through which our mind can penetrate into the inner kingdom.'

CHAPTER 47

ROY'S PASSING

Mavourneen and her husband, Roy Melville, had decided to go on holiday to the Gold Coast in Queensland. Roy had been receiving treatment for cancer and was in remission, so they took the opportunity to have a restful break away to recharge their energy after the gruelling time they had been through.

I had just returned home from a luncheon. I glanced into Graham's office and noticed two messages on our answering machine. Just as I was about to listen to them the phone rang. It was Mavourneen, sounding very distraught.

'Thank goodness you're home; I have been trying to reach you. Roy has taken a turn for the worse and the doctor's prognosis is not good. Yvonne, his health is failing quickly.' Mavourneen went on to tell me the doctor advised her to fly Roy home as soon as possible as he wasn't expected to live very long.

She rang me again later to say that they had been able to get seats on a flight the next day and would be arriving late that night, and would I send energy to Roy to assist him during the flight home. I willingly agreed.

An ambulance met the plane at Perth Airport and quickly transported Roy to the hospital and into a private room.

When I arrived at around 8.30 a.m. the following day, a close friend of both of them, Liz Murt, was sitting with Mavourneen comforting her. Doctors had already advised her that Roy would not last the day. It was a very sad time.

Their only child, Andrew Melville, was working in Jakarta. He anticipated the plane would land in Perth around 8.30 p.m. and hoped to be at the hospital by 9 p.m. I began giving energy to Roy to support him. By noon Roy was in a coma.

Late afternoon, I happened to glance over to my left towards the window and to the right of the window stood four winged angels in white robes, standing close together in a corner of the room. From my past experience in supporting others to pass over, when I see four angels it is usually only a couple of hours before they pass over. I glanced down at my watch again; only five minutes had passed. The time was 4.10 p.m. *Oh no*, I thought, *we still have a minimum of four to five hours before Andrew arrives.* I kept focusing on Andrew's flight arriving on time and kept visualising him standing next to his father, holding his hand before he passed over.

I looked back at the angels and spoke to them mentally, saying, *Please don't take Roy just yet. Andrew is coming and will be here soon.*

I stood at the foot of the bed, gently holding Roy's ankles, giving him energy. Another hour passed and the angels were still standing in the corner of the room. I started to feel a little anxious. Liz, Mavourneen and I would occasionally glance at each other with concerned looks on our faces.

'Andrew will be here soon. He is coming very soon,' I said gently. I sensed he could hear me. The three of us kept glancing at our watches, willing the time to miraculously fly to 9 p.m. Unfortunately, the afternoon went very slowly. I kept focusing on seeing Andrew arrive before Roy passed over. I thought to myself, *Well, the angels haven't moved, so that is a good sign.*

I continued holding Roy's ankles, giving him energy, then occasionally moving to give direct energy over his heart area, reminding Roy with increased enthusiasm, 'Andrew will be here real soon.'

Just before 6.30 p.m., I saw a very pale pulsating blue light surround Roy. Seeing the pulsating light around a person is showing me their soul is preparing to leave.

I told Liz and Mavourneen everything I had been seeing and they joined in voicing encouraging words to Roy. Mavourneen had been one of my students in Jakarta and understood.

By 7.30 p.m. I could see that the pale-bluish pulsating light surrounding Roy had intensified.

Roy's breathing changed and a nurse came into the room checking on Roy and said to Mavourneen, 'It won't be long now.'

The three of us looked at each other and started vocally encouraging Roy, telling him, 'Andrew is almost here. Any moment now he's going to walk through the door.'

By 8.40 p.m. Mavourneen received a call from her son saying the flight had just landed and he would be there in half an hour. I could see the pulsating blue light around Roy's body had not changed. We all sighed with relief when Andrew rushed quickly into the room and the relief was evident on his face when he saw his father was still alive.

The angels were still standing in the corner of the room. A short while later, I suddenly saw Roy leave his body. In a flash, he was standing by the bed about three metres in front of the angels. I was mesmerised as Roy stood watching Mavourneen and Andrew, who were each holding one of his hands and talking to him. His body was still breathing in and out sporadically. I wished I could have been able to take a video of what I was observing. It was one of the most beautiful and touching experiences I had ever encountered when supporting someone passing over.

Roy's blue eyes, instead of appearing dull and lifeless, were once again sparkly and bright. The radiance of love that was emanating from him was beautiful to experience. My eyes filled with tears of appreciation as I looked at Roy's spiritual body and I was seeing for myself firsthand Spirit's gift to each of us – 'eternal life' (Refer to chapter 19 – Insightful Vision). Roy stood there in a hospital gown with a gentle smile on his face and his energy had a very soft bluish-whitish glow radiating outwards from around his spiritual body. He was looking at his family with such love. I could actually feel the love he had for both of them.

I said to Mavourneen and Andrew, 'Would you two like some time alone with Roy?'

They both nodded their heads, unable to speak. Liz and I walked out of the room and I told Liz what I had just seen.

Liz, who had been a nurse, nodded and quietly said, 'I can tell by his breathing that it will happen very soon.'

Liz and I sat in the visitors' waiting room.

A short while later, I glanced up at the entrance to the waiting room and there stood Roy! I was surprised and actually amused to see him standing there. Cheeky Roy was obviously happy as a spiritual being again. He was indicating for us to come back into the hospital room.

I smiled and told Liz what I was seeing and said, 'Okay, we can go back in now.' As soon as we got up and started walking towards him, he disappeared. We walked down the corridor and turned to step back into the room and I bumped straight into Andrew and Mavourneen, who both said almost in unison, 'We were just coming to get you.'

'You are both too late. Roy beat you to it. He has already called us back to the room.' We gave each other a knowing nod. Roy enjoyed surprising people with his actions. They both told me later how comforting and supportive it was to them to hear about what I had seen and how peacefully Roy passed over.

A month later, Mavourneen came to my home for an energy treatment as she had been feeling quite unwell and listless since the funeral. During a treatment, information sometimes flows in to support a person. The energy guides my hands and my right hand often raises up and slowly begins to move over a person's body while my left hand usually remains steady in contact with their body. I will share here the relevant portion of the treatment directly relating to Roy.

Towards the end of the treatment, I said to Mavourneen, 'I am sensing that the connection remains strong between the two of you and you have both been together before in a previous life cycle.'

What happened next, I wasn't ready for and it has never happened to me again. My knees buckled and I found myself kneeling on the floor due to a sudden, powerful surge of energy that passed straight through me and then Roy appeared, surrounded by a soft light. Although his body was very difficult to see clearly, the warmth his energy carried touched me and the impact of the connection caused me to feel emotional.

Spirit's consciousness is there to support us all, not only in this physical life but also to help those who have passed over to heal as well.

Roy spoke to me, saying, 'Tell Mavourneen I understand it all now. I understand everything. Mavourneen, be happy – I now understand what you had been trying to tell me all these years.'

Then he was gone.

I relayed the message and Mavourneen said, 'Yvonne, I knew something was happening because I am covered in goosebumps.' She paused before adding, 'Roy had a very difficult time showing love as a result of his upbringing and it saddened me.'

Roy was letting her know he finally understood the difference between unconditional love and conditional love.

Maybe in Roy's situation when he was alive, he closed the door to his heart to avoid feeling because while growing up the only love he understood was a 'love that hurt'. Sadly, I have come across this pattern so often and that belief can bury itself deep into our psyche, lowering our self-worth.

I could clearly relate to Roy because that's what I did until I chose to deal with my hurts. The only person I was really hurting and shutting myself off from was myself. That approach didn't help me; it only caused me more heartache. My approach towards life in the past was self-destructive and I am so glad I made the decision to live with an open heart.

I have mentioned before, if we have not known or experienced unconditional love for ourselves growing up, it's difficult to easily express it to others. In saying that, our nature is love and deep within us we all have this inbuilt knowing (our truth indicator). Some call it our conscience; others call it Spirit of truth. Buddha called it becoming enlightened. It's that part of our nature that indicates to us what we are thinking of doing is either a right or wrong choice for us. I knew deep in my heart when my actions did not resonate with my authentic nature. The negative words spoken to others at times used to make me feel better for a short time. I had been unknowingly feeding more energy into my own ignorance and for a brief time, it made me feel powerful. However, that type of empowerment used to leave me feeling very uncomfortable afterwards until I chose not to live my life that way any longer.

I am so glad I focused on a more positive approach to life; I expanded my awareness, opening a door for the energy to feed my whole being. I realised for many years I had shut myself away from the one thing that could really support me – inner guidance.

When we are unable to open our hearts to loving ourselves, we can inadvertently cause sadness to the ones we care about the most. Our loved ones, who have difficulty showing love in this area, need even more love. Of course, I didn't realise that for many years because I was still struggling to love myself.

I understand that our loved ones outpouring frustration towards us on occasion may cause us pain and sadness. Being able to 'see' the bigger picture regarding our own and others' behaviour gives us the opportunity to grow in wisdom, understanding and compassion towards ourselves and those around us. I realised I couldn't express unconditional love towards others until I unconditionally loved myself. One of the benefits of expanding our conscious awareness is that we 'see' life more clearly and know the best course of action to take in a situation we face.

Conditional love – I love you if you comply with my expectations, wishes and beliefs, or I love you when you...

Conditional love is 'I' – self-centred. When our behaviour is conditional towards others, our heart is closed off to love in some way. Each of us has our challenges to learn from and overcome in this life.

Unconditional love is a beautiful vibration to experience and is all-encompassing, embracing and accepting. We may not agree with the words someone has spoken, their behaviour towards us, nor accept their actions. Being able to send forth unconditional love to someone who has caused us heartache and pain is a sign we have forgiven them.

Why is it important to forgive others and ourselves? The act of forgiveness frees us from holding onto an emotional hook connected to a distressing incident we have with another person, e.g., through resentment, guilt, hatred, anger, bitterness, heartache, a grudge, wanting revenge or experiencing a traumatic tragedy.

Forgiveness is basically being able to 'accept' what happened and it opens a door for us to let go of the emotional pain we have held onto and to see with clarity what is the best step forward for us to take. It doesn't mean we forget about the incident and for many that is impossible, but sadly if we continue holding onto our pain, eventually the only person we are hurting unknowingly is our self as in Carol's experience, who lost her grandson in tragic circumstances. Refer to chapter 31 – The Power of Love.

Emotional blockages affect our health. We may never forget what transpired but it's important to free ourselves of the painful mental/emotional connection we have with that person or situation. Forgiveness frees us and can help us to move on. We forgive others and/or ourselves for our own wellbeing.

Sometimes the act of forgiveness can be a slow and very difficult process for many, depending on the severity of what took place, e.g.

losing a loved one or, through mental abuse. Through the act of forgiveness, we can gently peel away the layers of hurt, letting go of the emotional pain we carry. Refer to chapter 40 – A Journey from Misery to Contentment.

Unconditional love at its essence is an energy that is pure love. Choosing to have this positive vibration flowing through us is 'real' empowerment. It is an energy that can heal our pain, uplift us, comfort and nourish our whole being.

When we act and speak from the energy flowing forth from our authentic nature (a loving kind vibration – our intrinsic nature), we feel light, open, genuine and whole. It just bubbles up out of us. It's effervescent.

If someone is desiring to forgive another and move on with their life, yet are having difficulty forgiving for whatever reason, I recommend they talk to their doctor or seek out a counsellor to help them.

There are many people out there who have experienced the pain associated with losing a loved one in some way and have gone on to use their experience as a stepping-stone towards helping others. Many have set up a foundation in their loved one's name. What a blessing these people are who have used their painful experiences to highlight issues that require addressing, bringing awareness to situations and giving hope, encouragement and healing to others through the support they selflessly offer.

CHAPTER 48

MANIFESTING A HEART'S DESIRE

In October 2005, the project Graham was working on near the coastal town of Dampier was coming to an end. Graham was approached and offered another management position with another company to work on a nearby gas plant project to be built close to the town of Karratha, approximately 1525 kilometres north of Perth.

Graham purchased a four-wheel drive car for me that was suitable for the rough conditions up north, leaving my car in our garage. We made the decision to keep our apartment readily available for whenever we flew to Perth.

I remained in Perth with our now eighteen-month-old fluffball Karza, who had turned into a mischievous little rascal, while Graham sought out a partially furnished house that would allow a pet. As our current property overlooked the Swan River and city, we desired to live on the coast in a township in the small community of Dampier, 21 kilometres west of Karratha. With the mining and gas boom happening up north, it was very difficult to find suitable accommodation in and around Karratha.

One morning, Graham rang feeling disappointed and frustrated. 'I have been looking but it's very hard to get suitable rental housing, so it may take quite a while.'

'I understand the situation. It's all over the newspapers and TV news down here, especially the soaring rental costs. Don't worry, I will focus on us acquiring suitable accommodation. It will happen – we just have to be patient.'

After getting off the telephone, I sat down and immediately made a detailed list of all our requirements; I focused on using the Reiki second degree (symbols students learn to utilise) coupled with using my imaging and senses to envision seeing the three of us together. I then sent out my request 'three' times before blowing it away, knowing the highest good would transpire for us.

Every morning and night, I re-read my list of requirements for our rental home, adding my gratitude and thanks for bringing to us the perfect place to live. I refused to allow myself to become despondent. I made a point of ignoring the various media reports that continued circulating regarding the lack of housing and the daily report of the escalating cost of living up north. Instead, I focused on the end result we both desired – the three of us living together and taking evening walks along the beach.

It was harder for Graham to ignore the negative reporting, as it was all everyone around him was talking about. He was working long hours and it was my desire to be there to support him.

A couple of weeks later, I woke up early one morning, opened my eyes and instead of seeing our bedroom windows in front of me, I was looking at an image of a house. I sat up in bed, watching the vision playing out before my eyes, just like a movie scene.

In the vision, *I saw my husband and me looking at a property overlooking the ocean. I then saw a retired couple talking to us. I could see Karza, our little white bundle of mischief, surprisingly, sitting angelically beside us. I saw glimpses of white trelliswork at the front of the house, which I assumed was the front boundary fencing.*

The owners said to us, 'We will leave anything that you would like to use in the house and the dog is welcome.'

The vision left me with a 'strong impression' *that the house was in Dampier and someone from his office was going to tell him about a house becoming available and that we had to wait.*

Then as quickly as it had appeared before me, it disappeared and I was once again looking at the familiar surroundings of our bedroom. Unable to go back to sleep, I lay in bed, battling with my thoughts as my logical mind started bombarding me with doubts.

Thoughts kept creeping in: *You just dreamt that. This is too good to be true. A three-bedroom house overlooking the water... Furniture offered to you... A place that will accept your dog... Get all this within your budget... What planet are you living on? Wake up, girl, this is just wishful thinking on your part. You are just dreaming about the desire you are hoping for.*

The chatter went on until I stopped the negative feedback by remembering how a house in Jakarta had come to us once. Refer to chapter 23 – A Lesson in Letting Go.

I gave thanks to Spirit that attracts and links together all like-minded ideals. Often, I found my logical mind very challenging to ignore. When that happened, I found myself arguing with my brain. I overcame the diversity of my thoughts by allowing the negative chatter to have its voice clearly listened to, then I simply let them go, refocusing on the 'reality' I chose to come into my life.

Later that morning, I rang Graham and told him about the vision I received. In a frustrated voice, he replied, 'Well, I can't just sit around and wait; I have to continue looking.' Again he reminded me just how hard it was to get anything suitable for us and I in turn reminded him...

'Remember how the house in Jakarta came to us. Spirit has given us a glimpse of the house we are going to be living in. We just have to trust the energy to bring it to fruition.'

In order to support the desire I was focusing upon to happen, I made a list of the belongings we would take with us and boldly invited three removal companies to give us quotations. I then forwarded the quotations to Graham. Remember, it's important to 'be the change' in support of our desire happening.

Whenever doubts crept in, I quickly refocused on the vision, saying, 'Thank you for providing the perfect home for us,' and I'd imagine the three of us in Dampier together, walking along the beach.

A couple of weeks later, Graham rang me from work. 'I have just been given the address of a house for rent in Dampier by a work colleague. The house has just been listed on a noticeboard in the shopping centre today. Unfortunately, I was not given a phone number.'

Graham waited until 6.45 a.m. the next morning before arriving at the house as he didn't want to disturb the owners too early. Unfortunately, when he arrived someone else was being shown through the house. After they left, Graham viewed the house and the owners said they would let him know as there was someone ahead of him and they had to check out the applications.

When Graham called, I asked him to describe the front of the house and he said, 'It has a wide front veranda which runs the full length of the house and is enclosed by white trellis panelling and the house overlooks the ocean.'

Goosebumps appeared all over me from my head to my toes and I said excitedly, 'It's happened. I am going to book a flight for tomorrow. I'm sure by your description it's the house I saw.'

'No, no, Yvonne, don't come up. We haven't been offered it yet,' Graham replied sternly.

'Graham, it's ours. I just know it.' Did I obey my husband? Of course not! All I could hear echoing in my head was one word repeating itself over and over in my head. *YES, YES, YES!*

Early afternoon the next day, I left an extremely unhappy and very sulky Karza at the kennels. It took all my strength not to look back at her; I ran to my car teary-eyed and drove to the airport.

I was waiting in line at the check-in counter when my mobile phone rang; it was Graham letting me know the house was ours. I said excitedly, 'I am so glad to hear that because I was going to ring you once I was sitting in the Qantas Club lounge.'

'What did you just say? Where are you?'

'At the airport, of course, darling, just getting my boarding pass. My plane arrives at four p.m.' I heard Graham let out a loud exasperating sigh so I hastily added, 'Oops, I must go. See you soon.' I quickly hung up before he could say anything else to me.

Graham picked up one very excited wife at the airport and he informed me we had an appointment with the owners the next morning to see the house. Pictures popped into my head as I proceeded to describe to Graham what the owners looked like and I sensed the wife enjoyed painting. Graham confirmed my description but didn't know if she was an artist.

Of course, I couldn't wait until morning. I had to see the house immediately from the outside. So off we drove to Dampier and as we slowly drove past the house twice, the owners noticed us. How could they not? The house was located in a small cul-de-sac. We hadn't noticed them but they had been sitting watching us from their front veranda as they enjoyed their pre-dinner cocktail. The husband recognised Graham's company car and ran out onto the road, waving us to come back.

We went in and as soon as the wife and I met, we both burst into tears. It was an emotional meeting. We both felt as if we already knew each other. It felt bizarre. We joined them on the front veranda, talking about the house whilst sharing a drink and watching the sun go down over the ocean. They knew we were the right people to look after their much-loved property while they went on a well-earned world cruise. The owners kindly offered to leave their furniture and any white goods we might require and what we didn't need go into their lockup garage and yes, our little Karza was welcomed with open arms. We also acquired the three-bedroom house within our budget.

As the wife showed me through the house, I stopped and admired a painting. She smiled and said, 'Thank you, I painted that.'

Some friends with whom I have shared this experience have said 'that was a miracle.'

I know from experience some 'so-called' miracles happen in our life when we consciously delve deep into our hearts, connecting with Spirit, which gives 'life' to our desires, as long as we do our part in supporting it to manifest. One really important thing to remember is that our desired result is for the highest good for all people.

As you will have read, trusting Spirit has been a slow process for me, even with all the support I have received. These days I am much more open and trusting towards our intangible inner world.

Our inner world is alive just as our physical world 'appears' to be. The difference between our inner and outer worlds is that our inner world is our true reality and is made up of frequencies, vibrations and billions of subatomic particles, and our physical world is made up of the same energy although appearing very dense and solid to the human eye. Yet, it is still the same vibrating energy that is a 'reflection' only of how our soul expresses itself into physicality, our beliefs for experiencing, evaluating and learning from.

I have a favourite saying... **Anything you can *imaginise* you can actualise.**

Graham said to me when he was editing a newsletter for me back in 1994, which I sent out to students in Jakarta... 'Yvonne, there is no such word as "imaginise".'

'There is now, I've just created it!'

CHAPTER 49

OUR NORTHWEST ADVENTURE

In December 2005, Karza (seated in cargo between another dog and a large container of fish) and I flew to join Graham in the northwest of Western Australia and we all moved into the house I had seen earlier in my vision.

After settling in, Karza and I became used to seeing two large monitor lizards with their wrinkly skin, long tongues and very long nails. They stared at us almost daily through the glass doors into the dining room, which opened onto the back patio area and spa. Months later, they had a baby who joined in gazing in at us. Now I know what animals feel like when we stare at them through their glass enclosures. The owners had pre-warned us the lizards had taken up residence.

I was writing a couple of days a week for as long as I could until I felt the anxiety rise up. Then I would walk outside or do some chores around the house to ease the built-up tension inside me.

We lived in the house for just over a year. During that time, we experienced five cyclones. I regularly saw kangaroos in our front garden or hopping down our street along with the occasional emus, echidnas, snakes *(yikes)* and other furry creatures. I didn't mind if I saw wild animals outside of our property but I know I would have freaked out if they had managed to sneak in. I was warned by neighbours to be careful when Karza was outside as she was still very little and eagles had been seen to swoop down grabbing fully grown rabbits, chickens and other small animals.

I was in the laundry early one morning when my inner senses went on alert. I knew something was about to happen. I dropped the wet sheets I was about to place in the laundry basket and ran outside. Karza thought she had found a new playmate; to her delight, she was happily chasing a small deadly dugite snake across our back lawn. I yelled out to Graham as I raced across the lawn before taking a flying leap forward in the air, managing to grab hold of the end of Karza's furry tail, and landing stomach-first onto the lawn. Fortunately, I had put on a little weight, cushioning my landing.

Karza gave a loud yelp, turned and looked at me in shock. I again called – no, I screeched out the word 'snake' to Graham, who was about to leave for work. By the time our hero arrived with gloves and boots on with a rake in hand, the snake was nowhere to be seen. I'm sure my screeching scared the snake away. Later that day I was told by our next-door neighbour (who probably heard my screeching) if I come across one not to scream out – to instead stand very still and remember to keep breathing until the snake moves away, watching where it slithers off to so a snake handler can come and remove it.

After the episode of seeing Karza chasing the snake that morning, I was still a little jumpy when we retired to bed. During the night, I woke up needing to go to the toilet. I didn't bother to put on the light. I sat and then heard a splashing sound (no, it wasn't coming from me) and I felt something slap my bottom. I jumped up, screaming, and Graham came staggering, half-asleep, switching on the light. He scowled at me standing up against the wall, both of us naked as the day we were born with Graham wearing a grumpy expression and I wearing a terrified look. My head was turned away and my shaking finger was pointing at the toilet. I didn't want to see what had slapped my bottom as it swam around in the bowl. He looked in.

'Oh, for goodness' sake, Yvonne. It's just a little lizard,' Graham grumpily said in a tired and exasperated voice.

'Well, I didn't know what it was. I thought it might be another snake,' I replied shakily. He just gave me an eye roll and retrieved it out of the toilet bowl, putting it outside. When he came back inside, he ignored me as we both climbed back into bed.

I added, 'And furthermore, Graham, it wasn't just a little lizard as you said. It had a long tail. It frightened me.'

He gave me another annoying eye roll before turning off the light.

From then on, I remembered to turn the light on if I needed the toilet during the night and I also put white light around our home morning and night. I never saw another snake on our property that I was aware of, although the lizards kept finding their way inside, which kept Karza entertained.

CHAPTER 50

DIVINE INTERVENTION

I received a phone call from our property agent one Tuesday evening in 2006. The following morning, instead of playing golf as planned with my golfing buddy Maxine, I was sitting on a plane heading to Perth. The tenant in our rental house had been using the oven's grill, causing a small fire in the kitchen. Fortunately, the fire was easily contained by the quick action of the fire brigade.

After a busy week organising repairs, I was looking forward to returning to Dampier to be with Graham and our still very mischievous bundle of joy, Karza. It was about 9 p.m. on Thursday night. I was upstairs in our South Perth apartment packing my suitcase when I started feeling an uneasiness stirring in my heart. I was experiencing the now-familiar inner pressure in my heart which meant Spirit desired my attention. I sensed I was to stop what I was doing and go sit somewhere quiet. The logical voice in my head piped up, saying, *no, finish your packing first, then go downstairs and have some quiet time.* I continued to pack. The more I attempted to focus on the job at hand, the more agitated I became.

I finally gave in to the disturbing feelings and walked downstairs and out onto our balcony, which overlooked the picturesque Swan River and the city skyline. It was a pleasant and clear night and the city lights were dancing playfully across the water. It was one of my favourite places to sit, meditating. I sat down, relaxing my body as my mind slowly stopped its busy chatter. I continued to slowly breathe in and out, gently expanding my awareness to understand why I was drawn downstairs to meditate. I then experienced a deep peace flowing into me and I became aware of a tiny speck of gold light that appeared in my third eye and I was quickly drawn to it. As I observed this light, it grew larger expanding rapidly in size. The gold light grew so large it could no longer be contained behind my eyes and an image burst forth. I watched a swirling mass of gold energy spinning very fast a few feet in front of me.

On cue, my logical mind questioned it and then suddenly all thoughts abruptly ceased. Literally in the blink of an eye, the mass of energy had formed into a gold being (as I named it). I remembered a similar occurrence in 2003 on a flight from Dubai to Bangkok when a gold being appeared in the aisle near me. That being's body was fully formed before popping into me. This being's body remained a beautiful twinkling gold vibrational form.

I have seen a few angels, messengers and various beings, all of which differed slightly in appearance depending on their purpose. This being did not have wings, nor was it fully formed as other gold beings I've seen. Refer to chapter 41 – The Messenger.

I sat there fascinated. Its gold energy twinkled like the stars at night and each time its energy twinkled, its presence sent forth a soft glowing mist of light. It was one of the most beautiful and mesmerising spiritual energies I have been blessed to experience. It reminded me of the lights we put up around our home at Christmas time, except these lights were made up of very tiny dots. Not one aspect of this being's presence appeared solid. It was made up of very tiny dots of twinkling gold lights; from the outline of its body to its face, eyes, nose and lips. All were tiny twinkling gold dots.

The being smiled at me and then stretched out its arms towards me lovingly. I likened the action to someone who was greeting an old friend. I sensed a familiarity with its energy which I found extremely comforting.

I smiled back at the gold being and spoke to it via my thoughts. *I acknowledge you and I welcome your presence.* I can only speculate that my return greeting and my openness towards this being was an invitation because, in a flash, the being's gold energy popped in through the top of my head, merging with my energy. That was definitely something I was not expecting and it shocked me. For a few seconds, I felt frightened.

Looking down at my arms resting on the chair, I wondered if there was a slight gold glow through my skin? *No, it couldn't be. That's impossible. It's just my imagination,* I told myself. I sat for quite some time, reliving the event over and over in an attempt to logically come to terms with what I had experienced. Then on cue, my brain started its usual tirade of self-doubts. *Did I imagine this? Am I going crazy? Did this really happen? Gosh, no one will believe this one. I am finding it hard to believe it myself.*

I touched my skin. I glanced down at my arms. I still felt the same. The inner pressure I felt in my heart earlier had dispersed. I smiled and shook my head. After all the support I've received over the past 50-plus years, my self-doubt still raises its voice and often loudly at times.

In my attempt to suppress the rising apprehension, I spoke to myself aloud, reassuring myself there was nothing to be afraid of. 'I'm okay. It means me no harm. Its presence feels comfortable. Only good will come out of this. I still feel peaceful.' I stayed sitting in the chair, nodding my head in agreement with my positive self-talk. After a while, I went back upstairs to complete packing before retiring for the night.

As I lay in bed, I knew this being's appearance didn't happen by chance; its energy had attached itself to mine for a specific purpose. *What purpose?* I thought excitedly to myself. *Am I going to receive more interesting and insightful information to stretch my mind?* I confess, I did end up sleeping with the bedside table light on all night for reassurance.

Why? Because somewhere in the recesses of my mind, I am still surprised that these experiences come through me. Why not come through someone who would willingly welcome them? I knew I trusted the inner guidance and support, yet these incidents still unnerved me, leaving me feeling somewhat vulnerable and out of control. The being's presence stayed for a very short time and the reason had nothing to do with imparting knowledge to me.

I woke up the next morning feeling fully refreshed after a surprisingly peaceful sleep. The two-hour flight from Perth passed quickly and I arrived late Friday afternoon at the Karratha airport. Graham and Karza greeted me with open arms (and paws!) and kisses (and licks!)

That evening, the three of us dined outdoors on the front patio. It was a warm night and the striking sunset reflected its colourful hues over the vast Indian Ocean. After we discussed my meeting with the insurance assessor and the repair work scheduled to commence the following Monday, I told Graham about my experience the night before.

'Nothing has happened so far and I don't feel any different,' I grumbled.

Graham remained quiet.

'No messages. No visions. Nothing. I just don't understand why the gold being has attached itself to my energy,' I explained in a disheartened voice.

Over the years I have come to realise Graham is my anchor. I sense, at times, part of his role in my life is to keep me grounded.

'Yvonne,' Graham said loudly. 'Did you hear what I just said?'

'No, I didn't. I'm sorry. What did you just say?'

'Yvonne, just let it be.'

'That's easy for you to say – you didn't have the experience. It's frustrating and you are so pragmatic. That's not what I was hoping you would say. I'd like to keep discussing the encounter in the hope we might solve the mystery.'

Graham stretched one arm up into the air then brought it back down as if he was pulling at something and then just stared at me for a moment with a glint in his eye. 'Earth calling, Yvonne. Earth to Yvonne, can you hear me?'

My eyes narrowed and my lips turned into a disgruntled smile and our discussion on that particular subject matter ceased.

On Sunday night I checked the refrigerator and freezer, realising we were in desperate need of replenishing our food supply. I decided to do a food shop first thing the next morning before the temperature reached its predicted peak of 38 degrees Celsius. My plans to go shopping early were delayed by a number of telephone calls relating to the fire at our rented property. When I finally looked at the clock it was almost 11.30 a.m.

'Okay,' I said to Karza, who looked up at me, pricking up her little white ears. 'Let's go to plan B. Let's have lunch then I'll go shopping.'

At the mention of food, Karza's fluffy white tail wagged excitedly up in the air and we headed off to the kitchen with her keenly leading the way.

After lunch, I collected my shopping list and as I reversed my car out of the carport, I again thought that my hands and arms had a glow to them.

I said, 'Oh, hello there. I thought you had deserted me. You have been very quiet these past three days.'

My memory of the being's presence brought a warm smile to my face.

I turned onto the main road, which would take me into the town of Karratha. I thought I could see the gold glow again. Has this glow become stronger or is it my imagination? Then I thought, *Oh, silly me. It's because I am out in the bright sunshine.*

The road was cut through granite rock and its shoulder slightly narrowed with the rough rock face jutting straight up on either side of the road. In some places where the road curved, there were crash barriers on both sides. I reduced my speed to 80 kilometres as stipulated from 110 kilometres per hour, steering my car around the long winding stretch of road.

My thoughts were partly on the errands I needed to do in town while in the background, the car's radio softly played. As I drove around a bend, I was shocked to see, on my side of the road, a ten-tonne truck careering towards me with only its right-side wheels touching the road. The truck's left-side wheels were lifted off the ground, spinning in the air.

My thoughts instantaneously stopped their chatter. My mind went blank; I felt numb. I distinctly remember how still I became. My whole awareness zoomed in, focusing on what was happening directly in front of me. I could clearly see the truck driver's horror-struck face looking back at me through his windscreen. Our eyes locked on each other in confusion and disbelief. For a second, I couldn't fully comprehend what was happening. We both mentally registered at the same time what was about to occur and we both took evasive action.

I remember saying to myself: *I've got to get out of the path of this oncoming truck to avoid a head-on smash. I've got to move over to his side of the road and hopefully miss colliding with him.* I was definitely fully aware the moment I started to turn the wheel to the right to cross over onto the other side of the road, when suddenly everything before my eyes began happening in slow motion, exactly like when watching a video and you press the button to slow the picture down. Instead of my car going to the right as I thought I was directing it, my car went to the left and came to a stop adjacent to and within a couple of centimetres of the rough rock face. I know I had my hands firmly on the wheel yet at the same time, I felt like I was the passenger and not the one steering the car. I can only surmise the gold being had been directing my actions because it definitely wasn't me.

The truck driver wrenched the wheel of his truck back to his side of the road so hard he overcorrected. His left-side wheels drove up over the crash barrier and travelled along the wall of the rock face before crashing back down onto the road, taking a small section of the crash barrier with him, becoming lodged under his truck.

Travelling behind me were two men in a four-wheel drive vehicle who witnessed the near miss. They stopped and the driver ran over to see if I was okay, whilst his passenger went over to the stunned truck driver.

I sat in my car feeling extremely disoriented. I could hear tapping and when I looked up, a man was indicating for me to unlock my car door. When my brain finally registered, I reached over, unlocking it.

The kind man opened my door, asking, 'Are you hurt?'

'No,' I replied in a quivering voice. 'I just feel a little disoriented.'

As I stepped out of my car, my legs had the wobbles and I felt lightheaded. I began to sway, and the man grabbed my arms and helped me to sit back down as my body started to shake and he said, 'You will be okay. You've just had a nasty shock.'

I leaned my head back against the car's head restraint and closed my eyes.

'You are one lucky lady. That truck was so close to hitting you.'

The reality of his words hit me, causing emotion to rise up as I realised just how close I had come to being seriously injured or possibly killed. Upon hearing his words I looked up at him and burst into tears. He took hold of my hand and squeezed it, reassuring me it was a shock reaction. All was okay.

His gaze moved to his friend, who was supporting the truck driver as they made their way slowly towards us. It was obvious the truck driver had hurt his shoulder and was in pain.

The truck driver said, 'I lost control of my vehicle after falling asleep at the wheel and I drove straight into the bend, causing my truck to veer sharply onto your side of the road. I am a contractor and I have been travelling back and forth picking up loads of sand since early this morning. I was so tired I fell asleep. I'm so glad you didn't cross onto the other side of the road because you would have ended up under my truck,' he admitted quietly. The relief on his face that I was okay was clearly evident.

The gentleman who assisted me said, 'That was some clever thinking and driving you just did, as most people's instinct would be to cross over to the other side, hoping to avoid a collision.'

I started to respond 'But I wa—' but stopped myself. How could I tell them it hadn't been me directing the car? They would have thought I was crazy. Even I think I'm crazy at times with some of the things I have experienced because I still don't understand how or why they happen to me. In so many ways, especially where Spirit is concerned, I am extremely naïve.

The passenger from the car that stopped to help turned to the truck driver, adding, 'And if you had been carrying a full load, the truck would have rolled. Your truck would not have been able to avoid crashing into the lady's car.'

After reassuring the three men I was okay to drive, they left to join another person who had stopped to help remove the debris from the road and from under the truck. I settled back into my car, briefly closing my eyes and running my hands over my face, when I sensed the being's energy leave my body. I leaned my head back against the headrest and said a prayer of thanks to the beautiful being who had just saved my life.

I have mentioned before a prayer I started saying years ago and as a result, I truly believe Spirit is always watching over me... 'I am always guided, always protected and always supported by Spirit.'

I understand many may question the validity of the being and this experience as I have also done so many times. I have had many experiences over the years, but none as phenomenal or mind-blowing as this one. I do not have a clear understanding as to how I saw and experienced an evolved gold being protecting me in that way.

Why did I see everything slow down in front of my eyes? Someone told me it is a common phenomenon in a situation like that to see everything slow down before your eyes. Was Spirit showing me, yet again, everything is energy and is flexible and pliable? Reminding me nothing is solid, even though we can physically see everything around us appear to be in a solid form.

How did Spirit know I was going to be in danger? If I had gone shopping that morning as planned, I don't believe I would have experienced that incident. Then I remembered this intrinsic power is all-knowing.

Why did this incident happen to me? Besides being protected from harm, maybe Spirit was attempting to encourage me to let go of the perceived control I thought I needed and trust. The answers to this experience were explained to me by The Voice years later. Refer to chapter 58 – The Voice's Powerful Revelations.

My mother used to worry about every little thing. She used to say, 'I am a born worrier.'

Not true! No one is a born worrier. Incessant worrying is an acquired habitual way of thinking. When we turn a concern into a worry, we are inviting our mind to dwell on difficulties and then we become mentally troubled, opening the door for fear-based thoughts and anxiety to take hold. When that happens, we lower our energy's vibrations, making it difficult to receive clear guidance.

Unfortunately, when young I inherited my mother's habit of worrying. I thought by worrying, I could control my life or if I worried about it, it wouldn't happen! That was definitely not a logical way of looking at life! By worrying about things, I narrowed my outlook on life. My mind became locked within an insular world. I was seeing life through a filter of trepidation and fear. I was 'sending forth' into the environment around me what I was focused upon continuously in my mind. Constant worrying can unfortunately attract to us the very things we worry about. E.g. like attracts like. Then we say, 'See, I told you this would happen to me.' Having that belief in my earlier years caused me much grief and stress along with health issues. My life in general and my body were only 'reflecting' back to me what I had been sending forth.

There is a big difference between worrying and being concerned. Worrying over a situation means we cannot let the problem go, we repeatedly focus in on it, often causing us stress. Being concerned allows us to logically analyse a situation. If a concern is valid, see what we can do to resolve it. If unable to easily find a solution, share the concern with someone or ask for inner guidance and then hand it over. I assure you the guidance will come. The key is to trust.

How do we learn to trust in a power we cannot see? It can be challenging and takes inner strength and courage to step over our fears, let go and simply trust and be open to sensing the inner guidance to assist us. It may help to reread the experiences from chapter 23 – A Lesson in Letting Go, chapter 24 – Why We Ask Three Times and chapter 48 – Manifesting A Heart's Desire.

We can gain so much more in life by 'believing' in this power and then 'seeing' the results. It's important to keep our focus ahead on the end result we would like to 'see' happen, not on what we 'don't' want to happen. Refer to chapter 15 – Work Was Suffocating Him. The key for us all is to choose wisely what we intentionally focus our thoughts upon.

I often have to remind myself to create the reality I choose to have in my life instead of wasting energy focusing on what I don't want to happen by worrying. Unfortunately worrying lowers our vibrations and can affect our physical body in a negative way.

For me, this is a challenging process due to my insecurity issues. In saying that, I am grateful that I am more focused in the 'now' as spiritual guidance can more easily penetrate my awareness.

I remember seeing a movie once where two friends were walking along a street and one of the men was sharing a problem that was worrying him and his mate turned to him, asking, 'Does worrying help?'

'No,' he answered.

'Then let it go.'

Energy follows thought.

CHAPTER 51

A MOTHER'S CONCERN

One morning I woke up with a close girlfriend, Jill, on my mind. We met and became friends not long after arriving in Jakarta and had enjoyed a holiday in India together amongst other holidays away with our husbands. Jill kept coming in and out of my thoughts and I wondered if she was all right. Before I had a chance to call her, she rang me, telling me her mother wasn't expected to live much longer and could I send energy to both of them. Jill and her mum had always had an extremely close relationship.

In Jill's own words:

Some years ago, my mother was dying in hospital. At that time, my friend Yvonne was in Dampier, Western Australia and had not been told of what was happening as the health of my mother had deteriorated quite quickly. In a phone call to Yvonne to explain what was going on, she said she had a feeling to call me as I had been coming in and out of her thoughts. My mother died soon after and Yvonne immediately booked a flight to Perth to give me the support and love she knew I would need.

The night before the funeral, Yvonne was sitting in our home reading. My husband Bevan and I were working on the eulogy. Suddenly Yvonne broke the silence.

'Your mother just appeared in front of me. She is standing over there, waving a piece of paper.'

We both looked over to where Yvonne was pointing but couldn't see anything. We were both aware of Yvonne's gift and were unfazed by her comment. We all queried as to what it meant and after a lot of back-and-forth questioning, we finally came to the conclusion that my mother was trying to make me aware that I had missed including the names of two of our grandchildren in the eulogy I was intending to read.

The next morning Yvonne again saw my mother waving a piece of paper. Bevan and I quickly checked through the eulogy once more before leaving for the funeral but couldn't find anything wrong with it. It left Yvonne confused and querying as to why my mother appeared for the second time. Something was still disturbing her.

As weeks went by it became clear to us that the paper my mother was waving at us was none other than her will. Sadly, that little piece of paper caused a ten-year standoff between my brother and me, which has only just now healed. To this day I have no idea what caused my brother's reaction regarding the will.

Jill Oakes

CHAPTER 52

KEEPER OF THE LAND

I spent some days at home writing and allowing ideas and thoughts to flow freely until I started to feel the dreaded build-up of anxiety and then I would stop and take a break.

Some evenings I often walked down to the end of the cul-de-sac not far from the house we were renting in Dampier. I would sit and meditate on a ledge opposite a small section of natural bushland where I could look out over the Indian Ocean. Most nights the sunsets were stunning and the reflection from the sun sent a myriad of pink, purple and red hues stretching out as far as I could see.

One particular evening, I was sitting quietly, enjoying the peaceful surroundings when out of the corner of my eye I saw an Aboriginal lady suddenly appear on my right. I turned and faced her. She was dressed in a black skirt and floral blouse. Her thick black wavy hair rested on her shoulders. She was standing on the other side of the road near a large group of trees about twenty metres away. We smiled at each other and I was about to say hello to her when she vanished.

Oh, I thought, *I wonder why she is here?* As I continued sitting there, I couldn't help but think about her and wonder why she had appeared before me. About fifteen minutes later she reappeared, smiling at me again.

I sensed her say to me telepathically, 'I am the keeper of this land and its inhabitants.'

I smiled, nodding my head, acknowledging her before she again disappeared.

A few months had passed since my first encounter with the lady. Nearly every afternoon when the heat of the sun had lessened its sting, I would walk Karza through the narrow natural bushland track at the end of our cul-de-sac, winding our way down through the natural scrubland and trees to the road adjacent to the beach.

This particular day, Karza was slowly sniffing her way down, frequently stopping to leave her 'reservoir' of visiting cards on every fascinating smell. The same Aboriginal lady suddenly appeared on my right and put her hand up and out in front of her in an action that indicated for me to stop. I immediately stopped walking and reigned in Karza's lead, wedging her body in tightly between my sandaled feet. The woman kept her hand up. I knew I didn't see spiritual beings by chance, so I waited. Then, out from the bush half a metre in front of us and on our left came two small yet deadly dugite snakes approximately 40 centimetres in length each. I watched as they quietly slithered across the track in front of us into the bush on the other side. *Phew,* I thought. *That was close.*

The woman disappeared and we moved off quickly, walking down the track to the road, not wanting to linger in case other snakes were lurking around too.

I waited by the roadside, looking back, hoping she would reappear so that I could thank her but she stayed elusive. As I walked onto the beach, I realised the spiritual being had protected us from possible harm. If she hadn't stopped us and with Karza sniffing nearly every leaf in sight we may have walked straight into them with dire consequences. Karza always liked to lead the way and my first reaction would have been to save her. She was still tiny and didn't weigh very much.

After enquiring with the vet on one occasion regarding venomous snakes, I was aware of how quickly a small dog Karza's size could die if bitten.

I silently gave thanks to this precious spiritual being I named 'The Keeper of the Land' for saving us from possible harm. I stood on the beach processing the occurrence and wondered why I kept on seeing her. I had never experienced recurring visits from someone who had passed over, especially someone I didn't know. There was something about her that touched my heart; it was the warm loving vibration emanating from her.

After that close encounter, whenever I took Karza for a walk I wore long pants, socks and sneakers instead of open-toed sandals and shorts. I also became very vocal, making lots of noise and stamping my feet to keep the snakes from coming out. A neighbour told me snakes prefer to keep out of our way.

The soil in the northwest is a deep orange-red-coloured fine dust. I looked at Karza one morning and instead of seeing her all white and fluffy, she had turned into a fluffy redhead. Her coat had taken on a strong red tinge. I gave her a bath and was happy to see the red earth go down the drain and the white softness return.

Later that afternoon, I decided to take her to the oval adjacent to the beach for a quick play with the ball. I wanted to keep her white and fluffy until her daddy saw her looking and smelling gorgeous when he arrived home from work, knowing he would make a bigger fuss of her than he usually did.

I had a plan of action to keep her clean. Instead of letting her walk through the track, I picked her up and carried her, much to her dismay. We were halfway along the track when the Aboriginal woman appeared once again just ahead of me and again on my right.

I am not sure why I always see spiritual beings on my right or walk away from me on my right. My only logical conclusion is that they are continuing on their evolution, moving forward as the 1992 message indicated with the arrow moving clockwise. Refer to chapter 19 – Insightful Vision.

She was laughing at me, shaking her head back and forth and I sensed her say to me, 'Why are you bothering to carry her?' Then she disappeared.

I was really surprised as it was the first time I had seen a spiritual being laughing and I laughed out loud as well. Her delightful antics were contagious. I felt light and happy seeing her again.

On the oval, I started throwing the ball for Karza to chase and after about ten minutes, her little legs appeared to be changing colour. Sure enough, when she came back her legs, ears and whiskers around her mouth were again turning bright orange. The wind the previous night had carried the fine red soil across the oval, becoming attached to the blades of grass.

'Damn,' I said.

I looked down at Karza with her newly acquired orange legs and beard, who was impatiently jumping up and down, eagerly waiting for me to throw the ball again. I checked the time and decided to let her play a little longer, then when we returned home, I'd give her another quick wash.

I picked her up, carrying her back through the track with her little orange legs pointed straight up in the air. I was pleasantly surprised to see the Aboriginal lady appear once again. This time she was clapping her hands together and laughing at me. Her mannerism was infectious.

I laughed too and said out loud, 'You knew this was going to happen, didn't you?'

She smiled once again before disappearing. That was the last time I saw her.

How did this spiritual being know what was going to happen? Because they can see clearly what is going to transpire through their interconnection to all life. Refer to chapter 51 – A Mother's Concern.

Our lease expired on the house in Dampier in December 2006 to coincide with the owners' return from their world trip. We decided, after experiencing five cyclones during that year, I would return to Perth and Graham would continue working up north on a fly-in fly-out basis.

The night before we left, I walked down and sat at my favourite spot and thanked the beautiful spiritual being for looking after us while we'd been living there. Sadly, she didn't appear. I still laugh when I think of her and wonder if she is still protecting the land, the people and the native animals around Dampier.

After we returned to Perth to live, my inner work and commitment to healing my life opened another inner door for me to receive more in-depth visions relating to the Room of Knowledge as you will read in chapter 53 – Informative Vision.

CHAPTER 53

INFORMATIVE VISION

It had been five years since the last vision I experienced in 2003, relating to the Room of Knowledge. I was sitting in my office writing again when I paused in thought, looking out the window at the Swan River. Suddenly a vision formed in front of my eyes. This cluster of visions is the most lengthy and in-depth I have received to date.

The first thing I saw was *light-coloured fine gritty sand before a woman appeared dressed in a simple robe with a sash tied loosely around her waist. She walked down stone steps into the same main room I had entered in a previous vision, where the walls are covered in simple symbols.*

The woman was holding the hand of a small boy, who was wearing light-coloured clothing which hung loosely from his shoulders, stopping just above his knees. After a conversation, she handed him over to a man. He took the boy's hand and the woman left. My focus was drawn to the small boy and I felt a stirring of sadness.

At the time I thought my feeling of sadness towards the boy was because he appeared too young to be separated from what I assumed was his mother.

The vision quickly changed to another image. I saw that the young boy was now a strong young man sitting facing a much older man. I then saw the young man carving a symbol onto a large stone. When the symbol was completed, it was filled in with a blackish substance.

I sensed, after seeing this vision, the young man had been trained to connect with Spirit to receive a symbolic image and then draw and finally he connected the associated frequency and vibrational message to that symbol.

I saw many symbols all slightly different in appearance adorning the walls of this Room of Knowledge.

Another vision appeared and I was shown how the people accessed the support and inner guidance they were seeking.

I saw a woman with a shawl over her head, standing in the centre of the room until she felt drawn to walk over to and stand in front of one particular symbol.

The woman held her left hand out at chest level, palm facing outwards a couple of centimetres in front of the symbol without touching it. Closing her eyes, she stood in that position before withdrawing her hand, then placing her hand over her heart for a few seconds before quietly retreating.

During that ancient era, I sensed there were no churches as such where these people lived. It was not required; they trusted and believed the vibrations they felt coming from the symbol(s) was coming from a good uplifting power to support them.

The scene changed again and I saw boatloads of people arriving on their shores.

I sensed, over time, these people slowly introduced their own ideas, which differed greatly from the original people's simplistic philosophy of life.

Then in a flash, the vision changed. I saw the same young man a lot older.

The words I received were 'The man became the leader and keeper of the records.' *I saw him sitting in a meeting with other leaders. It was at this meeting the majority of men decided to close off access to the Room of Knowledge.* I sensed their intent was to gain power and control over the people, making them come to them for guidance instead of having one-on-one direct contact with Spirit.

When the visions stopped, I pondered over why a deep fear rose up within me as a result of the visions and again I felt sadness in my heart for the man.

I had no idea why I continued spasmodically to have visions related to what I called this Room of Knowledge. I wondered if the man I have seen being killed by a large boulder was the same man. If so, was he killed for refusing to close the Room of Knowledge? I couldn't understand or sense any connection between the man and me, except for the fear and deep sadness I felt for him. I now know I was not ready to go within to connect the memory threads to experience the truth.

As I typed up this vision in 2017 from my notes, I thought the action these men took closed the door to the 'light', so to speak, causing the people over time to doubt their inherent ability to have direct contact with Spirit to receive guidance. They were slowly conditioned to look outside of themselves for guidance instead of within, where each individual's power resides.

I thought to myself, *Wow, wouldn't it be wonderful if everyone had access to the Room of Knowledge again, just as those people did so long ago?* Then I realised we already have this one-on-one direct contact available.

I remember thinking in 1992, that the vision (chapter 19 – Insightful Vision) and the Room of Knowledge vision (chapter 20 – Stepping Forward) in 1993 were somehow interconnected. This last vision confirmed it.

The visions I've received over the years relating to the Room of Knowledge slowly started linking together.

Being back home again in Perth from living up in Dampier proved invaluable, becoming a time of contemplation and an opportunity to consolidate all my learnings to date with the intention of continuing my writing. The following three chapters explain my understanding of our energetic connection and how we can communicate to receive spiritual guidance.

CHAPTER 54

A SOUL'S ASSOCIATED FREQUENCIES AND VIBRATIONS

The information below is based on a symbol I was shown in 1993, giving me a simple framework of how I see our spiritual and physical composition.

Our **soul** resides beyond our third-dimensional physical reality and all our decisions are stored in our soul's **energy body.** Our **physical body** is a 'reflection' only of our soul's energy body's vibration.

Our inner spiritual world is made up of energy and the information flows, in the form of impressions/impulses into our 'master computer' – 'our soul'. It is our soul's strongly held beliefs that filter all incoming information and decide to either accept or repel the frequencies and vibrations the soul 'attracts' via its conscious thoughts and subconscious patterning using its energy body's electromagnetic field (some scientists call it a 'biofield').

The information we choose to retain is stored in our soul's energy body, also referred to as our subconscious mind, including our frequency of learning(s) for this life cycle, our past knowledge accumulated over many life cycles and any parental patterns necessary for supporting and triggering our learnings in this life cycle.

Our soul's energy body 'radiates' forth, adapting to accommodate the environment it moves into, manifesting as our physical body into third-dimension reality, 'appearing' to the human eye as a solid dense form.

Consciousness gives the soul and its physical body the ability to observe, interact, and understand subjectively and objectively at the soul's current level of openness to support the evolution of our soul.

What happens when the physical body dies?

The non-physical aspect of 'us' – that is, our immortal soul – detaches from the physical body and we once again live on in our natural form as a spiritual being. We simply step out of the physical body we occupied on earth. I was blessed to witness this transformation take place. Refer to chapter 47 – Roy's Passing.

Spiritual body – After we pass over, our soul retains three main features: firstly, our past life cycle experiences; secondly, aspects of our soul where our truths have aligned with our inherent nature and thirdly, the fragmented compartmentalised parts of our soul still requiring healing.

Prior to returning to Earth to begin another life cycle, a spiritual being receives its 'frequency of learning' for further evolvement, imprinted within the energetic configuration of their soul's energy body and the complex structure of their DNA. This frequency of learning is decided upon by the individual under the guidance of more advanced spiritual beings.

When I give an energy treatment to someone and my hands are often raised up above a person's body, the vibrations I feel in my hands are coming from a person's energy body, which can sometimes give me either a picture show, an image or a message.

How come? Because our energy body is the soul's body which in turn forms the physical body and from my understanding and my years of working with clients and students, our soul's expressive nature is always communicating back and forth between the desires of our heart and brain.

Our brain controls our cognitive abilities and many other complex processes that regulate our physiological function – including deciphering the frequencies and vibrations sent to it via our soul and outside environment.

Some messages flowing into our soul often bypass the brain and the information drops straight into our hearts. There are times when we definitely 'know' something without knowing it, so to speak, or we hear the voice of intuition speaking to us. That's when the brain may say, 'Where did that come from? I didn't authorise that.' It's also where we can bring balance between any disturbing opposing energies, e.g. sometimes our mind wants to retain a position of safety and control, which could relate to a fearful mental pattern, whereas the heart is saying 'yes, give it a go. Be bold, step outside of the square.' E.g. write a book!

I mentioned in the foreword that each of us is supported by a hierarchy of spiritual beings/guardian angels assigned to assist us through each life cycle. Our inner spiritual guidance can see the big picture and knows why we chose the life we are living now and for what purpose and offers us support and encouragement for achieving our goal/s.

What can hinder us from achieving our life purpose? Our fear patterns and negative beliefs carry a strong vibration and activate our inner resistance to change to protect us from harm and our fears can close the door to accepting positive changes, as in my case until I faced my fears and distorted beliefs.

The different aspects of our learnings in this life cycle come together as one single frequency (similar to a rainbow, with many colours all flowing from the one white prism of light) and align with our soul's physical body's dense vibrations. An individual's actions will continually be measured and adjustments made where necessary. This is where our inner guidance system helps us by offering encouragement to an individual to follow the pathway towards the goal they chose to achieve in this life cycle. That is, if they are willing for change to occur. Our freewill plays an important role in our soul's evolution. Each spiritual being has the freewill to give up on the goal they are aiming for. Unfortunately, if the goal is not achieved in this life cycle, they will have to return and repeat the same lessons before they can evolve further.

Why? Because the lessons a soul has chosen to learn in this life cycle are the next step forward in the soul's development.

You may recall I wrote about the inner driving force I sensed spurring me on, encouraging me not to give up on the frequency of learning(s) I chose to achieve in this life cycle. The driving force within me was my soul crying out for the pain I have harboured over eons to be healed.

One afternoon when Kouchi was six months old, we were out the front of our house in Perth doing some gardening when she snuck away and took herself off on a little adventure. We did not give up our search until we found her and she was home again.

It's the same with our soul; it will not rest until all the fragmented aspects of our soul are all reunited back to wholeness. It's our soul we can feel deep inside when we sense there is something missing or we feel unfulfilled. So often we continue looking outside of ourselves for answers and fulfilment in an attempt to comfort our unmet needs.

I often remind students who become despondent and impatient with their spiritual growth, 'It doesn't serve us to attempt to leap ahead to the next step before successfully accomplishing the previous steps.'

Our soul is learning to build a firm solid foundation aligning with innate universal truths from which to continue building upon in future life cycles, if required. It's important to live our lives with an open heart at our current level of understanding. When we do, our growth naturally progresses as designed.

Why? Because Consciousness is able to step in and guide us. We will experience unforeseen 'coincidences' taking place. We will find ourselves being guided to someone to assist us.

A soul living on Earth gravitates to an environment and works in a field(s), and associates with people who will challenge and/or support them to achieve their chosen goal(s). The people and the environment around them will 'reflect' back to them their qualities and also areas in their life requiring attention so their soul's true nature can unfold and shine forth. People are attracted to each other through their energy body's vibrations. Like attracts like.

Some people come into our lives for only a short time to reflect something back to us for gaining understanding and clarity. Or come to show us areas in our life where we have been lacking in self-worth/respect. Or in some cases, they come to show us where our ego (self-concept) is standing in the way of our progressing and sometimes we are reluctant to let go. As you have read, it has been my own 'resistance' to life's challenges I have encountered that created my inner disturbances.

When people trigger our resistance, it gives us an opportunity to look within and deal with our resistance so as to expand our conscious awareness to 'see' life more clearly. Often it's our loved ones around us who 'trigger' our gifts for learning.

Or if you easily admire a 'quality' in someone else that you may believe is lacking within you, then how did you recognise it in the other person? It's not possible unless the vibrational imprint is within you otherwise you wouldn't have been able to sense and observe it in them. Their gift back to you is to recognise that the quality you admired in them simply requires you to acknowledge and nurture its presence so it can manifest and shine forth from within you too.

The frequencies and vibrations our soul receives are 'impressed' upon us with the aim of uplifting our vibrations, expanding our awareness and deepening our understanding of life. We may feel an inner desire to pursue a certain goal, as in my situation regarding writing this book. My frequency of learning kept nudging at me, encouraging me not to give up and I am so glad I didn't. I am healing a frequency of learning I chose to overcome in this present life cycle, with the intention of freeing my partly blocked self-expression and fear of life.

Once a soul has achieved a frequency of learning in its current life cycle and the intended goal is fully realised, another door opens and another frequency of learning is released for us to continue learning on earth for expanding our soul's awareness towards the ultimate goal of total unification.

Energy follows thought.

CHAPTER 55

OUR SENSING SYSTEM

Our soul has a 'two-way' function due to its finely tuned sensing and filtering system.

Its sensing system communicates continuously as it receives impulses coming from either our inner or our outside environment. Our soul then distributes the messages and impressions accordingly; they either drop directly into our heart or go to our brain for deciphering so we can make sense of what we are receiving.

Our 'external' sensing system supports us to smell, see, hear, taste and touch, so we can be more aware of life's happenings around us. These frequencies and vibrations flow in, continuously feeding information to us concerning our outside environment through our senses. Our body will either subtly contract or expand to whatever we are experiencing, whether we are aware of it happening to us or not. This is explained in more detail in chapter 56 – Reading the Incoming Impulses.

Our 'internal' sensing system works exactly the same way. The more we expand our awareness, the clearer we can hear/sense Spirit communicating with us. It's possible to sense a loved one who has passed over, connecting with our energy body, causing our physical body to react: e.g., goosebumps. Refer to chapter 63 – Sid's Farewell Hug. Or we can utilise our senses to receive guidance and/or to see clairvoyantly deeper into consciousness to support our self and others.

Some call this internal system our sixth sense – intuition. Dictionary.com defines intuition as a 'direct' perception of truth, fact etc., independent of any reasoning process. The Voice calls it our inner guidance system.

Intuition is a normal and natural aspect of nature and we hear the small inner voice in our heart, indicating we either have an imbalance that requires attention and/or offering guidance and support.

Intuition always speaks quietly and gently in our hearts, never speaks harshly or uses words like you 'must' or you 'should'. From my experience, if I hear harsh words it's coming from head knowledge, not from the wisdom flowing in from our inner world.

Or we may sense a subtle intuitive impression which is an indication to stop and feel what Spirit is saying as our brain attempts to decipher what our soul has sensed.

Have you ever observed an animal after it has given birth to its newborn? 99% of the time, it intuitively knows how to look after them; its instincts take over because it's imprinted in its soul's DNA. Nature can teach us a lot about taking the time to just be and flow with life.

What is the difference between our inner and outer worlds? Our inner world is equally alive, vibrant and real as our outer world, although there is a big difference between the two. Our inner world's energy is not dense and solid in appearance. Earlier in this book, I spoke of Graham's deceased uncle (Refer to chapter 4 – A Life-Changing Experience) who manifested in front of me. At first, his form appeared as a swirling mass of energy before manifesting briefly. In contrast to our inner world's vibrational energy, our current physical world on earth holds a very dense vibration where everything appears solid to the physical eye, including us. Yet everything we can see and touch is the same energy appearing in a different form, vibrating so fast that it portrays an 'illusion' of solidity.

Some of our false belief patterns can also appear solid and unmovable until we realise they are only an illusion of solidity. Just as there are three aspects to the dissolving of an ice cube: e.g., from ice – solidity to water – liquidity, then it evaporates into 'air' – energy. There are three main aspects to our configuration too. Physical (solidity), energy body (liquidity) and spiritual – our soul (energy).

I visited Jakarta in 2007, sharing freely the information I had received with groups of students. Towards the end of a session, the students were sitting/lying quietly in meditation. I prayed, asking Spirit to bless and touch each one of them. I saw the spiritual energy descending on all the students. The energy particles flowing down looked similar to snowflakes, except these very tiny flakes floated down very slowly and gently. A couple of the students came to me afterwards asking if I knew what it was they had seen floating down in their mind's eyes. They left feeling very blessed to have seen the energy descending for themselves.

In another incident whilst still in Jakarta, I was shown one afternoon how everything forms on Earth. It had been a busy couple of weeks visiting friends and sharing with groups of students. Before leaving to fly back to Perth, my friend Marilyn Ardipradja and I went to Puncak for three days to a friend's holiday home to share time together prior to my returning to Perth.

We had just finished giving each other energy treatments. I ventured outside, sitting quietly under the shade of a tree, looking out at the surrounding countryside below from the hilltop. My eyes were drawn to a very large tree about 20–25 metres in front of me. Suddenly the solid tree disappeared and in its place was a huge mass of fast-moving vibrating energy surrounded by light, where the tree had stood. I could still vaguely make out a slight outline of the tree, even though the static-like energy was swirling around excitedly until suddenly the tree once again became a solid form. Spirit was reminding me; all of life is energy and our beliefs are not 'fixated' nor unchangeable – they are only 'liquidity', no matter how challenging some things may appear to us to overcome.

All the incoming impressionable impulses are intended to provide information, offering us support to move forward and expand our awareness of life. Spirit is always imparting wisdom to us on our journey towards recognising the enormity of who we are.

If you suddenly sense to listen more intensely to what someone is saying or to what is happening around you, it could be of immense support to you. When that happens to me, I have found that by taking a deep breath, I still my mind of any thought and slowly expand my awareness, quietly and gently feeling within to understand what my senses have subtly picked up. Often, more information becomes available. Our power lies in our breath and in the silence of the moment.

When supporting a client to resolve an issue, I tune into their energy body and if the client's issue is ready for it to be dealt with, Consciousness shows me firstly through sensations in my hands, then I often see the issue (mental/emotional energy blockage) clairvoyantly through an image or a series of images that forms in front of my eyes. Core memory threads reside in the cells of our body and these vibrations can affect the healthy functioning of our physical body. Learning to listen to and trust the intuitive information flowing into our awareness is a wonderful tool to master. It's our inner guidance system. Information is in the 'air' all around us.

We are all unique and how Spirit communicates with us can differ greatly. All that is required of us is to have the willingness to open our heart, to 'sense/listen' to the wisdom flowing in.

Each one of us appears as an individualised being yet in the big scheme of things, we are all interconnected to one whole big unit of Consciousness.

Do not be put off or influenced by other people's words. Seek your own inner guidance; feel your own truth in each moment. The reason I have mentioned this is because if I had continued to listen to other people's advice without going within for clarity or confirmation, I could possibly have ended up more confused as every person sees a situation from their current level of understanding through their own viewing platform. How clear a person's viewing ability is will depend on how much they have expanded their conscious awareness.

We are the only ones who truly know the best course of action to take. We can receive advice but ultimately the decision is ours alone to make. Whatever decision we make, we can still learn and gain understanding from our choices. Some decisions bring us unforeseen challenges but ultimately there is always a gift of learning from the choices we make.

If our vibrations are very low due to illness, tiredness or being unable to dismiss a worrying thought, we are often unable to receive clear and accurate inner guidance. We can never lose our connection to Spirit; however, we can close the door to sensing its presence.

Another reason we can shut down our connection is if we choose to avoid accepting or dealing with a painful experience, then we can easily allow that experience to overwhelm us. If that happens, we can either feel isolated, depressed, hurt and/or alone. The pain comes from our own inner resistance. You will read further on how I did just that to myself after we moved to live in Tasmania. Refer to chapter 62 – Hobart, Tasmania.

One thing I would like to recommend is to strengthen your self-worth and its importance to establish a firm foundation. That's something I didn't put enough effort into, causing me much anguish. I struggled with trusting the inner guidance I received for myself, causing much uncertainty to rise up. I was so keen to get to the end of my journey, I neglected to take the time to make sure my foundation was steadfast and firmly in place. Our viewing platform can strongly affect how we perceive life.

When I start to feel pressured, I ask myself, 'Am I being the turtle right now or have I become the hare? Am I pushing and racing ahead of myself instead of embracing and enjoying this journey as I imagine the little turtle did? I wonder if the turtle stopped every now and then to smell the flowers, as it slowly meandered down the path to the finish line?'

We are all on an adventure here on earth, exploring the many different faces of consciousness, whether we are aware of it or not. The key element to our inner journey is to trust the process and in doing so, we will each experience the wonderful end result as it reveals our soul's beautiful and unique authentic self. We are all born with the ability to heal.

CHAPTER 56

READING THE INCOMING IMPULSES

If I hear an untruth... my soul's senses react to the information flowing from our outside environment and I can physically feel my body slightly contract; it's a very 'subtle' feeling. This happens only in circumstances when I sense my awareness heightens, and I focus in on what is being said or happening around me. I have mentioned earlier that every word we send forth either verbally or non-verbally carries a frequency and vibration. It's the 'energy' of the 'intent' behind the correlation of words that can heighten a person's senses. I have mentioned before: our words create a thought form, a mould for the energy pattern to build upon and carries the energy of our intent.

An impulse coming from the outside environment could be a warning to heighten our awareness to be alert for what is about to happen or what is going on around us. Refer to Hierarchy of Spiritual Beings.

If I speak from a tainted intention... my senses will indicate to me when I have either handled a situation wrongly or spoken in a manner that does not resonate with my inherent nature. Again, my energy contracts. I get a disturbing feeling in my heart and solar plexus.

The more I have expanded my awareness, the more I sense the frequencies and vibrations I send forth, automatically responding internally to how I communicate with other people. The disturbance feels like a slight heavy sensation in my heart, giving me an opportunity to gain clarity from that experience.

I choose to live and express myself in such a way that my words and actions are harmless to myself and others. Yes, I certainly still fail at times and my heart quickly lets me know. I forgive myself and seek to learn from it and where necessary, correct or apologise for my actions. I do not berate or judge myself as I used to; I pick myself up and move on towards my goal.

When I speak or hear truth... my body and heart feels open, light and clear and my energy body expands. It's a joyful and comforting feeling. There is no tainted frequency to lower my vibrations because a truth vibration is whole and pure. It's an uplifting vibration.

Impression – A new idea pops in, giving me information to assist a project I am working on, or with the aim of assisting me to refine my nature. When an impression drops straight into my heart, bypassing my brain, I can feel confusion and my brain might yell out 'Hey, what's going on here?' It's my ego feeling threatened. Its concern is about protection and survival.

Inner impulses – A slight pressure builds, creating discomfort in my heart, telling me to stop, step back and look again when Spirit desires me to listen to the voice in my heart and not my head. Refer to chapter 35 – A Timely Coincidence.

An inner alert – Goosebumps sometimes appear on my body and / or I sense to heighten my awareness to what is happening around me, e.g., Karza and the snake experience. Refer to chapter 49 – Our Northwest Adventure. Or it could be a strong impulse to suddenly get up and make immediate contact with someone.

Following an impulse one morning at work, I suddenly excused myself and stepped out of a meeting and sensed strongly to telephone my mother. She had managed to crawl to the phone before collapsing with heart trouble. I asked a work colleague to call for an ambulance as I rushed to my car. The ambulance arrived at the same time I did and the paramedics saved her life.

When Spirit has a message for us to either help another person or in answer to a request we have sent forth to the universe, it can drop into our mind, come via a friend or in some other way – even a book! The key is to anticipate an answer. All we have to do is keep an open mind as to how the answer will present itself. Refer to chapter 21 – The Unexpected Guest.

Energy follows thought.

CHAPTER 57

THE VOICE'S POWERFUL REVELATIONS

There were now four of us living in our apartment in South Perth. We had purchased a playmate for Karza in the form of a little black and white very chubby bundle of joy, a seven-week-old Maltese cross Shih-Tzu. We christened her Zoet Fogarty. Karza thought Zoet was another toy for her to play with; in fact, she thought Zoet was her pet and she was ours. From the moment they met, they were the best of mates. Much to Karza's delight, Zoet idolised her big sister and followed her everywhere.

Karza loved her large teddy bears and other fluffy toys and would play for hours, tossing them over her shoulder. One evening when Graham was home for a few days on some much-needed R&R from Karratha, the dogs were chasing each other around when Karza, in her excitement, suddenly grabbed hold of Zoet's collar, tossing her over her head. We both gasped in horror as this chubby bundle of fur landed with a thud on her back. I jumped up and before I could reach her, Zoet stood back up, gave herself a big shake from her head to the tip of her tail and then scampered off after Karza.

After Graham left early one morning to fly back to Karratha, I made myself a coffee and walked back upstairs with Karza racing ahead leading the way into my office with little Zoet bringing up the rear.

As I was editing, I thought about how the process of writing this book was slowly bringing 'light' and understanding to the darkest corners of my life, gently removing blindfold after blindfold of untruths for me to see and experience life more clearly. I suddenly felt a strong inner urge to open the door for the second time to converse with The Voice. The last time I initiated a conversation with The Voice took place years ago in 1995 where I referred to The Voice as God and because I was still fearful towards our spiritual world, I closed the door on initiating any further two-way conversations.

My questions to The Voice were asked telepathically and when The Voice speaks to me the answers are always concise.

I didn't know how to start the conversation so I said...

Hello, Voice. Are you The Voice of Consciousness I heard in 1995?

'I am one voice.'

Voice, are you my spirit guide in this life cycle?

'I am and have been through many cycles.'

I have never forgotten the words spoken to me in 1995. They still touch my heart, every time I recall that conversation.

Refer to chapter 58 – God be Real to Me.

'Yvonne, the resonance of Truth always leaves a deep and lasting impression.'

Why haven't I heard your Voice strongly all the time?

'It wasn't necessary.'

Why was it important at those times?

'If you recall, it happened at significant junctures. All happenings are connected to a soul's desired purpose and their frequency of learning in their current life cycle. All soul's connections differ in frequency and vibration.

When I feel inner urges/nudges or hear an inner voice speaking in my heart, is it still The Voice of Consciousness?

'Yes. There are many variants to the flow of frequencies. ALL Consciousness is one. There are many individualised aspects to it.'

Like the spiritual beings I have seen, received support or information from. Are they all variants of Spirit's consciousness?

'Yes, all souls are.'

I have one more question. Is everything predetermined?

'All have freewill choice to move towards or away from their prechosen destiny. There have been moments during your life cycle where interference has been necessary to protect, confirm or stimulate movement of energy. All happenings are part of vital adjustments to a soul's frequency of learning.'

... Do you mean like checkpoints?

'Consciousness guides and governs all aspects within species. It is the blueprint for past, present and variable future life cycles.'

The message is a confirmation to me that we are all interconnected and Consciousness is the vehicle for 'seeing' and experiencing 'all' life living and for those who have passed over.

I sat wondering why our experiences and connection to this power differs so greatly between souls... we are all here learning about life, which stem from our past experiences, individual perspectives, frequency of learning and beliefs. All these attributes distinguish us from each other and how we see the world either limits or expands our ability to see life clearly. Spirit's ability to support us depends on our 'intention' behind how we utilise this potent energy and basically, it comes down to our beliefs and actions. It's a force that 'responds' to the soul and heart of a person's inner values.

In the following chapter 58 – God be Real to Me, I would like to share something that means a lot to me. The day I received that 1995 message I had been seeking to gain a deeper understanding of life. The words came vibrating through, touching my heart deeply. Each time I started articulating a question in my mind, the answers poured in, overriding my thoughts...

CHAPTER 58

GOD BE REAL TO ME

God be real to me. I asked... Fill me with your light.
It is already within you, feeding and sustaining you.
God, please 'touch' me!
I am in every movement of life energy within you.
Be near me, God!
Yvonne, breathe.
Who are you really, God?
I am you in expression.
Can I see you, God?
I am in every form you see; look in the mirror at your reflection!
How may I hear you, God?
Yvonne, are you ready to listen and experience my presence?
Yes.
Yvonne, are you ready to realise me?
Yes.
**Yvonne, open your heart, accept my presence to 'unite'
and live as 'One'.**
God... Are you my Consciousness?
Yvonne... I AM.

Yvonne Fogarty, 1995

CHAPTER 59

MEDITATION

There is a lot of information out there so I will touch on this subject briefly, pointing out ways I have found that work for me. I'm sure you will find the right form of meditation that resonates with you.

Basically, one aim of meditation is to reduce the mind chatter and still the mind, as we can accumulate so much during the day. Regular meditation heightens and enhances our overall wellbeing and leaves our mind and body calm and peaceful.

When I first commenced sitting and meditating, I could focus only for a couple of seconds before my mind wandered off. In fact, I really struggled with meditating until I was told about two techniques I have personally found helpful...

Either lie flat or sit whilst keeping the spine straight. Breathing in, I focus on the tip of my nose, feeling my breath flow in and out slowly through my nostrils. An Indian friend taught me that technique. Thoughts still pop in. The difference is these days I don't berate myself or give up like I used to. I gently refocus my attention on the tip of my nose again as I continue to breathe in and out.

Focus on feeling your lungs expand and deflate as you inhale and exhale. If your mind wanders, as soon as you become aware you drifted off, your focus is instantly back in the 'present moment', observing your breath again.

Another valuable gift from using a breathing meditation is that our breathing is always happening whether we are conscious of it taking place or not. Sometimes we can get distracted, focusing our thoughts on a past incident, bringing it into the present moment and reliving it. Or we start thinking about a future event, bringing those thoughts into the present moment, which can cause our body to tense up. Whether we are reliving the past or pre-empting a future experience, we could be inviting stress and anxiousness into the now moment. Our mind doesn't know the difference between what is real and what is imagined. Have you ever sat watching a scary movie and become so caught up in the movie that it feels real?

Spiritual power is always in the SILENCE of the NOW moment, never in the past or future and when we meditate, we are automatically connecting to our 'home base'.

CHAPTER 60

OUR MOVE TO TASMANIA

Living in South Perth was comfortable and easy. We had many friends and family around the state. Graham and I could walk over the Narrows Bridge into Perth CBD in twenty minutes if we chose not to drive, or we could walk three minutes to the ferry terminal. Sixteen restaurants were within walking distance. We had access to the freeway not far from the corner of our street to take us easily in any direction we chose. The views from our penthouse apartment were picturesque, overlooking the Swan River and the city. Walking beside the river was a pastime the four of us enjoyed immensely. It was perfect in so many ways and a wonderful place to be residing. The energy stirred inside me, instilling within me deep unrest. *What was wrong with me?*

After much contemplation, I realised my strong inner connection had heightened my sensitivity to the environment around me. I felt uncomfortable living in such a busy environment. Perth had grown immensely during our many years away. With the mining boom up north of Western Australia, many things we had enjoyed about Perth had changed.

We had never envisaged that Perth would not remain our permanent home, but we both felt Perth had outgrown us in many ways and we desired a quieter lifestyle. We started looking at properties down the southwest of Western Australia, thinking it would give us a more laidback, peaceful environment. But nothing appealed. We even looked around Cairns, north of Queensland, during a brief holiday catching up with Jakarta friends.

One morning, almost simultaneously, we both had the same idea. Why don't we take a short trip to the island state of Tasmania? We had never visited that state before. Within a week of arriving, we knew we had found where we wanted to live in retirement. We fell in love with Tasmania.

Within a few months of our visit to Tasmania, Graham decided on an early retirement; all our belongings, cars and dogs were now on the northwest coast of Tasmania. Tasmania is very laid back, which makes for a peaceful and relaxing environment; it has a quaint innocence about it.

Friends who have visited us here are surprised at how welcoming the people are. Nearly everyone we meet is friendly and most people we pass by as we walk around doing our shopping say hello or nod to us. Hobart reminds us of how Perth was 30–40 years ago.

As for the food – oh dear, one look at my waistline says it all. The local, fresh chemical-free meats, fruit and vegetables are enticing. The landscape and countryside are lush and green most of the year. Within twenty minutes travelling south from the centre of the capital city Hobart, you find yourself amongst the picturesque countryside.

Most of the time we fill our lungs with crisp clean air, except when Tasmania experiences a destructive bushfire. Tasmania is a haven for us after living in heavily polluted environments for many years in cities with millions of people.

Another big plus is experiencing four distinct seasons again, something we missed while living in Asia. Acclimatising to Tasmania took me a while as it was challenging to adapt to a much cooler climate in winter. I do not miss the long hot summers in Perth anymore with its prolonged periods with the temperature often exceeding 37 degrees Celsius.

The other main city, Launceston, is in the north of Tasmania. The surrounding area is also beautiful; the soil is a deep red, perfect for growing vegetables, and they breed some very healthy stock.

After our move in 2010, the intensity of my anxiety was getting worse every time I thought I was getting somewhere with the book. Even though I received encouragement and inner guidance, unfortunately I continued to struggle with my writing. The anxiety I had previously felt when sitting to write now overwhelmed me. I couldn't understand what could still be in the way of totally clearing whatever fear was preventing my self-expression from flowing freely. I desired to write with the words flowing freely from heart knowledge, not coming from 'knowing of something' (head knowledge) but from living it.

In the end I decided to stop writing again because I had difficulty handling the intense feelings that rose up. I asked myself, *if I am to write this book, why is it so hard? Does it mean I am not meant to be doing this?*

On the spur of the moment, we purchased a beautiful block of land with 360-degree views from the ocean to the inland mountains and we set about designing our new home. We, unfortunately, started to miss the varied restaurants we were used to experiencing and the live theatre, amongst other things. Again, we started to feel unsettled and ended up selling our block of land.

One afternoon, before our move to Hobart, I decided to have a long-overdue massage at a wellbeing centre not far from where we were living ...

CHAPTER 61

FIONA'S BEST FRIEND

During the remedial massage, I was suddenly drawn out of my slumber, focusing in on where Fiona was massaging my back. As I observed her movements, I was surprised to see a small black dog sitting on top of her hands. As her hands moved slowly over my back, I watched in fascination as this little dog continued to move with them. I thought, *This is a first. What an unusual thing to see.*

Why am I seeing you? What are you attempting to show me? I asked the dog. I wondered if Fiona had recently lost a dog. I didn't say anything until her hands moved to my right leg and the dog followed. *This is wacky,* I thought. *I have to say something; I won't be able to enjoy my massage until I do.*

I hesitated slightly before blurting out, 'I hope I don't upset you by asking, but have you lost a dog recently? I have been observing a small black dog with a touch of white on its head and on one front paw. Every time you move your hands, the dog moves with them. It's as if the dog is attempting to get your attention. Does that make any sense to you?'

She stopped massaging me and walked around to the front of the massage table. I swivelled my head to face her as her eyes welled up with tears.

'Yes, my little dog Toby became ill and had to be put down a few months ago. He was fourteen years old. I miss him so much. I should have named him Shadow instead of Toby because he followed me everywhere. He was my best friend. We had such a strong bond between us. I had him from six weeks of age and I miss him terribly. I keep a photo of him on my refrigerator and another on my bedside table. I think I know why he is after my attention; I have been so busy lately he must be feeling neglected. I haven't told anyone else this but I still talk to him when I'm home. There are times when I look down at my feet because I feel as if he is sitting there beside me.' Then she added quickly, 'And I haven't been meditating like I usually do and I used to talk to him then too.' Tears spilled out, rolling down her face.

I took her hand and said, 'I think you have been sensing him around you and that's why you talk to him.'

She was quiet for a few moments, pondering over what I had just said, then she looked at me excitedly.

'I think you are right. I do feel as if I am sensing him, but I thought it might just be my imagination. I kept on talking to him anyway because it comforts me and it feels natural.'

'Toby is definitely around you. I don't think he has any plans to leave you. He is missing getting his usual attention from you and that's why I could see him following your hands. This is his way of letting you know he is around and you are not crazy talking to him. He loves it.'

We both laughed and she said, 'From the time I got him, there was a special heart connection between us. He was very demanding and always nudging me with his nose, wanting to be the centre of my world. It was as if he couldn't get enough cuddles from me. Tonight, I am going to light a candle, sit down and put his photo in front of me and have a long talk with him. Thank you for telling me what you saw. I thought if I told my friends I spoke to Toby and felt him around me, they might think I'm crazy.'

If you experience sensing someone around you, it could be a loved one. Acknowledge them and open your heart to feel/sense who they may be. Our loved ones are around us; welcome them, chat with them. They are still living, just not in their physical body anymore where they can easily be seen and acknowledged.

Our much-loved pets are especially close to us. The more open we are, trusting what we sense and feel, as in Fiona's experience, the more we can experience comfort and love. You may remember reading in chapter 31 – The Power of Love when Kouchi came to say goodbye. Since then, over the years, I have seen her three more times.

CHAPTER 62

HOBART, TASMANIA

In late 2012 we moved from the northwest of the state, renting a property twenty kilometres south of Hobart where we felt there was a better infrastructure for all our requirements now and in the future. I enjoyed living in Tasmania even though I missed my friends and family.

My inward journey had reached another level and without any warning, I woke up one morning feeling as if I had hit a massive impenetrable brick wall.

Within a week I felt as if I was stuck in a dark tunnel. I surmised; my inner connection had deserted me. I felt empty and hollow inside, lost and confused. I felt as if I had lost a vital part of myself.

I had no idea what was happening to me. My heart was heavy, I couldn't hear any inner guidance speaking to me in my heart. Nothing. I felt dead inside. I longed for the precious inner connection that had always been there since I was young to return. I wondered, *Had I taken this connection for granted? What have I done to lose this connection?*

I wallowed in bucketloads of self-pity. After all these years of inner development, it felt as if I had gone back years in my growth. I ended up getting a few illnesses. Firstly, I came down with the flu, then sinus infections and later debilitating vertigo, which I had never experienced before. I became depressed, isolating myself from others.

I realised my illnesses were due to my inner resistance. Ugh! I had not let go and accepted the decision we jointly made to move here and embrace all the wonderful offerings of Tasmania. My longing for Perth and friends had drained my energy, thus lowering my vibrations. I was homesick.

This heaviness and isolation lasted about six weeks; it was a very testing time (for Graham too!) One day while walking the dogs along the foreshore of the northwest bay inlet, I remembered how Mum couldn't come to me because her vibrations were too low. (Refer to chapter 18 – Healing for My Mother and Me.) I wondered, *have I done that to myself?* I knew instantly the answer. Of course, I had. How could I receive support when my vibrations were so low? By allowing my vibrations to drop so low, I had immersed myself in despair and feelings of hopelessness.

I recalled something I had shared with students and mentioned earlier in the book – 'If our energy is not "now-here" present, it is "no-where" to be able to fully support us.' My energy had been focused on the past. No wonder I went down in a heap. My energy wasn't where it could easily support and uplift me in the present moment.

I forgave myself and I asked for nothing, not even for my connection to return. I simply kept focusing on seeing the beauty of life around me and showing appreciation and gratitude for everything.

March 2013 came along and I woke up one morning realising the heaviness and isolation I had been feeling had completely gone. I felt alive again. My connection had returned. I was so relieved.

I hadn't lost my connection at all. In fact, it's impossible. We are all interconnected through Consciousness. I recalled words The Voice had spoken to me years earlier… *'The Voice you hear – it is you. It is I. We are really One.'*

Why do I keep forgetting that? *I am still not absorbing this truth in my heart, why? Is it my past mental conditioning that results in my slipping back into old habits of thinking? Am I still seeing Spirit's power* *as being separate from me in some way, instead of accepting I am an element of this power?* I wondered.

Spirit was quietly waiting for me to step over my feelings of hopelessness and raise my vibrations again. It was a really good lesson for me to remember to always consciously 'accept' the choices and decisions I make. Although I am a spiritual being, I am, for now, in a human body who can often mess things up, but Spirit understands and support is always available.

Through that experience, I realised it is so easy to take things for granted, so instead of my focusing on connecting 'to get', my focus had changed to a desire to connect to just 'BE' a vastly different intention, which is all-encompassing.

We are here to be creative, explore and experience life. It's our birthright to seek inner support. I learnt some very valuable lessons through that experience. We can never lose our inner connection; however, we can close the door to sensing guidance by lowering our vibrations through our thoughts and attitude.

For over twelve months we had been looking all around the surrounding areas of Hobart for a property to buy. One day I woke up with the idea to put our names down with a number of agents, with the intention of obtaining a property prior to it going on the open market.

The house we eventually purchased, and currently live in, came to us through a couple of visions. The house is perfect, although I didn't think so the first time I saw it. I was drawn to contemporary houses; instead, this spacious house is totally different. The design is very similar to an English Georgian manor house with a long oval driveway. The house is situated on one-and-a-half acres surrounded by gardens and lawns. It is nestled on top of a hill with sweeping views overlooking the Northwest Bay, Bruny Island and around to Mount Wellington. It is a beautiful and serene place to live. Graham likened finding our home to a British television show called 'Escape to the Country'. The last house a couple is shown is what they call the 'mystery house' – a quite different house to their specified criteria yet it fulfilled everything on their list of requirements and more.

We particularly enjoy seeing the different species of wildlife, namely rabbits, wallabies, bandicoots and the odd echidna, various species of birds, goannas and yes, snakes – *yikes!* I have seen one snake on our property as it took itself on an afternoon slither across our lawn. I quickly reminded myself to surround the whole area of our property in white light.

After a long rest from writing, I attempted once more to write and after a frustrating internal battle, I again became extremely anxious crippling my ability to think clearly. Disappointed and disgruntled after fifteen years of attempting to complete this book, I finally gave up in a flood of tears, disappointment and frustration. I had spat the dummy, so to speak. My dozens of notebooks, loose notes and umpteen files of documented information (recorded since the 1980s) were all stacked away in each of our office cupboards.

Friends would ask me, 'How's the book going?'

'It's not,' I would reply. 'I've come to the conclusion writing isn't for me.'

I could feel the sadness in my heart as I spoke.

Instead, I made a commitment to focus on my health. When we'd moved to live south of Hobart, I started feeling fearful and anxious whenever I drove around a large section of rock face on the southern outlet highway heading into Hobart. As soon as I approached that winding section of road, the discomfort would start. I knew my sensitivity easily absorbed things and I realised later I was subconsciously recalling the near-miss accident I'd experienced with a truck in Dampier. (Refer to chapter 50 – Divine Intervention.)

The memory from the 2006 incident was still resident in my energy body. It surprised me. I wasn't physically hurt but the frightening experience had buried itself in my subconscious mind, causing a fearful reaction every time I drove around the high rock face heading into Hobart.

Once I realised the cause, I was able to clear the fear from my energy body and now I can drive into Hobart without any inner discomfort. It's interesting how our psyche absorbs trauma and hides it away and if not dealt with can cause emotional blockages, stopping the natural flow of energy intended to sustain our mental, emotional and physical body's wellbeing.

CHAPTER 63

SID'S FAREWELL HUG

Our grandfather was one of the original settlers at Yoongarillup near Busselton, Western Australia and the dairy farm was handed over to my uncle before being handed down to my cousin, Sid Slee, who was eighteen years older than me (I was the last in a long line of cousins. Yes, I'm the baby of our extended family!)

Sid's health had been declining slowly and once again he was back in the hospital. Upon hearing this, I attempted to telephone him a few times without success.

Just before Christmas 2015, I again rang the hospital and this time he answered the phone. He was his normal, witty, cheeky self, although I could tell his voice sounded weary. I raised my voice and said, 'What have you been up to this time? If you don't get yourself well again and out of the hospital, I am going to have to fly over there and spank your bottom.'

'I'd like to see you try,' he replied, laughing.

Sid and his brother Brian were both over 1.8 metres tall and as a child, I used to tilt my neck right back to look up at my gorgeous cousins.

Sid was always full of life and we had such fun whenever we visited the farm. Sid and his wife Imelda's home was my safe haven when younger from my sometimes-turbulent home life. I have so many fond memories of holidays on their dairy farm.

During the telephone call with Sid, I told him I would ring again in a few days to check up on him to make sure he was still behaving himself and recovering.

On the 30th of December, my husband and I had been out for a long, leisurely lunch. That evening I was sitting, reading, when I felt a sudden uneasiness stirring in my heart. Before I had a chance to focus in on the feeling, our doorbell rang, announcing the unexpected arrival of some neighbours.

Later, we waved them goodbye. Graham ushered the dogs back into the house and I closed the front door. When I turned around, I was suddenly aware of someone's arms encircling me, giving me a hug and my whole body from head to toe broke out in goosebumps. I sensed the person was big in stature and the impression I received was that the person's energy felt 'larger than life'. I could feel love emanating from this person. Then the apparition disappeared. I couldn't see who it was as they didn't materialise; all I saw was the outline of a person whose body appeared to be made up of a slight bluish-grey energy with a gold tinge surrounding it.

Even after the person disappeared, I could still feel the deep impression made by the embrace as the goosebumps, love and warmth lingered on. The encounter left me with a huge smile on my face. I instantly knew the way the hug was given to me was specifically intended, to be experienced with a mischievousness attached to it. It was definitely not intended to be a too soon-to-be-forgotten embrace. *Oh!* I thought. *It could be Sid being his cheeky self.* I have always felt a very strong heart connection with Sid. I wanted to laugh because of how I felt when he hugged me.

I said to Graham, 'I think Sid just gave me a huge cheeky hug.' Then my smile turned to concern. 'Oh, maybe he has taken a turn for the worse and is in a coma.'

'Why don't you ring the farm and check on him?'

I thought about Graham's suggestion. 'No, I'll ring the farm in the morning, I don't want to disturb the family tonight.' I prayed for Sid before going to bed and sent him loads of love.

Before I had a chance to ring the farm the next morning, I received a call from my second cousin Wendy to say her father had died last night. They had decided to wait until the next morning to ring me as they knew I would be extremely saddened by the news. I was upset and didn't talk for long. I rang Wendy back later and shared with her that Sid had 'called in' last night and had given me the most beautiful goodbye hug. I knew she would understand.

Graham and I flew to Perth for the funeral. I was teary throughout the service, not only because of the situation but because I realised how much I missed all our family. Towards the end of the service, all the family walked up to say goodbye to Sid. The family placed things on his coffin. I didn't have anything. My intention was to lightly touch the coffin. When I reached out to touch the coffin, I shocked myself by spontaneously smacking the coffin lightly with my hand saying quietly, 'Sid, I told you I would come and smack you if you didn't get better.'

Wendy saw me do it and quietly laughed despite the somberness of the situation. 'It would have been just like him to tap back at you if he could,' she whispered.

The cousins later thanked me for changing a solemn moment to a joyous one as we remembered his fun personality. I was actually quite embarrassed by my spontaneous action.

After returning home to Tasmania, I was talking on the phone to Imelda when she said, 'You will never forget the day Sid died, will you?'

I continued holding the phone to my ear as I searched my blank mind in an attempt to grasp her meaning when she added, 'Yvonne, don't you remember? Sid died on your birthday.'

'Gosh, yes, so he did. I had forgotten that. Imelda, I definitely won't be sad on my future birthdays because Sid left a precious long-lasting birthday gift that will always remain deeply embedded in my heart – his mischievous hug.'

CHAPTER 64

PARIS, FRANCE, LATE 1700S – PAST LIFE REGRESSION SESSION

While living in Jakarta in 1996, Ida (a Reiki student) and a woman by the name of Gail asked me to help her heal Ida's friend, who was a very prominent person in Jakarta and had been affected by black magic.

Some people were seeking to destroy him with the intention of gaining a powerful and highly sought-after government position and had consulted a 'dukun' (commonly known as a witch doctor) to perform the task. Black magic, known as 'ilmu hitam', is found throughout Indonesia. Before being taken by car to meet him, we were advised that our healing work with this gentleman, his name and his position of power were never to be revealed.

I had no prior knowledge of black magic in Indonesia until I too felt the effects of it in a small way and I cleared it from my body myself. Later a close friend was also affected by this destructive energy, which can have a debilitating effect on a person's body.

There are many different reasons people go to see a 'dukun'. For some, they desire to learn to play with this energy to attract power and money; for others, it's to attract a husband or to punish someone. The most destructive is to use the energy with the intention of crippling or destroying a person's life.

I've been told by Indonesian friends it is common to use dukuns to stop the rain from hampering an important outdoor event in the country. Detailed experiences and healings as a result of this form of energy will be explained in my next book.

After supporting the gentleman to clear the energy from around his energy body, and prior to Gail returning to Europe, she casually asked me, 'Have you ever had a past life regression session?'

'No, I haven't,' I said.

I agreed to a regression session, partly out of curiosity, and I asked if it's possible to focus on an era, which could connect me to the cause of my still partly blocked self-expression and anxiety. Ida advised me it certainly is possible.

I felt strongly that there may be another layer to be cleared before my expression could flow freely. You may recall reading I remained anxiety free until 1999 when I began the journey of writing this book, which triggered anxiety again.

This session took approximately two hours, which was recorded as I relived a sad and painful past life in Paris, which I assumed, after doing some research, took place in the late 1700 and into the 1800s. I found the experience quite challenging emotionally...

In the first scene...

I saw and sensed his parents were of noble birth and taken away by horsemen in blue uniforms while the family was having a picnic by a lake in the gardens of their stately home. He was their only child (approximately 3–4 years of age) and was left on the lawn with the servants and he never saw his parents again.

I felt his pain at seeing his parents being taken away. He was traumatised and the shock and sadness of being abandoned so suddenly registered deep within his psyche.

The scene changed.

I saw him older, possibly twelve years of age, standing in the gardens of the same expansive family home at the edge of the small lake near where his parents had been taken away. He was a handsome boy, fair-

haired with deep blue eyes. He was playing with a reed, sweeping it back and forth across the top of the water, causing a rippling effect as he made a vow in honour of his parents.

He said, 'When I am in a position of influence to make a difference, I will strive for peace not war. Pain and sadness hurts too much.'

I sensed that his parents were executed as it was a time of great unrest in Paris. I cried out as I felt the deep anguish and pain he harboured.

When he became an adult, he inherited and/or was offered a position of power after his uncle died. He joined a large group of influential men. I saw him walking into a very large room where they held meetings. It was here where decisions were made that I sensed could greatly affect the country. I then saw a flash of red and soldiers fighting.

I sensed an aloofness about him, which I assumed was due to his status.

During one such meeting, he was too afraid to stand up and speak his truth in the hope of influencing for peace and not war. Instead, he stayed silent, fearing what would happen to him if he did speak up, exposing his views openly. He harboured a deeply embedded fear that he too might be killed as his parents were for their beliefs.

Leaving the meeting, he knew he had failed yet again to honour his parents' memory and the vow he had made when young. He had sat in on many meetings in the past and realised he had left it too late to have the courage and inner strength, to stand up and speak his truth.

He buried his pain and stopped feeling deeply by living a very shallow existence. He became a playboy. He wasted his life partying and drinking too much in the hope of dulling his pain.

I then saw an image of him as an old man sitting by the fire in his home. The last words he spoke were, 'I died with a tortured soul. I felt inadequate, a failure. Don't hide and waste your life. I was too afraid to stand up for what I believed in. I never fulfilled my purpose by following my heart and speaking my truths.'

Upon hearing his words, I let out a deep long heartfelt agonising moan and I wept for a soul in pain. I can only surmise by the last image I saw of him; he died alone, possibly while sitting in a chair by a fireplace.

Unfortunately, in conjunction with my beliefs and my ignorance at that time, I quickly dismissed the past life regression session as 'hoo-ha', or maybe his words hit too close to home and I wasn't emotionally ready to go there, or more likely I was in denial. I told myself I couldn't see the connection to what I experienced, other than his pain and emotions I experienced very strongly during the session. In saying that, deep inside I sensed what I had experienced was the truth. At that time, my mind had been unwilling to connect the memory threads to that experience, thus blocking me from connecting the dots to open a door for healing to take place.

As I am writing this, I can now understand the younger me in 1996. I believe my mind was closed off in an attempt to protect myself from delving too deeply. I was not mentally ready to handle the bottled-up emotions that were seeking release. I feared what I might uncover if I did.

The energy continued working quietly below the surface of my conscious awareness, gradually gathering all the loose memory threads together and preparing to bring them to the surface of my conscious awareness for healing to take place when the timing is right.

I am glad I had that unfulfilled experience back in 1996 because it helped me with my healing work to understand how important it is to only do regression work when the client is mentally ready to connect the memory threads together for healing to happen.

I would like to add here I will not do a past life regression if asked. The reason being that the past life recession I participated in left me in a state of flux. I had no memory threads readily available to link me clearly to the experience other than curiosity and the deep emotion I felt regarding his life and the word 'truth' that resonated with me. That experience actually left me floundering and continued to disturb me. There had been no closure. I was left hanging without threads tying together to complete a healing circuit. Since then, I often thought about that regression yet I still couldn't see a clear connection between that man's life and mine.

I know through my work the energy always completes a healing circuit during a session. I have no idea where a treatment is headed when I receive the first image or words. Slowly, Consciousness brings clarity to all the images, tying all the threads together to complete a healing circuit. The insights I receive clairvoyantly and pass on to the person can open a door in their mind. Finally, the energies come together, forming a deep inner knowing coupled with the understanding, as a new awareness/truth becomes embedded in their psyche.

I have worked with many clients and on occasion during a treatment when the timing was right, we have automatically connected back into a past life.

When that happens, a door automatically opens for the person. I only see the relevant connecting threads to their current issue connected to the relevant past life, playing out like flashes of small movie clips in front of my eyes.

How do I see these images? All our history is recorded in our soul's energy body and consciousness operates by showing me images that are relevant to the client's issue.

Clearing a specific issue heals and clears the blockage that was in the way of them moving forward. When the client's current issue has been connected back energetically to a core past life experience and mentally realised by the client, they know intuitively and understand the 'why and how' the two experiences are connected. When they let go of the pains of the past that had been influencing their lives, they are able to move on free of the encumbrance. It's wonderful to see the end result. Clients' actual experiences related to healing past life traumas will be explained in more detail in my next book.

The threads to my current issue and the 1996 regression all came together for release when I was in Paris in 2016...

CHAPTER 65

PARIS, FRANCE 2016

In early July, when my partly completed manuscript and notebooks were still packed away, we went on holiday, touring parts of Europe we hadn't yet visited before joining a river cruise from Budapest to Amsterdam and ending our holiday in Paris.

A couple of days before arriving in Amsterdam, I was lying on a deck chair on our balcony, enjoying the picturesque scenery and most of all enjoying how calm and peaceful it felt as the ship slowly glided over the calm waterways. I was excited; our final stop was to spend a few days in Paris. I had always felt a pull to go there; my heart was calling me.

In fact, while living in Jakarta I had a yearning to learn French instead of the Indonesian language. My husband couldn't see any logic to my desire. Ha, nor could I!

As I lay back dozing on the deck chair, The Voice spoke to me,

'Yvonne, write your intention of what you desire to achieve in the coming year.'

I hadn't heard from The Voice for a while and I was surprised. *Oh okay,* I thought. I picked up my notebook and pen and without any hesitation, I immediately wrote one sentence: *'my number one desire is to be free of my fear of writing and free my self-expression to complete the book.'*

I realised if I were to die tomorrow, my biggest regret would be that I hadn't fulfilled my desire to write books and share my simple wisdom and experiences of life.

On the third day of our holiday in Paris, I stepped off the tour bus in an old area of Paris and the instant my feet touched the ground, I turned to the tour guide and said to her in a surprised voice, 'Oh! I am suddenly feeling such emotion for Paris.'

'Yes, many do have that feeling when visiting Paris,' she replied.

I thought, *Okay I'm just having a normal reaction.* As we were led through an archway to the area where Louis XIV had once resided, I became more emotional; I could feel a deep discomfort rising up from my abdomen moving into my heart. I turned my head away from the Palais Royal and glanced to my left. I could see a park enclosed by a wrought iron fence. People were walking around the grounds, some were sitting on seats reading and/or eating, whilst others sat looking around soaking in the sunshine. As I continued absorbing the scene before me, the pain and emotion in my heart became stronger, causing my body to shake slightly as tears began trickling down my face. I thought, *What's happening to me? What's this reaction I'm having?*

I briefly glanced back to see where Graham was, I guess for reassurance, and in that brief moment just as I turned to look back at the park, a vision appeared and the park transformed before my eyes, becoming much larger...

I was looking out at another era. I could see well-dressed people, the men in fancy attire and women wearing elegant long dresses, either walking or riding around on horseback.

Suddenly, an elegantly dressed man appeared on the pathway. He wore a deep blue outfit and a top hat. As he rode towards me on a beautiful white horse, he was staring at me. I sensed a deep familiarity about this man, not physically but a deep heartfelt connection, especially when we locked eyes on each other. We both continued holding eye contact with such intensity, I felt as if his blue eyes and my eyes were fused together. In that moment, something happened between us, causing even more emotion to rise up.

As he passed by, a shiver vibrated throughout my body. A deep intimate connection and knowing passed between us. It felt as if we both understood our hidden pain and why we had both closed ourselves off to life, locking our feelings away deep inside. I stood watching him as he continued riding towards the Palais Royal before vanishing.

I realised, in that nanosecond of time, my past and present life cycles had merged briefly. It's very difficult to find the words to express with clarity this interaction; the transference of energy that passed between us was an extremely deep knowing that reached into 'our' soul and I felt deep heartfelt compassion towards him. I closed my eyes, taking a deep breath in an attempt to control my emotions and when I reopened them all the surroundings were as before. I immediately thought this had to be the same man I saw during the regression session in 1996.

I turned away, walking back to the archways, resting my hand on one of the large round columns for support. Flashes of scenes appeared before me so I quickly removed my hand from the column to stop the images from appearing in an attempt to regain control. I purposely slowed down my breathing as I battled to pull my emotions together.

Graham came over as he could see I was visibly distressed. The emotion and pain flowing out of me were something I had never experienced before. I was releasing the buried pain and grief stored in 'our' soul that I had carried with me from that past life cycle. I intuitively knew things about the park and the area in general.

I shared the experience with Graham. He then walked over and spoke to the guide who confirmed that the park used to be quite large and at one time was used only by people of a higher status.

As Graham went to walk away, she added, 'and it's not far from here where they beheaded people,' then she quickly added as an afterthought, 'including nobility!'

By the time we arrived at the Eiffel Tower, all the pain and emotion I experienced had completely dissipated. Although I felt drained emotionally, the connection was gone. The distraction was good for me and we did what most tourists do – we went to the top of the Eiffel Tower and had our photo taken, despite my husband's grumbles.

As our group was slowly making its way back to our coach, one of the ladies approached me. 'How are you feeling now? I hope you don't mind me asking as I was watching you earlier. Do you think you may have had a past life experience this morning?'

I was surprised. I thought I had hidden my reaction well, turning and walking far away from the group and hiding behind my sunglasses but obviously, I hadn't. She went on to say it reminded her of a similar experience she had years before while on a visit to Italy.

'I haven't delved into my feelings as yet, but it certainly shook me up,' I told her.

I chose not to talk about the past life experience at that time as I was still attempting to come to terms with what happened myself. I thanked her for her concern before gently redirecting our conversation.

That evening I documented what had transpired and recalled as much as I could remember of the past life regression session back in 1996. I felt confident it was definitely the same man with fair hair and blue eyes that I had seen.

The following morning, the day before we were to fly home, I felt lighter. I chose not to focus in on my feelings at that time and my thoughts were soon focused elsewhere as we set out to enjoy our last day in Paris.

Upon arriving home, we received a warm welcome from our friend Christine who looks after our dogs whenever we are away and we always received a very vocal welcome from our fur kids, filling our hearts with joy, whether we've been away for a few hours or weeks.

I woke up a few days later feeling extremely light and joyful.

I excitedly dug out the notes I had transcribed from the tape of the 1996 regression session and sat, feeling the past and recent experiences. After rereading everything carefully a couple of times, I knew without any doubt I had come face-to-face with myself from a past life and it wasn't an aloofness I had sensed around him; it was a protective barrier.

Consciousness brought about this healing and I reminded myself yet again that Consciousness knows 'no' boundaries. A big shift had taken place within my conscious awareness. I realised in that brief moment in Paris, I had merged together a past and a present life cycle. The interaction of energies in that moment healed the pain buried deep within my psyche that had been holding me back through fear until the pain was able to be acknowledged and healed in this cycle.

THE CONNECTING THREADS BETWEEN OUR LIVES

- We both experienced psychological trauma when very young that led us to believe life was dangerous and found it difficult to trust people.

- Our experiences as children, although different, meant pain and sadness, and he became oversensitive to life's hurts, as I also had done.

- We both feared exposure by speaking our heartfelt truths.

- Neither of us had the inner strength to stand in our own power through fear. We buried our pains and stopped feeling life deeply. As a result, he chose to live a shallow life to protect himself out of fear of consequence. I, for the first 20-plus years of my life, did the same until I chose to face my fears.

- He died unfulfilled and with a tortured soul, whereas I healed 'our' past trauma by following inner guidance and delving deep within, which resulted in freeing my blocked self-expression; I had opened a door for my authentic voice to finally 'have' a voice.

Unresolved memories of any past trauma can be felt as a disturbing frequency and vibration (in my situation anxiety) and when all the threads are linked and ready, a door opens and both past and present energies find a way of merging together for healing to take place. It's wonderful to see the change in a person when they understand the reason for a certain condition or ongoing inner discomfort. I have witnessed this level of soul healing when working with clients and now I have experienced it for myself.

We returned to Paris again in June 2017 and we purposely went back to the same area. This time I experienced a slight reaction, which quickly passed. I also caught up with the same tour guide at the hotel and she said to me, 'I have never forgotten you and I often recall what you experienced whenever I take a group to that area of Paris.'

All beings are interconnected via Consciousness, which encompasses all life and everyone's experiences come together in a higher realm as one whole Powerhouse of Consciousness. Many call this Powerhouse of Consciousness 'the Mind of God'.

Some scientists believe that out there in the universe, there exists a unified field of pure intelligence. Stephen Hawking, in his book 'A Brief History of Time', describes a 'field' as something that exists throughout space and time.

Could this Powerhouse be what many call the Akashic records, where everyone's many life cycle experiences are retained and brought together as one whole unit of Consciousness as each of our souls progress on our individual pathways, towards total unification? I wonder.

The more I clear my misperceptions, the deeper I journey into consciousness. Through my work I sense that our soul is pivotal and the more we expand our conscious awareness, we 'see' life more clearly in all directions, past, present and future.

Is this how a past life cycle of fragmented unresolved issues supports the soul's energy body to attract those memory threads together to bring about healing in our current life cycle, even if the core issue happened in a past life? I believe so. In fact, we use our minds in a similar way to attract and create a desire to manifest in our life.

This idea could also explain our telepathic ability to think of someone, then within a short time, we hear from them or receive a message for a friend whose loved one has passed over, as you may have read in chapter 42 – Message for Loraine and chapter 51 – A Mother's Concern.

In the bigger scheme of things, we are all one whole unit of Consciousness and...

Energy follows thought.

The quality of our life is determined by the quality of our awareness.
Our input equals our output in life.

Yvonne Fogarty

CHAPTER 66

UNCOVERING MY AUTHENTIC VOICE

In late October 2016, I was down on my hands and knees, happily retrieving my many notebooks and files out of storage, eager to start writing again when The Voice came through and simply said, *'One Voice, One Flow, "One" Expression.'*

Since my first attempt to write in 1999, The Voice was reminding me, yet again, that all of life is one whole unit of Consciousness with many aspects to it.

I'm happy to say I soon discovered I could now sit working on this book for many hours comfortably without any anxiety.

I believed my days of experiencing annoying niggles from the past were now behind me. That was a very naïve thought of mine. In fact, we never stop learning.

After completing the manuscript, I emailed it to my assessor, Dr Rosie Dub, again in 2017. Upon receiving it back with lots of advice and encouraging words, the feedback suggested there were still many areas that required development.

After Christmas a couple of incidents took place. Karza required emergency surgery in 2018 to remove her gall bladder to save her life. A 'specialist' veterinary surgeon had flown into Hobart, visiting with our own vet for a few days. She performed the operation the night before she flew to America to give a series of lectures at a university. For a time, Karza's recovery required our full attention. Instead of her nickname being 'little rascal', it became 'our little miracle'.

I settled back into writing again until my years of playing various sports finally caught up with me and I underwent knee replacement surgery in April 2019. I nearly died twice due to unexpected complications. Firstly, my body reacted to medications. Secondly, a few days after leaving the hospital I was feeling quite unwell and when I was able to get out of bed and move around, I almost passed out a few times. The Voice intervened one morning, urging me to get up and go to a doctor. I rang my doctor, who told me to come straight in as she was in her office catching up on paperwork. Graham and I walked into her office; after I sat down, I passed out. I could feel myself floating away and I felt I was wrapped in a beautiful cocoon of love. An ambulance was called and I was quickly readmitted to the hospital where multiple pulmonary embolisms were discovered in both my lungs.

When I caught up with my doctor a couple of weeks later, we hugged and she said, 'If you hadn't come to see me when you did, you could easily have died in your sleep.'

My doctor knew of and had experienced for herself my gift and I told her, 'Thanks to you and The Voice intervening, I am still here. I don't think I am meant to go just yet. I have a manuscript to finish.'

As a result, the manuscript lay dormant on my desk until late December 2019. During a short holiday away, I received two very clear messages advising of adjustments to the book. *Oh,* I thought, *Am I ready to go back to it again?* The break from writing and editing was a blessing. I came back to it with a renewed vigour.

In January 2020, whilst working on the book, I noticed the words were flowing easier than before, although I was conscious of a subtle niggle in my solar plexus. I ignored the discomfort and continued on, confidently knowing this time I would complete the book.

There were times during the re-editing process I could sense myself hesitating/holding back. I asked myself, *Why am I still holding back?* As I questioned what could still be in the way, I felt the niggle again. This time I was able to connect with the sensation, then suddenly all went quiet and still. It was a strange feeling. Without any understanding coming into my conscious awareness, I asked for guidance and continued editing.

A short time later, I felt emotion rising up into my heart. Then thoughts popped up one after another

What are you doing to us?

Other negative words that reinforced my insecurities and self-doubts came pouring out. Fear rose up again. I briefly saw two images, both of me when young, probably between the ages of two and four along with other thoughts. *Don't expose yourself. It's too dangerous. You might get hurt. Life isn't safe. You're bad and no good.*

I had an extremely exciting 'aha' moment… *There reside the two inhibiting factors,* I thought. *I have at last uncovered two 'core' memory protector patterns.* (It's quite possible one of the memory patterns began forming while I was still in the womb.)

I had tapped into belief patterns that had been attempting to protect me from harm. Although I had peeled away so many layers, these root-core belief patterns were still running like a recording repeatedly playing in the background of my subconscious mind.

Then other thoughts rose up, challenging my negative beliefs, saying,

Hey, ask yourself this… Who said you can't? Who said you are unlovable? Who said you are bad? Who said you are not good enough to?

I was ecstatic. A child's painful experiences can leave an indelible imprint in our psyche. Sadly, if not rectified early, it can attract similar and like thoughts and experiences, reinforcing the painful memories. In turn, destructive patterns can have a strong influence over our ability to function rationally at times until confronted and cleared.

I had been chipping away for years until finally, I had broken down my tough wall of resistance. At last, a door had opened for the distorted memories to rise to the surface of my conscious awareness, enabling me to release the suppressed 'core' memories that had formed when young. In a split second, a massive shift of power had taken place.

As anger rose up, I heard myself saying out loud, 'Those negative words I've clung onto and believed for all these years are **bullshit! THEY REALLY ARE!'**

I had 'allowed' other peoples' negative words to cripple my ability to function effectively as they became mine too, 'embodying' them deep in my subconscious mind. These powerful negative memory threads had been subtly influencing my life in a destructive way.

Since the late 1970s, I had removed many layers of misperceptions until I finally exposed the root causes. More deep-seated anger-filled emotions flared up, releasing their load, as realisation after realisation came tumbling out. The negative words my mother used at times were out of a need to protect and control her own life. My mother had offloaded her pain, frustrations and disappointments in life onto me.

Why? Mum was unhappy, sad and needy. I too became needy. I am sure my mother regretted her outbursts afterwards, as I too have felt deep remorse after speaking from anger or pain, which hurt me more than the other person.

I was seeing everything very clearly; my sensibilities and insecurities had created some dysfunctional memory patterns I experienced daily and continued believing these destructive thoughts that rose up.

From childhood into adulthood, I had developed some strong coping mechanisms.

Protector patterns:

1. Helped me to cope with the pain of my unmet needs and my fear of being rejected. To compensate, I worried about what other people thought of me and I became a people pleaser.

2. If an aspect of me thought I might be in danger of exposing myself, or whenever I triggered a protector pattern, such as when I was serious about my writing, *WHAM*, anxiety would rise up to warn me. If I didn't listen to the warnings, I would

experience a panic attack, all with the intention of protecting me from harm.

Reaction pattern: The inner feelings of panic I experienced, which triggered a fight, flight or freeze reaction to the build-up of discomfort inside me, was to either withdraw into myself, look for a way to escape or stop whatever I was doing that caused me fear. My varied reactions fed my insecurities.

I now understood with clarity why the article by Jeremy McAlister mentioned in the introduction resonated and carried such a deep thread of truth for me, yet at that time I didn't fully comprehend how true his words would prove to be in my circumstances. I have repeated it here...

> ... *A missing experience creates an inability to heal, <u>yearning for unmet needs</u> while <u>protecting against them</u>. Just as we internally separate parts that seek connection from parts that seek safety, we push externally against whatever we need most in life because there is no agreement. At some level, we wait for the elusive experiential safety that will release us and reverse the process, bringing everything together.*

I came across another article that sheds some light on Emotional-Behavioural Patterns...

> *Emotional-behavioural patterns are <u>habitual and defensive reactions to past events</u> that are <u>projected in the field of present time,</u> so that all that is happening is effectively a repetitive, individual pattern of manipulation and unconscious beliefs.... We discover our mechanical nature through '<u>inner work</u>'. Our mechanical behaviour is based on the relationship of action to reaction. It is the opposite of response... It is born of the victim mentality... By becoming aware of how you react, from the very first interaction to the last, you become aware of the protective predictability of your unconscious patterning.*

Ref: Richard Harvey. https://www.linkedin.com/pulse/what-emotional-behavioral-patterns-richard-harvey

These self-sabotaging fearful patterns I harboured were aimed at ensuring my safety. The more I succumbed to them, the more I continued reinforcing my shield of protection, thus increasing their hold over me. These many fearful experiences buried over time had slowly gathered together, building upon each other as each life cycle passed over. Painstakingly, the memory threads came together, healing my inner fears. I have slowly over the years removed layers of barriers, leaving the protector and defensive reactive patterns with nothing left to hide behind.

I had opened a very deep wound inside me. I continued seeing flashes of my younger self over the following days as waves of anger, sadness and discomfort washed over me as I continued to release the pains from my past. I admit, it was a difficult time. Afterwards, I felt empty and drained yet, at the same time, a deep peace had settled inside me.

I had blindly been self-sabotaging my own life until slowly the ingrained emotional hooks and blockages I committed myself to overcoming in this life cycle were finally exposed and cleared away, and I could 'see' clearly.

Why did it take me a very long time to realise the damage I was inflicting on myself? Because subconsciously fear blocked certain thought patterns from rising to my conscious mind and I never thought to question the beliefs – e.g. *'not good enough'* – because at a deep level I still naïvely believed them to be true.

A few days later, another realisation poured in. I had been playing a game, only 'pretending' I was writing a book to appease my desire.

Why? Because deep in my heart I never believed I would actually complete it. If we don't believe something, feeling it in our hearts without harbouring any doubt, it's difficult to manifest a goal the way we desire. Refer to chapter 23 – A Lesson in Letting Go.

I can easily understand where people are coming from when they say hurtful things, criticise or judge others, withhold support, don't tell the truth through fear of confrontation or are jealous of others. We have heard or read that people belittle others through social media, being a bully, or in some other way. Somewhere deep inside them, they could be feeling 'deficient' or 'deprived' in some way. Some people feel better for a little while by offloading/projecting their own inner wounds and hurts onto others in an attempt to ease their own pain.

Sadly, it is their 'own unmet needs or disappointments in life' they are expressing to ease their own pain. It's **'not our issue'**, it's theirs.

Why do I understand where people are coming from when they hurt others? Because I used to be like that. I was jealous of other people's happiness. It's important that we do not allow negative beliefs to continue holding our heart prisoner. Loving our self unconditionally is the most precious and rewarding gift we can give to our self and in turn, we reflect that warm vibration outwardly to others. Unconditional love is a healing vibration.

Unfortunately, I am not alone in experiencing a dysfunctional upbringing. I'm grateful for the journey I have undertaken because I sure do love who I have become.

Once we can embrace our interwoven negative belief patterns about our self and see them clearly in the light of understanding, our perception of that pattern changes and we make more room for the vibration of love to flow in more easily, each time we heal a negative destructive pattern. Once a negative memory/belief is recognised and cleared, it dissolves.

How come? Because we have eliminated a negative behavioural pattern from influencing our life anymore.

Does any of this sound familiar? You may have on occasion felt fearful to take a step forward or heard a voice in your mind, telling you that you are perhaps 'not good enough'. Comments like that can restrict us from living a more fulfilling life.

Derogatory words repeatedly spoken to us since young and retained in our minds are **bullshit.** Actually, I checked the dictionary for clarification. Bullshit means 'to lie, exaggerate or speak nonsense'. It certainly is a very fitting word; in fact, I think it is a perfect word. I am simply highlighting the point here to anyone reading this book who has been on the receiving end of demeaning mental abuse – the abuse is truly bullshit.

If you are reading this book, I would like to say to you... You are an amazing incredible being. Nothing is impossible, especially when able to keep our hearts and minds open to possibilities.

You might wonder ... how can I say that about you? Because you are as I am, a direct offspring of Spirit's powerful attributes and its vibrational essence is pure love, just as our essence is, and Spirit's vibrations are always offering help encouraging us to recognise the enormity of who we are. It's wonderful to know that there is a power greater than us that truly cares.

As the man from my past life said... 'Don't hide and waste your life. I was too afraid to stand up for what I believed in. I never fulfilled my purpose by following my heart and speaking my truths in favour of a peaceful solution.' Refer to chapter 64 – Paris, France, Late 1700s – Past Life Regression Session.

It's important to show love and compassion to the disowned aspects we shut away, our inner fears need to know they are loved and it's safe to come out into the open.

All through my years of clearing to free my self-expression, I had always said to Spirit, 'I only ever desire to write books with the words "flowing freely" from the depths of my heart.' At the time I didn't understand the depth of what I was requesting but Spirit understood. Inside, my soul was crying out for release, for inner freedom. I desired to set myself free from the chains I first sensed around me in 1987. I knew deep down I would never give up on this journey to free my self-expression. Our tenaciousness can be a positive weapon to keep us focused on a desired goal.

A girlfriend, Jill Oakes, once said to me while we were walking our dogs along the foreshore in South Perth, 'Your attempts to write a book remind me of a dog with a bone; you will not let it go. You keep on gnawing at it.'

I answered Jill with a smile on my face, a nod of my head and a cheeky, 'Woof, woof.'

We laughed and Jill was right – I have kept at it, just like the little tortoise, or maybe after all these years I'm possibly more like a little snail, slowly making its way along the road to the finish line.

My life experiences and happenings, coupled with the unfolding of inner gifts, have been a wonderful catalyst of growth for me. All played a role in encouraging me to keep searching to heal my life to reconnect parts of my consciousness that were fragmented.

I could feel bubbles of joy rising up from within my heart as tears of joy ran freely down my cheeks when I realised what I had finally achieved. I have at last uncovered my soul's authentic voice and my self-expression is flowing just as The Voice's message to me said in 2016, *'One Voice, One Flow, "One" Expression.'*

When we open the door of our hearts, requesting guidance to support our 'inner work', we sense the impressions/messages flowing to us in support of our desire to heal our life. It was through following the threads of inner guidance I came to understand the driving force behind my journey – it was my soul seeking freedom of expression and as a result, I uncovered my soul's authentic voice.

I felt such deep gratitude and love when I finally understood with clarity the purpose behind the psychic gifts available and our 'inner guidance system'. It's Spirit's qualities carried by Consciousness that truly cares about the welfare of all of us. Importantly, these qualities support our soul to heal and, in my case, to clear the fears that blocked the way of me expressing my deepest truths.

I also sensed that there are a number of pathways our soul walks before 'fully' uncovering our soul's authentic self. This frequency of learning I completed is one of those pathways.

Spirit honoured my desire for freedom of expression. I have received what I had been asking for and so much more. I often remind myself when writing or talking to stop and feel. Flow comes through sensing what my soul's inner senses have to say to me for expressing my deepest truths. When we ask, we will always receive an answer.

Why? Because...

Energy follows thought.

Through my direct experience with Spirit,
I empowered my life,
building a foundation of truths that resonate
in harmony with spiritual truths.
These truths became the embodiment of my life.

Yvonne Fogarty

CHAPTER 67

COLLATING THE ROOM OF KNOWLEDGE VISIONS

Before you turn to the next chapter, I have brought all these related visions together connected to the Room of Knowledge for easy recall. A couple of the visions below have not been mentioned in the book before.

You may remember reading in chapter 19 – Insightful Vision, which took place in 1992, that I received the message relating to impressions, understanding and knowledge.

Then in chapter 20 – Stepping Forward, I spoke about a vision I received the morning prior to my initiation as a Reiki Master on the 3rd of October 1993. In that vision I was led down some steps into an underground room I named the Room of Knowledge, where all the walls were covered in simple symbols. I felt an unseen presence guiding me over to just one of the many symbols I saw. I sensed the 1992 'Insightful Vision' and 1993 visions were connected.

In 1996 while receiving a treatment from a friend, Marilyn Ardipradja, a vision appeared.

I saw a very large boulder suspended above a man. The boulder was light in colour and I could see strong ropes attached to it. The ropes went from the boulder to what appeared to be a tripod structure with men in ancient clothing holding onto the ropes, keeping the boulder suspended in the air. A man was lying on the ground, tied up, directly under the suspended boulder. The men holding the ropes let go of the boulder, fatally crushing the man's chest.

This vision has recurred a number of times over the past twenty-plus years.

In mid-2001, in chapter 36 – Kundalini Awakening, I again saw a vision of a man being stoned to death.

Late 2001 I was upstairs resting when The Voice spoke, saying, **'Yvonne, go downstairs and turn on the television.'**

As I proceeded to walk down the stairs I thought, *What channel am I to turn to?* We had Indovision (similar to Foxtel) installed in Jakarta. As I flicked through the channels, I stopped on the History channel and on the screen in front of me was a sketch showing a tripod with ropes holding a large boulder suspended above a person lying on the ground. He was being held down by four ropes connected to stakes in the ground.

Spirit had given me confirmation the visions were true. I sensed the man had a strong connection to the Room of Knowledge and was subsequently killed because of it. Over the following years, a series of more detailed visions took place after my Kundalini energy opened, all relating to the Room of Knowledge.

Mid 2003, one of my Masters, Sangeeta Jaggia, who had been with me when my Kundalini energy awakened in 2001, flew in from Jakarta to spend ten days with us in Bangkok. On our last day together, she was giving me a treatment when I saw myself back in the Room of Knowledge again after almost ten years since the 1993 vision. Refer to chapter 20 Stepping Forward and chapter 39 – Bangkok, Thailand, where the man said,

'Yvonne, it's important this information is preserved. This symbol represents the manifestation of life.'

2008, I received another more detailed vision (refer to chapter 53 – Informative Vision) explaining how the Room of Knowledge was utilised and the young boy eventually became the leader and keeper of the records. I realised many years later that the symbol I was shown in 1993 was a focusing tool for me to gain insight and understanding regarding our spiritual and physical composition.

Symbol – Focusing on a symbol, which could even be a book we are guided to, directs a person to go within to seek spiritual understanding, which can link us to receive the symbols' associated frequency and vibrational information giving the person an understanding and/or answer to what they are seeking help or guidance for.

Some people use tarot cards as symbols and are intuited to share what they sense.

If you seek guidance, quiet your body and as you breathe out, feel as if your energy is expanding outwards and focus into 'the nothingness' within, sensing/feeling for an answer, the depth and meaning of a symbol can slowly reveal itself. As it did for me after I sought understanding as to why I was guided to focus on the one symbol in the Room of Knowledge. After doing my Reiki training, I had a strong inner desire to understand our spiritual-physical structure and the symbol slowly revealed its meaning to me. Refer to chapter 54 – A Soul's Associated Frequencies and Vibrations.

September 2019, I continued editing the book while recovering from knee replacement surgery. A friend, Angela Whayman, and I had been giving each other intuitive energy treatments for a few weeks.

During one treatment, I experienced a series of flash visions, the first taking me back into the womb, for clearing a residual of trauma left in the mitochondria cell membranes called mtDNA. The other DNA found in the rest of our body's cells are called nuclear DNA.

Then in three flash visions, I again saw the Room of Knowledge, followed by the same image I had seen before of a man being crushed to death by a huge boulder and then finally an image of a triangle. I sensed more information may emerge when the timing is right. Refer to chapter 41 – The Messenger, where one of the visions refers to a pinecone (pineal gland).

November 2019, when no more information was forthcoming

relating to why I had these visions, I sent my manuscript to a publisher – fortunately it was not accepted. In 2020 I was finally shown the full picture of my connection to the man in the Room of Knowledge, thus completing a circuit of healing...

CHAPTER 68
COMPLETING A FREQUENCY OF LEARNING

Marilyn Ardipradja and I have been friends since first meeting in Jakarta in December 1990. We spoke often on the phone and I always kept her up to date with my journey and writings. I again mentioned I still had no idea why I continued having these visions occasionally connected to the Room of Knowledge. We decided we were overdue for another catch-up.

Late February 2020, Marilyn, whom I had the pleasure of training in Jakarta, flew in from Melbourne for five days. We gave each other treatments and during one of the treatments I received, I again saw an image of the man from the Room of Knowledge being crushed to death.

I relayed what I was observing to Marilyn and she said, 'I remember you had this vision once before when I treated you back in Jakarta and again when we went to Puncak when your Kundalini energy opened. I believe the man and you are the same person and you continue seeing him because you have unfinished business.'

'Yes, I have never forgotten that vision. It was in 1996, actually, when I first experienced the man being killed because it scared me.'

Marilyn's comment triggered a thought. I said, 'I am aware of a slight discomfort hovering around but I have no idea what it is related to because I am feeling great since I uncovered my authentic voice.'

On the 4th of March, another friend, Anna Travers, who is a Reiki

Master and medium, telephoned me one evening not long after Marilyn left, saying, 'Spirit has been very persistent I give you a soul retrieval treatment tonight to heal the remaining fragmented parts from a past life so you can connect it back to wholeness.'

I was very surprised. I said to Anna, 'I thought I had already achieved that.'

'Not quite, Yvonne.'

I willingly agreed to the session.

During the treatment I once again found myself back in the Room of Knowledge and in the vision, *I saw the same man I had seen on previous occasions, only this time he was extremely upset.* The scene changed. *I saw five angry men walking around the Room of Knowledge. They then took hold of him, dragging him away.*

I felt the man's anguish very strongly and I cried out as the pain from that long-ago era was finally acknowledged. I accepted what my soul and heart had been attempting to tell me – I was that man in that very ancient life cycle. The unresolved pain we held in 'our' soul was carried forward, affecting the life of man in the late 1700s until resolved in this life cycle. Refer to chapter 64 – Paris, France, Late 1700s – Past Life Regression Session.

A short time later, waves of energy surged strongly through my body, starting from my head, moving down and out through my feet. The energy caused my body to shudder in jerking movements for about ten minutes until all the built-up energy from the past was released.

Why had I mentally blocked accepting that the man in the Room of Knowledge and I were the same person? Because I had been subconsciously attempting to avoid feeling his pain and I still held a strong belief I was unworthy. As my mind lingered over those thoughts, I saw a quick glimpse of the man from the Room of Knowledge and I felt deep remorse rise up within me before quickly subsiding.

Later that night my body felt light although I also felt exhausted.

The following day I saw a glimpse of the man again and I instantly understood the reasons behind his reaction to the closure of the Room of Knowledge. He felt ashamed of his defiant behaviour. It pained his heart when he realised he could have handled the closure differently. He responded to the closure reactively instead of seeking another way to continue supporting the people.

He felt deep remorse that he had failed Spirit, his mentor, the people and lastly, he had failed himself. He died a horrible death with his heart full of pain.

Clearing the pains, I encountered in this life and from that past life experience in Paris had opened another door for further healing to take place, linking me back to a previous life cycle with the man in the Room of Knowledge. Both men had died harbouring guilt, anguish and deep remorse; the Paris man for his 'inaction' and the other man for his 'reaction'.

I felt a deep peace inside me as the fragmented aspects from those past life traumas were finally clearing, reuniting those fragmented aspects of my consciousness back to wholeness in conjunction with completing this frequency of learning. I was filled with gratitude for my life and my parents as they were the catalyst activating my learnings in this life when I was in my mother's womb. I am so glad I chose to persevere and not give up on this shrouded journey.

Spirit showed me through those experiences how we can build upon negative frequencies and vibrational patterns, carrying them with us through many life cycles until we have the courage to deal with our past traumas. As in my situation, the pain of hanging onto them finally became too much to bear on all levels of my being. Dealing with them was the only way to free myself from the layers of pain my soul had accumulated. One thing I am sure of, these visions were repeated with the intention of encouraging me to keep opening doors until I had achieved my goal.

A couple of months later I woke up with The Voice saying to me... **'Full surrender'.**

It had been a while since I last heard The Voice. I lay in bed for some time, unable to sleep as thoughts popped up. *What does The Voice mean by full surrender? How do I fully surrender and what am I surrendering to? I feel unburdened, light and free! I'm obviously missing something. What is it?*

I said to The Voice, 'I am willing to surrender but please give me the clarity and understanding.'

I let The Voice's words float around in my mind, knowing the answer would come.

Upon waking one morning, a realisation slowly came into my conscious awareness in answer to my request. I was elated. I had trusted in the inner guidance 100% to support others but not so willingly for myself. I had been selective. At the 'core' of my being, I was resisting fully letting go of the control I thought I had over my life and I felt undeserving of having that same powerful depth of connection again that I had access to eons ago.

All Spirit had been asking me to do when I heard the words 'full surrender' was to have the 'willingness' to open my heart without any resistance, let go and fully trust myself to life again and live in the moment.

Back in the 1980s, I thought all I had to deal with were the anxiety attacks and my blocked self-expression that I experienced in this life cycle. I had no idea that was only the tip of the iceberg, so to speak, of the depth of healing I was required to undertake to heal my fragmented soul.

When The Voice suggested in 1999 that I write a book, I had no idea the shrouded inner journey I would undertake, as door after door slowly opened healing many interwoven fears through writing. Doors slowly opened for me to access the depth of expression I desired.

I have undertaken a wonderful journey of self-healing by challenging the hand-me-down and distorted beliefs, along with the unacknowledged past pains.

My life experiences are an example of how Spirit can support us when we hold a deep yearning in our hearts for inner freedom, along with a heartfelt desire. Spirit never gave up on me as I struggled for many years to accept the whole reality of my existence.

Although I have come a long way, I'm definitely still 'in training' and learning every day and my training wheels often fall off. The difference is these days I know and understand from personal experience how great it feels when I remember to keep an open-hearted approach to life to the best of my ability.

The Voice's words '*full surrender*' gave me a glimpse of the new frequency of learning I will undertake. I realised letting go and trusting myself to all of life and living in the moment, for me, is an ongoing learning process.

Spirit has demonstrated through the various experiences in this book the power available to each of us, giving us a glimpse of the 'enormity' of who we are and what we are capable of achieving when we choose to open the door to listen to the inner voice of wisdom and truth to guide our way.

As you go about your day, please keep in mind that...

Energy follows thought

Living in tune with our inner guidance, we can change our 'ignorance' to 'illumination' and our 'illusions' to 'clarity'. The end result is we experience ourselves, expressing freely and openly, our own authentic voice.

Yvonne Fogarty

CHAPTER 69

IN CLOSING

We are all interconnected and living within a vast ocean of Consciousness sometimes referred to as the Mind of God or as the psychologist Carl Jung named it, The Collective Unconscious. Our consciousness is interconnected to more vastly advanced levels of inner guidance – our mentor's – and their wisdom is always available to support us.

Why? Because Consciousness is always flowing within, around and through us. It is a natural aspect of our nature to experience these frequencies and vibrations interacting directly with us.

Consciousness knows no boundaries whether we are living on Earth or have passed over. The only mental boundaries we encounter are held within our soul's subconscious mind.

To me, spirituality means recognising, sensing and believing in something much greater than myself. Caroline Myss said in her book 'Defy Gravity', 'Divine Light has no religion and that's the cosmic truth.' Religion is more a specific set of organised beliefs and practices.

It's important to respect other people's choices to follow their heart, whichever way their journey directs them. Some go it alone, as I have done, whilst others find comfort through fellowship within a church – either way, it is very uplifting and supportive.

I see living authentically as 'grounding' my spirituality and living with an open heart and that my thoughts, words and actions are harmless to myself and others. It also means choosing to let go of living by other people's negative hand-me-down beliefs or behavioural patterns, by establishing and living in alignment with our own inherent truths. At our core essence, we are all One. If we hurt another person, we are also hurting ourselves.

As individuals, it is important to realise that we are responsible for the **evolution of our soul** and our uplifting positive vibrations touch and assist the whole world towards the survival of our planet and advancement of humanity.

We are all on a journey towards reuniting the fragmented parts of our consciousness back to wholeness with the intention of fully uncovering every aspect of our souls' authentic self.

These days when challenges confront me, I still experience the vibrations of love, joy, peace and contentment bubbling up from deep within me. I like to think these bubbles of joy is my soul singing out, saying, 'Yay. My soul's authentic voice is free at last.'

All that is required of us is to simply go about our daily life 'living consciously', our truths at our level of understanding in each moment, listening within and in each of those insightful 'aha' opportune moments, we will experience ongoing awakenings and the expansion of our consciousness for seeing more clearly **the enormity of who we are.**

This book is finally completed. I am appreciative for my life and the shrouded journey I have undertaken. I'm looking forward to new adventures and sharing more of my life experiences and wisdom. I'm sure the next book will not take as long as this one did; otherwise, I could be writing it perched on a cloud.

I could say here that this is **'The End'**, or is it **'The Beginning'** – actually, it's **BOTH!**

Shawline Publishing Group Pty Ltd
www.shawlinepublishing.com.au

SHAWLINE
PUBLISHING
GROUP

More great Shawline titles can be found here:

New titles also available through Books@Home Pty Ltd.
Subscribe today - www.booksathome.com.au

CPSIA information can be obtained
at www.ICGtesting.com
Printed in the USA
BVHW052113090223
658229BV00010B/141